Black Looks

Black Looks

Race and Representation

bell hooks

South End Press
Boston, MA

Printed in the U.S.A. on recycled, acid-free paper.
Text design and layout by the South End Press collective.
Cover design by Julie Ault and Gloria Watkins.
Cover photo from *The Black West* by William Loren Katz,
Open Hand Publishing Inc., 1987. Used with the kind
permission of William Loren Katz.
Grateful acknowledgment is made to the following publications for
permission to use previously published material: *Black American
Literature Forum; Z Magazine;* and the book *Cultural Studies,*
edited by Lawrence Grossberg, Cary Nelson, and Paula Treichler,
New York: Routledge, 1992.

Library of Congress Cataloging-in-Publication Data
Hooks, Bell.
Black looks : race and representation / Bell Hooks.
p. cm.
Includes bibliographic references.
ISBN 0-89608-433-7 : $12.00
1. Afro-American women. 2. Afro-Americans—Social conditions—
1975- 3. Racism—United States. 4. United States—
Race relations. I. Title
E185.86.H734 1992   92-6954
305.48'896073—dc20   CIP

South End Press, 116 Saint Botolph Street, Boston, MA 02115
9 8 7 6 5 4 3   93 94 95 96 97 98 99

Table of Contents

I dedicate this book to all of us who love blackness,
who dare to create in our daily lives
spaces of reconciliation and forgiveness
where we let go of past hurt, fear, shame
and hold each other close.
It is only in the act and practice
of loving blackness
that we are able to reach out
and embrace the world
without destructive bitterness
and ongoing collective rage.

Holding each other close across differences,
beyond conflict, through change,
is an act of resistance.
I am especially grateful to those
who hold me close and do not let me go;
to those of you who challenge me
to live theory in a place beyond words
(to you Angela, Anthony, Anu, Gwenda,
Julie, Karen, Paul, Susan, Valeria,
and those unnamed
whom my heart remembers).

Introduction

Revolutionary Attitude

*Decolonization...continues to be an act of confrontation with a hege-
monic system of thought; it is hence a process of considerable historical and
cultural liberation. As such, decolonization becomes the contestation of all
dominant forms and structures, whether they be linguistic, discursive, or
ideological. Moreover, decolonization comes to be understood as an act of
exorcism for both the colonized and the colonizer. For both parties it must be
a process of liberation: from dependency, in the case of the colonized, and from
imperialist, racist perceptions, representations, and institutions which, unfortunately, remain with us to this very day, in the case of the colonizer...Decol-
onization can only be complete when it is understood as a complex process
that involves both the colonizer and the colonized.*

—Samia Nehrez

If we compare the relative progress African Americans have made
in education and employment to the struggle to gain control over how
we are represented, particularly in the mass media, we see that there
has been little change in the area of representation. Opening a magazine or book, turning on the television set, watching a film, or looking
at photographs in public spaces, we are most likely to see images of
black people that reinforce and reinscribe white supremacy. Those
images may be constructed by white people who have not divested of
racism, or by people of color/black people who may see the world
through the lens of white supremacy—internalized racism. Clearly,
those of us committed to black liberation struggle, to the freedom and
self-determination of all black people, must face daily the tragic reality

1

that we have collectively made few, if any, revolutionary interventions in the area of race and representation.

Theorizing black experience in the United States is a difficult task. Socialized within white supremacist educational systems and by a racist mass media, many black people are convinced that our lives are not complex, and are therefore unworthy of sophisticated critical analysis and reflection. Even those of us righteously committed to black liberation struggle, who feel we have decolonized our minds, often find it hard to "speak" our experience. The more painful the issues we confront the greater our inarticulateness. James Baldwin understood this. In *The Fire Next Time,* he reminded readers that "there has been almost no language" to describe the "horrors" of black life.

Without a way to name our pain, we are also without the words to articulate our pleasure. Indeed, a fundamental task of black critical thinkers has been the struggle to break with the hegemonic modes of seeing, thinking, and being that block our capacity to see ourselves oppositionally, to imagine, describe, and invent ourselves in ways that are liberatory. Without this, how can we challenge and invite non-black allies and friends to dare to look at us differently, to dare to break their colonizing gaze?

Speaking about his recent film *The Camp at Thiaroye,* African filmmaker Ousmane Sembene explains: "You must understand that for people like us, there are no such things as models. We are called upon to constantly create our models. For African people, Africans in the diaspora, it's pretty much the same. Colonialism means that we must always rethink everything." Challenged to rethink, insurgent black intellectuals and/or artists are looking at new ways to write and talk about race and representation, working to transform the image.

There is a direct and abiding connection between the maintenance of white supremacist patriarchy in this society and the institutionalization via mass media of specific images, representations of race, of blackness that support and maintain the oppression, exploitation, and overall domination of all black people. Long before white supremacists ever reached the shores of what we now call the United States, they constructed images of blackness and black people to uphold and affirm their notions of racial superiority, their political imperialism, their will to dominate and enslave. From slavery on, white supremacists have recognized that control over images is central to the maintenance of any system of racial domination. In his essay "Cultural Identity and Diaspora," Stuart Hall emphasizes that we can properly understand the traumatic character of the colonial experience by recognizing the connection between domination and representation:

> The ways in which black people, black experiences, were positioned and subjected in the dominant regimes of representation were the effects of a critical exercise of cultural power and normalization. Not only, in Said's "orientalist" sense, were we constructed as different and other within the categories of knowledge of the West by those regimes. They had the power to make us see and experience *ourselves* as "Other"…It is one thing to position a subject or set of peoples as the Other of a dominant discourse. It is quite another thing to subject them to that "knowledge," not only as a matter of imposed will and domination, but by the power of inner compulsion and subjective conformation to the norm.

That the field of representation remains a place of struggle is most evident when we critically examine contemporary representations of blackness and black people.

I was painfully reminded of this fact recently when visiting friends on a once colonized black island. Their little girl is just reaching that stage of preadolescent life where we become obsessed with our image, with how we look and how others see us. Her skin is dark. Her hair chemically straightened. Not only is she fundamentally convinced that straightened hair is more beautiful than curly, kinky, natural hair, she believes that lighter skin makes one more worthy, more valuable in the eyes of others. Despite her parents' effort to raise their children in an affirming black context, she has internalized white supremacist values and aesthetics, a way of looking and seeing the world that negates her value.

Of course this is not a new story. I could say the same for my nieces, nephews, and millions of black children here in the States. What struck me about this little girl was the depths of her pain and rage. She was angry. And yet her anger had no voice. It could not say, "Mommy, I am upset that all these years from babyhood on, I thought I was a marvelous, beautiful gifted girl, only to discover that the world does not see me this way." Often she was "acting out"—behaving in a manner that in my childhood days would have made older "colonized" black folks talk about her as evil, as a little Sapphire. When I tried to intervene and talk with her mother about the need to directly address issues of race and representation, I sensed grave reluctance, denial even. And it struck me that for black people, the pain of learning that we cannot control our images, how we see ourselves (if our vision is not decolonized), or how we are seen is so intense that it rends us. It rips and tears at the seams of our efforts to construct self and identify. Often it leaves us ravaged by repressed rage, feeling weary, dispirited, and sometimes just plain old brokenhearted. These are the gaps in our psyche that are the spaces where mindless complicity, self-destructive rage, hatred, and paralyzing despair enter.

To face these wounds, to heal them, progressive black people and our allies in struggle must be willing to grant the effort to critically intervene and transform the world of image making authority of place in our political movements of liberation and self-determination (be they anti-imperialist, feminist, gay rights, black liberation, or all of the above and more). If this were the case, we would be ever mindful of the need to make radical intervention. We would consider crucial both the kind of images we produce and the way we critically write and talk about images. And most important, we would rise to the challenge to speak that which has not been spoken.

For some time now the critical challenge for black folks has been to expand the discussion of race and representation beyond debates about good and bad imagery. Often what is thought to be good is merely a reaction against representations created by white people that were blatantly stereotypical. Currently, however, we are bombarded by black folks creating and marketing similar stereotypical images. It is not an issue of "us" and "them." The issue is really one of standpoint. From what political perspective do we dream, look, create, and take action? For those of us who dare to desire differently, who seek to look away from the conventional ways of seeing blackness and ourselves, the issue of race and representation is not just a question of critiquing the *status quo*. It is also about transforming the image, creating alternatives, asking ourselves questions about what types of images subvert, pose critical alternatives, and transform our worldviews and move us away from dualistic thinking about good and bad. Making a space for the transgressive image, the outlaw rebel vision, is essential to any effort to create a context for transformation. And even then little progress is made if we transform images without shifting paradigms, changing perspectives, ways of looking.

The critical essays gathered in *Black Looks: Race and Representation* are gestures of defiance. They represent my political struggle to push against the boundaries of the image, to find words that express what I see, especially when I am looking in ways that move against the grain, when I am seeing things that most folks want to believe simply are not there. These essays are about identity. Since decolonization as a political process is always a struggle to define ourselves in and beyond the act of resistance to domination, we are always in the process of both remembering the past even as we create new ways to imagine and make the future.

Stuart Hall names this process eloquently in this powerful statement, again from the essay "Cultural Identity and Diaspora":

> Cultural identity...is a matter of "becoming" as well as "being." It belongs to the future as much as to the past. It is not something which already exists, transcending place, time, history, and culture. Cultural identities come from somewhere, have histories. But, like everything which is historical, they undergo constant transformation. Far from being eternally fixed in some essentialized past, they are subject to the continuous "play" of history, culture and power. Far from being grounded in a mere "recovery" of the past, which is waiting to be found, and which, when found, will secure our sense of ourselves into eternity, identities are the names we give to the different ways we are positioned by, and position ourselves within, the narratives of the past.

In *Black Looks*, I critically interrogate old narratives, suggesting alternative ways to look at blackness, black subjectivity, and, of necessity, whiteness.

While also exploring literature, music, and television, many of these essays focus on film. The emphasis on film is so central because it, more than any other media experience, determines how blackness and black people are seen and how other groups will respond to us based on their relation to these constructed and consumed images. In the essay "Black Feminism: The Politics of Articulation," filmmaker Pratibha Parmar states, "Images play a crucial role in defining and controlling the political and social power to which both individuals and marginalized groups have access. The deeply ideological nature of imagery determines not only how other people think about us but how we think about ourselves."

Many audiences in the United States resist the idea that images have an ideological intent. This is equally true of black audiences. Fierce critical interrogation is sometimes the only practice that can pierce the wall of denial consumers of images construct so as not to face that the real world of image-making is political—that politics of domination inform the way the vast majority of images we consume are constructed and marketed. Most black folks do not want to think critically about why they can sit in the darkness of theaters and find pleasure in images that cruelly mock and ridicule blackness. That is why many of the essays in *Black Looks* focus on spectatorship.

I ask that we consider the perspective from which we look, vigilantly asking ourselves who do we identify with, whose image do we love. And if we, black people, have learned to cherish hateful images of ourselves, then what process of looking allows us to counter the seduction of images that threatens to dehumanize and colonize. Clearly, it is that way of seeing which makes possible an integrity of being that can subvert the power of the colonizing image. It is only as we collectively change the way we look at ourselves and the world that we can change how we are seen. In this process, we seek to create a world where everyone can look at blackness, and black people, with new eyes.

In 1962, at the age of thirty-two, only a few years before her unexpected death from cancer, black woman playwright Lorraine Hansberry wrote a letter in response to a "white farm boy living on a rich, fertile farm on the Mason-Dixon line" who was concerned that black people were becoming too militant. She answered that "the condition of our people dictates what can only be called revolutionary attitudes." In the letter she also declared, "The acceptance of our present condition is the only form of extremism which discredits us before our children." Many black folks refuse to look at our present condition because they do not want to see images that might compel them to militance. But militancy is an alternative to madness. And many of us are daily entering the realm of the insane. Like Pecola, in Toni Morrison's *The Bluest Eye,* black folks turn away from reality because the pain of awareness is so great. Yet it is only by becoming more fully aware that we begin to see clearly.

We experience our collective crisis as African American people within the realm of the image. Whether it is the face of homeless folks encountered in city streets or small town alleyways, the wandering gaze of the unemployed, the sight of our drug addicted loved ones, or some tragic scene from a film that lingers in the mind's eye, *we see that we are in trouble.* I can still see the images of young black men brutally murdering one another that were part of the fictional narrative of John Singleton's film *Boyz 'N The Hood.* These images were painful to watch. That is how it should be. It should hurt our eyes to see racial genocide perpetuated in black communities, whether fictional or real. Yet, in the theater where I saw this film, the largely black audience appeared to find pleasure in these images. This response was powerful testimony, revealing that those forms of representation in white supremacist society that teach black folks to internalize racism are so ingrained in our collective consciousness that we can find pleasure in images of our death and destruction. What can the future hold if our present entertainment is the spectacle of contemporary colonization, dehumanization, and disempowerment where the image serves as a murder weapon. Unless we transform images of blackness, of black people, our ways of looking and our ways of being seen, we cannot make radical interventions that will fundamentally alter our situation.

This struggle needs to include non-black allies as well. Images of race and representation have become a contemporary obsession. Commodification of blackness has created a social context where appropriation by non-black people of the black image knows no boundaries. If the many non-black people who produce images or critical narratives about blackness and black people do not interrogate their perspective, then they may simply recreate the imperial gaze—the look that seeks to dominate, subjugate, and colonize. This is especially so for white people looking at and talking about blackness. In his essay "The Miscegenated Gaze," black male artist Christian Walker suggests, "If white artists, committed to the creation of a non-racist, non-sexist and non-hierarchical society, are ever to fully understand and embrace their own self-identity and their own miscegenated gaze, they will have to embrace and celebrate the concept of non-white subjectivity." Their ways of looking must be fundamentally altered. They must be able to engage in the militant struggle by black folks to transform the image.

As a radical intervention we must develop revolutionary attitudes about race and representation. To do this we must be willing to think critically about images. We must be willing to take risks. The essays in *Black Looks* are meant to challenge and unsettle, to disrupt and subvert. They may make some folks get mad, go off, or just feel upset. That is the idea—to provoke and engage. Like that photographic portrait of Billy Holiday by Moneta Sleet I love so much, the one where instead of a glamorized image of stardom, we are invited to see her in a posture of thoughtful reflection, her arms bruised by tracks, delicate scars on her face, and that sad faraway look in her eyes. When I face this image, this black look, something in me is shattered. I have to pick up the bits and pieces of myself and start all over again—transformed by the image.

Chapter 1

Loving Blackness
as Political Resistance

We have to change our own mind... We've got to change our own minds about each other. We have to see each other with new eyes. We have to come together with warmth...

—Malcolm X

The course I teach on black women writers is a consistent favorite among students. The last semester that I taught this course we had the usual passionate discussion of Nella Larson's novel *Passing*. When I suggested to the class (which had been more eager to discuss the desire of black folks to be white) that Clare, the black woman who has passed for white all her adult life and married a wealthy white businessman with whom she has a child, is the only character in the novel who truly desires "blackness" and that it is this desire that leads to her murder, no one responded. Clare boldly declares that she would rather live for the rest of her life as a poor black woman in Harlem than as a rich white matron downtown. I asked the class to consider the possibility that to love blackness is dangerous in a white supremacist culture—so threatening, so serious a breach in the fabric of the social order, that death is the punishment. It became painfully obvious by the lack of response that this group of diverse students (many of them black people) were more interested in discussing the desire of black folks to be white, indeed were fixated on this issue. So much so, that they could not even take seriously a critical discussion about "loving blackness."

9

They wanted to talk about black self-hatred, to hear one another confess (especially students of color) in eloquent narratives about the myriad ways they had tried to attain whiteness, if only symbolically. They gave graphic details about the ways they attempted to appear "white" by talking a certain way, wearing certain clothing, and even choosing specific groups of white friends. Blonde white students seized the opportunity to testify that they had never realized racism had this impact upon the psyches of people of color until they started hanging out with black friends, taking courses in Black Studies, or reading Toni Morrison's *The Bluest Eye*. And better yet, they never realized there was such a thing as "white privilege" until they developed non-white connections.

I left this class of more than forty students, most of whom see themselves as radical and progressive, feeling as though I had witnessed a ritualistic demonstration of the impact white supremacy has on our collective psyches, shaping the nature of everyday life, how we talk, walk, eat, dream, and look at one another. The most frightening aspect of this ritual was the extent to which their fascination with the topic of black self-hatred was so intense that it silenced any constructive discussion abut loving blackness. Most folks in this society do not want to openly admit that "blackness" as sign primarily evokes in the public imagination of whites (and all the other groups who learn that one of the quickest ways to demonstrate one's kinship within a white supremacist order is by sharing racist assumptions) hatred and fear. In a white supremacist context "loving blackness" is rarely a political stance that is reflected in everyday life. When present it is deemed suspect, dangerous, and threatening.

The oppositional black culture that emerged in the context of apartheid and segregation has been one of the few locations that has provided a space for the kind of decolonization that makes loving blackness possible. Racial integration in a social context where white supremacist systems are intact undermines marginal spaces of resistance by promoting the assumption that social equality can be attained without changes in the culture's attitudes about blackness and black people. Black progressives suffered major disillusionment with white progressives when our experiences of working with them revealed that they could want to be with us (even to be our sexual partners) without divesting of white supremacist thinking about blackness. We saw that they were often unable to let go the idea that whites are somehow better, smarter, more likely to be intellectuals, and even that they were kinder than black folks. Decolonized progressive black individuals are daily amazed by the extent to which masses of black people (all of whom would identify themselves as anti-racist) hold to white supremacist ways of thinking, allowing this perspective to determine how they see themselves and other black people. Many black folks see us as "lacking," as inferior when compared to whites. The paucity of scholarly work looking at the issue of black self-hatred, examining the ways in which the colonization and exploitation of black people is reinforced by internalized racial hatred *via* white supremacist thinking, is awesome. Few black scholars have explored extensively black obsession with whiteness.

Black theologian James Cone has been one of the few insurgent black intellectuals who has consistently called for critical interrogation of "whiteness" while simultaneously problematizing constructions of white identity within white supremacist culture. In his early work, *A Black Theology of Liberation,* Cone urges folks to understand blackness as an "ontological symbol" that is the quintessential signifier of what oppression means in the United States. Cone calls upon whites, blacks, and all other non-black groups to stand against white supremacy by choosing to value, indeed to love, blackness. Boldly stating his case, Cone suggests:

> Most whites, some despite involvements in protests, do believe in "freedom in democracy," and they fight to make the ideals of the Constitution an empirical reality for all. It seems that they believe that, if we just work hard enough at it, this country can be what it ought to be. But it never dawns on these do-gooders that what is wrong with America is not its failure to make the Constitution a reality for all, but rather its belief that persons can affirm whiteness and humanity at the same time. This country was founded for whites and everything that has happened in it has emerged from the white perspective…What we need is the destruction of whiteness, which is the source of human misery in the world.

Not surprisingly, many of Cone's readers were disturbed by his evocation of a binary approach. At first glance it can appear to be a mere reversal of white racist paradigms. Blackness in much of his early work is identified with that which is good, righteous, positive and whiteness with all that is bad, negative, sinful.

Cone wanted to critically awaken and educate readers so that they would not only break through denial and acknowledge the evils of white supremacy, the grave injustices of racist domination, but be so moved that they would righteously and militantly engage in anti-racist struggle. Encouraging readers to break with white supremacy as an epistemological standpoint by which they come to know the world, he insisted that "whiteness" as a sign be interrogated. He wanted the public to learn how to distinguish that racism which is about overt prejudice and domination from more subtle forms of white supremacy. In his early work, he frequently chose a rhetoric that would "shock" so as to forcefully impress on the reader's consciousness the seriousness of the issues. Unfortunately, many readers were turned off by his rhetorical stance, his emphasis on binary opposition, and could not hear the wisdom in his call for a critique of whiteness. By focusing on his personal style, many readers willingly allowed themselves to dismiss and/or ignore the extent to which (all polemical rhetoric aside) his discourse on whiteness was a necessary critical intervention, calling for ongoing interrogation of conventional ways of thinking about race or about strategies to eradicate racism.

Cone was suggesting the kind of shift in positionality that has become a crucial and widely accepted tenet of anti-racist struggle advocated in much recent critical work on the subject of race, especially the work that emerges from feminist theory, cultural studies, and postcolonial discourse. Whether they are able to enact it as a lived practice or not, many white folks active in anti-racist struggle today are able to acknowledge that all whites (as well as everyone else within white supremacist culture) have learned to over-value "whiteness" even as they simultaneously learn to devalue blackness. They understand the need, at least intellectually, to alter their thinking. Central to this process of unlearning white supremacist attitudes and values is the deconstruction of the category "whiteness."

It is much more acceptable nowadays, and even fashionable, to call for an interrogation of the meaning and significance of "whiteness" in contemporary critical discussions of race. While Cone's analysis was sometimes limited by a discourse that invested in binary oppositions (refusing to cut white folks any slack), the significant critical intervention that he made was the insistence that the logic of white supremacy would be radically undermined if everyone would learn to identify with and love blackness. Cone was not evoking the notion of racial erasure, that is, the sentimental idea (often voiced by religious folks) that racism would cease to exist if everyone would just forget about race and just see each other as human beings who are the same. Instead he insisted that the politics of racial domination have necessarily created a black reality that is distinctly different from that of whites, and from that location has emerged a distinct black culture. His prophetic call was for whites to learn how to identify with that difference—to see it as a basis for solidarity.

This message can be heard in current feminist writing on race. Moving away from the notion that an emphasis on sameness is the key to racial harmony, aware feminist activists have insisted that anti-racist struggle is best advanced by theory that speaks about the importance of acknowledging the way positive recognition and acceptance of difference is a necessary starting point as we work to eradicate white supremacy. Critically discussing Richard Rorty's book *Contingency, Irony and Solidarity,* philosopher Ron Scaap, in his essay "Rorty: Voice and the Politics of Empathy," makes the point that liberals often give lip service to a vision of diversity and plurality while clinging to notions of sameness where we are all one, where (to use Michael Jackson's lyrics) "it doesn't matter if you're black or white." Scaap suggests,

> Liberals may pride themselves in their ability to tolerate others but it is only after the other has been redescribed as oneself that the liberal is able to be "sensitive" to the question of cruelty and humiliation. This act of redescription is still an attempt to appropriate others, only here it is made to sound as if it were a generous act. It is an attempt to make an act of consumption appear to be an act of acknowledgment.

Many unlearning racism workshops focus on helping white individuals to see that they too are wounded by racism and as a consequence have something to gain from participating in anti-racist struggle. While in some ways true, a construction of political solidarity that is rooted in a narrative of shared victimization not only acts to recenter whites, it risks obscuring the particular ways racist domination impacts on the lives of marginalized groups. Implicit in the assumption that even those who are privileged *via* racist hierarchy suffer is the notion that it is only when those in power get in touch with how they too are victimized will they rebel against structures of domination. The truth is that many folks benefit greatly from dominating others and are not suffering a wound that is in any way similar to the condition of the exploited and oppressed.

Anti-racist work that tries to get these individuals to see themselves as "victimized" by racism in the hopes that this will act as an intervention is a misguided strategy. And indeed we must be willing to acknowledge that individuals of great privilege who are in no way victimized are capable, *via* their political choices, of working on behalf of the oppressed. Such solidarity does not need to be rooted in shared experience. It can be based on one's political and ethical understanding of racism and one's rejection of domination. Therefore we can see the necessity for the kind of education for critical consciousness that can enable those with power and privilege rooted in structures of domination to divest without having to see themselves as victims. Such thinking does not have to negate collective awareness that a culture of domination does seek to fundamentally distort and pervert the psyches of all citizens or that this perversion is wounding.

In his work, Cone acknowledges that racism harms whites yet he emphasizes the need to recognize the difference between the hurt oppressors feel and the pain of the oppressed. He suggests:

> The basic error of white comments about their own oppression is the assumption that they *know* the nature of their enslavement. This cannot be so, because if they really knew, they would liberate themselves by joining the revolution of the black community. They would destroy themselves and be born again as beautiful black persons.

Since it is obvious that white folks cannot choose at will to become "black," that utopian longing must be distinguished from a solidarity with blackness that is rooted in actions wherein one ceases to identify with whiteness as symbol of victimization and powerlessness.

Recently, I gave a talk highlighting ways contemporary commodification of black culture by whites in no way challenges white supremacy when it takes the form of making blackness the "spice that can liven up the dull dish that is mainstream white culture." At the end of the talk a white woman who sounded very earnest asked me: "Don't you think we are all raised in a culture that is racist and we are all taught to be racist whether we want to be or not?" Note that she constructs a social framework of sameness, a homogeneity of experience. My response was to say that all white people (and everyone else in this society) can choose to be actively anti-racist twenty-four hours a day if they so desire and none of us are passive victims of socialization. Elaborating on this point, I shared how I was weary of the way in which white people want to deflect attention away from their accountability for anti-racist change by making it seem that everyone has been socialized to be racist against their will. My fear is that this often becomes another apology for racism, one which seeks to erase a vision of accountability and responsibility which could truly empower. It was apparent that the white woman who asked the question was dissatisfied with my response. When I suggested that she was less interested in what I had to say and perhaps had her own agenda, she stated that the point she really wanted to make was that "blacks are just as racist as whites—that we are all racists." When I critically interrogated this statement, explaining the difference between prejudicial feelings (which blacks and white alike harbor towards one another as well as other groups) and institutionalized white supremacist domination, she promptly left.

A vision of cultural homogeneity that seeks to deflect attention away from or even excuse the oppressive, dehumanizing impact of white supremacy on the lives of black people by suggesting black people are racist too indicates that the culture remains ignorant of what racism really is and how it works. It shows that people are in denial. Why is it so difficult for many white folks to understand that racism is oppressive not because white folks have prejudicial feelings about blacks (they could have such feelings and leave us alone) but because it is a system that promotes domination and subjugation? The prejudicial feelings some blacks may express about whites are in no way linked to a system of domination that affords us any power to coercively control the lives and well-being of white folks. That needs to be understood.

Concurrently, all social manifestations of black separatism are often seen by whites as a sign of anti-white racism, when they usually represent an attempt by black people to construct places of political sanctuary where we can escape, if only for a time, white domination. The ideas of conservative black thinkers who buy into the notion that blacks are racist are often evoked by whites who see them as native informants confirming this as fact. Shelby Steele is a fine example of this tendency. I believe that his essays were the most xeroxed pieces of writing by white folks in the academy who wanted to share with black colleagues that they have been right all along when they suggested that black folks were racist. Steele suggests that any time black people choose to congregate solely with one another we are either supporting racial separatism because of deeply ingrained feelings of inferiority or a refusal to see racial differences as unimportant (i.e., to accept the notion that we are all the same). Commenting on the issue of self-segregation in *The Content of Our Character*, he declares: "There is a geopolitics involved in this activity, where race is tied to territory in a way that mimics the whites only/colored only designations of the past." At no point in his analysis does Steele suggest that blacks might want to be away from whites to have a space where we will not be the object of racist assaults.

Every aware black person who has been the "only" in an all white setting knows that in such a position we are often called upon to lend an ear to racist narratives, to laugh at corny race jokes, to undergo various forms of racist harassment. And that self-segregation seems to be particularly intense among those black college students who were often raised in material privilege in predominately white settings where they were socialized to believe racism did not exist, that we are all "just human beings," and then suddenly leave home and enter institutions and experience racist attacks. To a great extent they are unprepared to confront and challenge white racism, and often seek the comfort of just being with other blacks.

Steele's refusal to acknowledge this pain—this way that white supremacy manifests itself in daily social interaction—makes it appear that black individuals simply do not like socializing with whites. The reality is that many black people fear they will be hurt if they let down their guard, that they will be the targets of racist assault since most white people have not unlearned racism. In classroom settings, I hear so many narratives of black students who accepted the notion that racism did not exist, who felt there was nothing wrong with being with white friends and sharing similar interests, only to find themselves in circumstances where they had to confront the racism of these people. The last story I heard was from a young black woman talking about always being with white buddies in high school. One day they were all joy-riding in someone's car, and they came across a group of young black males crossing the street. Someone in the car suggests they should "just run those niggers down." She talked about her disbelief that this comment had been made, her hurt. She said nothing but she felt that it was the beginning of an estrangement from white peers that has persisted. Steele's writing assumes that white people who desire to socialize with black people are not actively racist, are coming from a position of goodwill. He does not consider the reality that goodwill can co-exist with racist thinking and white supremacist attitudes.

Throughout my tenure as a Yale professor, I was often confronted with white students who would raise the issue of why it is black students sit together in the cafeteria, usually at one table. They saw this as some expression of racial separatism, exclusion, etc. When I asked them why did they never raise the issue of why the majority of tables are white students self-segregating, they invariably said things like, "we sit together with folks with whom we share common interests and concerns." They were rarely at the point where they could interrogate whether or not shared "whiteness" allowed them to bond with one another with ease.

While it has become "cool" for white folks to hang out with black people and express pleasure in black culture, most white people do not feel that this pleasure should be linked to unlearning racism. Indeed there is often the desire to enhance one's status in the context of "whiteness" even as one appropriates black culture. In his essay "A Place Called Home: Identity and the Cultural Politics of Difference," Jonathan Rutherford comments:

> Paradoxically, capital has fallen in love with difference: advertising thrives on selling us things that will enhance our uniqueness and individuality. It's no longer about keeping up with the Joneses, it's about being different from them. From World Music to exotic holidays in Third World locations, ethnic tv dinners to Peruvian hats, cultural difference *sells*.

It makes perfect sense that black people/people of color often self-segregate to protect themselves from this kind of objectifying interaction.

Steele never sees the desire to create a context where one can "love blackness" as a worthy standpoint for bonding, even if such bonding must take the form of self-segregation. Luckily, there are individual non-black people who have divested of their racism in ways that enable them to establish bonds of intimacy based on their ability to love blackness without assuming the role of cultural tourists. We have yet to have a significant body of writing from these individuals that gives expression to how they have shifted attitudes and daily vigilantly resist becoming reinvested in white supremacy. Concurrently, black folks who "love blackness," that is, who have decolonized our minds and broken with the kind of white supremacist thinking that suggests we are inferior, inadequate, marked by victimization, etc., often find that we are punished by society for daring to break with the *status quo*. On our jobs, when we express ourselves from a decolonized standpoint, we risk being seen as unfriendly or dangerous.

Those black folks who are more willing to pretend that "difference" does not exist even as they self-consciously labor to be as much like their white peers as possible, will receive greater material rewards in white supremacist society. White supremacist logic is thus advanced. Rather than using coercive tactics of domination to colonize, it seduces black folks with the promise of mainstream success if only we are willing to negate the value of blackness. Contrary to James Cone's hope that whites would divest of racism and be born again in the spirit of empathy and unity with black folks, we are collectively asked to show our solidarity with the white supremacist *status quo* by over-valuing whiteness, by seeing blackness solely as a marker of powerlessness and victimization. To the degree that black folks embody by our actions and behavior familiar racist stereotypes, we will find greater support and/or affirmation in the culture. A prime example of this is white consumer support of misogynist rap which reproduces the idea that black males are violent beasts and brutes.

In Nella Larsen's *Passing,* Clare chooses to assume a white identity because she only sees blackness as a sign of victimization and power-lessness. As long as she thinks this, she has a sustained bond with the black bourgeoisie who often self-segregate even as they maintain contempt for blackness, especially for the black underclass. Clare's bond with Irene, her black bourgeois friend, is broken when she seeks to define blackness positively. In *Passing* it is this bourgeois class and the world of whiteness Clare's husband embodies that turns against her when she attempts to reclaim the black identity she has previously denied. When the novel ends we do not know who has murdered her, the black bourgeois friend or the white husband. She represents a "threat" to the conservative hierarchical social order based on race, class, and gender that they both seek to maintain.

Despite civil rights struggle, the 1960s' black power movement, and the power of slogans like "black is beautiful," masses of black people continue to be socialized *via* mass media and non-progres-sive educational systems to internalize white supremacist thoughts and values. Without ongoing resistance struggle and progressive black liberation movements for self-determination, masses of black people (and everyone else) have no alternative worldview that affirms and celebrates blackness. Rituals of affirmation (celebrating black history, holidays, etc.) do not intervene on white supremacist socialization if they exist apart from active anti-racist struggle that seeks to transform society.

Since so many black folks have succumbed to the post-1960s notion that material success is more important than personal integrity, struggles for black self-determination that emphasize decolonization, loving blackness, have had little impact. As long as black folks are taught that the only way we can gain any degree of economic self-suf-ficiency or be materially privileged is by first rejecting blackness, our history and culture, then there will always be a crisis in black identity. Internalized racism will continue to erode collective struggle for self-determination. Masses of black children will continue to suffer from low self-esteem. And even though they may be motivated to strive harder to achieve success because they want to overcome feelings of inadequacy and lack, those successes will be undermined by the persistence of low self-esteem.

One of the tragic ironies of contemporary black life is that individuals succeed in acquiring material privilege often by sacrificing their positive connection to black culture and black experience. Paule Marshall's novel *Praisesong for the Widow* is a fictional portrayal of such tragedy. A young black couple, Avey and Jay, start their family life together empowered by their celebration and affirmation of black culture, but this connection is eroded as Jay strives for material success. Along the way, he adopts many mainstream white supremacist ways of thinking about black folks, expressing disdain for the very culture that had been a source of joy and spiritual fulfillment. Widowed, her children grown, Avey begins a process of critical remembering where she interrogates their past, asking herself:

> Would it have been possible to have done both? That is, to have wrested, as they had done over all those years, the means needed to rescue them from Halsey Street and to see the children through, while preserving, safeguarding, treasuring those things that had come down to them over the generations, which had defined them in a particular way. The most vivid, the most valuable part of themselves!

To recover herself and reclaim the love of blackness, Avey must be born again. In that state of rebirth and reawakening, she is able to understand what they could have done, what it would have called for: "Awareness. It would have called for an awareness of the worth of what they possessed. Vigilance. The vigilance needed to safeguard it. To hold it like a jewel high out of the envious reach of those who would either destroy it or claim it as their own." To recover herself, Avey has to relearn the past, understand her culture and history, affirm her ancestors, and assume responsibility for helping other black folks to decolonize their minds.

A culture of domination demands of all its citizens self-negation. The more marginalized, the more intense the demand. Since black people, especially the underclass, are bombarded by messages that we have no value, are worthless, it is no wonder that we fall prey to nihilistic despair or forms of addiction that provide momentary escape, illusions of grandeur, and temporary freedom from the pain of facing reality. In his essay "Healing the Heart of Justice," written for a special issue of *Creation Spirituality* highlighting the work of Howard Thurman, Victor Lewis shares his understanding of the profound traumatic impact of internalized oppression and addiction on black life. He concludes:

> To value ourselves rightly, infinitely, released from shame and self-rejection, implies knowing that we are claimed by the totality of life. To share in a loving community and vision that magnifies our strength and banishes fear and despair, here, we find the solid ground from which justice can flow like a mighty stream. Here, we find the fire that burns away the confusion that oppression heaped upon us during our childhood weakness. Here, we can see what needs to be done and find the strength to do it. To value ourselves rightly. To love one another. This is to heal the heart of justice.

We cannot value ourselves rightly without first breaking through the walls of denial which hide the depth of black self-hatred, inner anguish, and unreconciled pain.

Like Paule Marshall's character Avey, once our denial falls away we can work to heal ourselves through awareness. I am always amazed that the journey home to that place of mind and heart, where we recover ourselves in love, is constantly within reach and yet so many black folks never find the path. Mired in negativity and denial we are like sleep-walkers. Yet, if we dare to awaken, the path is before us. In *Hope and History,* Vincent Harding asks readers to consider: "In a society increasingly populated by peoples of color, by those who have known the disdain and domination of the Euro-American world, it would be fascinating to ponder self-love as a religious calling." Collectively, black people and our allies in struggle are empowered when we practice self-love as a revolutionary intervention that undermines practices of domination. Loving blackness as political resistance transforms our ways of looking and being, and thus creates the conditions necessary for us to move against the forces of domination and death and reclaim black life.

Chapter 2

Eating the Other

Desire and Resistance

This is theory's acute dilemma: that desire expresses itself most fully where only those absorbed in its delights and torments are present, that it triumphs most completely over other human preoccupations in places sheltered from view. Thus it is paradoxically in hiding that the secrets of desire come to light, that hegemonic impositions and their reversals, evasions, and subversions are at their most honest and active, and that the identities and disjunctures between felt passion and established culture place themselves on most vivid display.

—Joan Cocks
The Oppositional Imagination

Within current debates about race and difference, mass culture is the contemporary location that both publicly declares and perpetuates the idea that there is pleasure to be found in the acknowledgment and enjoyment of racial difference. The commodification of Otherness has been so successful because it is offered as a new delight, more intense, more satisfying than normal ways of doing and feeling. Within commodity culture, ethnicity becomes spice, seasoning that can liven up the dull dish that is mainstream white culture. Cultural taboos around sexuality and desire are transgressed and made explicit as the media bombards folks with a message of difference no longer based on the white supremacist assumption that "blondes have more fun." The "real fun" is to be had by bringing to the surface all those "nasty" unconscious fantasies and longings about contact with the Other embedded in the secret (not so secret) deep structure of white supremacy. In many ways it is a contemporary revival of interest in the "primitive," with a distinctly postmodern slant. As Marianna Torgovnick argues in *Gone Primitive: Savage Intellects, Modern Lives:*

> What is clear now is that the West's fascination with the primitive has to do with its own crises in identity, with its own need to clearly demarcate subject and object even while flirting with other ways of experiencing the universe.

Certainly from the standpoint of white supremacist capitalist patriarchy, the hope is that desires for the "primitive" or fantasies about the Other can be continually exploited, and that such exploitation will occur in a manner that reinscribes and maintains the *status quo.* Whether or not desire for contact with the Other, for connection rooted in the longing for pleasure, can act as a critical intervention challenging and subverting racist domination, inviting and enabling critical resistance, is an unrealized political possibility. Exploring how desire for the Other is expressed, manipulated, and transformed by encounters with difference and the different is a critical terrain that can indicate whether these potentially revolutionary longings are ever fulfilled.

Contemporary working-class British slang playfully converges the discourse of desire, sexuality, and the Other, evoking the phrase getting "a bit of the Other" as a way to speak about sexual encounter. Fucking is the Other. Displacing the notion of Otherness from race, ethnicity, skin-color, the body emerges as a site of contestation where sexuality is the metaphoric Other that threatens to take over, consume, transform *via* the experience of pleasure. Desired and sought after, sexual pleasure alters the consenting subject, deconstructing notions of will, control, coercive domination. Commodity culture in the United States exploits conventional thinking about race, gender, and sexual desire by "working" both the idea that racial difference marks one as Other and the assumption that sexual agency expressed within the context of racialized sexual encounter is a conversion experience that alters one's place and participation in contemporary cultural politics. The seductive promise of this encounter is that it will counter the terrorizing force of the *status quo* that makes identity fixed, static, a condition of containment and death. And that it is this willingness to transgress racial boundaries within the realm of the sexual that eradicates the fear that one must always conform to the norm to remain "safe." Difference can seduce precisely because the mainstream impo-

sition of sameness is a provocation that terrorizes. And as Jean
Baudrillard suggests in *Fatal Strategies:*

> Provocation—unlike seduction, which allows things to come into
> play and appear in secret, dual and ambiguous—does not leave
> you free to be; it calls on you to reveal yourself as you are. It is
> always blackmail by identity (and thus a symbolic murder, since
> you are never that, except precisely by being condemned to it).

To make one's self vulnerable to the seduction of difference, to
seek an encounter with the Other, does not require that one relinquish
forever one's mainstream positionality. When race and ethnicity become commodified as resources for pleasure, the culture of specific
groups, as well as the bodies of individuals, can be seen as constituting
an alternative playground where members of dominating races, genders, sexual practices affirm their power-over in intimate relations with
the Other. While teaching at Yale, I walked one bright spring day in the
downtown area of New Haven, which is close to campus and invariably
brings one into contact with many of the poor black people who live
nearby, and found myself walking behind a group of very blond, very
white, jock type boys. (The downtown area was often talked about as
an arena where racist domination of blacks by whites was contested on
the sidewalks, as white people, usually male, often jocks, used their
bodies to force black people off the sidewalk, to push our bodies aside,
without ever looking at us or acknowledging our presence.) Seemingly
unaware of my presence, these young men talked about their plans to
fuck as many girls from other racial/ethnic groups as they could "catch"
before graduation. They "ran" it down. Black girls were high on the list,
Native American girls hard to find, Asian girls (all lumped into the same
category), deemed easier to entice, were considered "prime targets."
Talking about this overheard conversation with my students, I found
that it was commonly accepted that one "shopped" for sexual partners
in the same way one "shopped" for courses at Yale, and that race and
ethnicity was a serious category on which selections were based.

To these young males and their buddies, fucking was a way to
confront the Other, as well as a way to make themselves over, to leave
behind white "innocence" and enter the world of "experience." As is
often the case in this society, they were confident that non-white people
had more life experience, were more worldly, sensual, and sexual
because they were different. Getting a bit of the Other, in this case
engaging in sexual encounters with non-white females, was considered
a ritual of transcendence, a movement out into a world of difference

that would transform, an acceptable rite of passage. The direct objective
was not simply to sexually possess the Other; it was to be changed in
some way by the encounter. "Naturally," the presence of the Other, the
body of the Other, was seen as existing to serve the ends of white male
desires. Writing about the way difference is recouped in the West in
"The 'Primitive' Unconscious of Modern Art, or White Skin, Black
Masks," Hal Foster reminds readers that Picasso regarded the tribal
objects he had acquired as "witnesses" rather than as "models." Foster
critiques this positioning of the Other, emphasizing that this recognition
was "contingent upon instrumentality": "In this way, through affinity
and use, the primitive is sent up into the service of the Western tradition
(which is then seen to have partly produced it)." A similar critique can
be made of contemporary trends in inter-racial sexual desire and
contact initiated by white males. They claim the body of the colored
Other instrumentally, as unexplored terrain, a symbolic frontier that will
be fertile ground for their reconstruction of the masculine norm, for
asserting themselves as transgressive desiring subjects. They call upon
the Other to be both witness and participant in this transformation.

For white boys to openly discuss their desire for colored girls (or
boys) publicly announces their break with a white supremacist past that
would have such desire articulated only as taboo, as secret, as shame.
They see their willingness to openly name their desire for the Other as
affirmation of cultural plurality (its impact on sexual preference and
choice). Unlike racist white men who historically violated the bodies
of black women/women of color to assert their position as colo-
nizer/conqueror, these young men see themselves as non-racists, who
choose to transgress racial boundaries within the sexual realm not to
dominate the Other, but rather so that they can be acted upon, so that
they can be changed utterly. Not at all attuned to those aspects of their
sexual fantasies that irrevocably link them to collective white racist
domination, they believe their desire for contact represents a progressive change in white attitudes towards non-whites. They do not see
themselves as perpetuating racism. To them the most potent indication
of that change is the frank expression of longing, the open declaration
of desire, the need to be intimate with dark Others. The point is to be
changed by this convergence of pleasure and Otherness. One dares—
acts—on the assumption that the exploration into the world of difference, into the body of the Other, will provide a greater, more intense
pleasure than any that exists in the ordinary world of one's familiar
racial group. And even though the conviction is that the familiar world

will remain intact even as one ventures outside it, the hope is that they will reenter that world no longer the same.

The current wave of "imperialist nostalgia" (defined by Renato Rosaldo in *Culture and Truth* as "nostalgia, often found under imperialism, where people mourn the passing of what they themselves have transformed" or as "a process of yearning for what one has destroyed that is a form of mystification") often obscures contemporary cultural strategies deployed not to mourn but to celebrate the sense of a continuum of "primitivism." In mass culture, imperialist nostalgia takes the form of reenacting and reritualizing in different ways the imperialist, colonizing journey as narrative fantasy of power and desire, of seduction by the Other. This longing is rooted in the atavistic belief that the spirit of the "primitive" resides in the bodies of dark Others whose cultures, traditions, and lifestyles may indeed be irrevocably changed by imperialism, colonization, and racist domination. The desire to make contact with those bodies deemed Other, with no apparent will to dominate, assuages the guilt of the past, even takes the form of a defiant gesture where one denies accountability and historical connection. Most importantly, it establishes a contemporary narrative where the suffering imposed by structures of domination on those designated Other is deflected by an emphasis on seduction and longing where the desire is not to make the Other over in one's image but to become the Other.

Whereas mournful imperialist nostalgia constitutes the betrayed and abandoned world of the Other as an accumulation of lack and loss, contemporary longing for the "primitive" is expressed by the projection onto the Other of a sense of plenty, bounty, a field of dreams. Commenting on this strategy in "Readings in Cultural Resistance," Hal Foster contends, "Difference is thus used productively; indeed, in a social order which seems to know no outside (and which must contrive its own transgressions to redefine its limits), difference is often fabricated in the interests of social control as well as of commodity innovation." Masses of young people dissatisfied by U.S. imperialism, unemployment, lack of economic opportunity, afflicted by the postmodern malaise of alienation, no sense of grounding, no redemptive identity, can be manipulated by cultural strategies that offer Otherness as appeasement, particularly through commodification. The contemporary crises of identity in the west, especially as experienced by white youth, are eased when the "primitive" is recouped *via* a focus on diversity and pluralism which suggests the Other can provide life-sustaining alternatives. Concurrently, diverse ethnic/racial groups can also embrace this sense of specialness, that histories and experience once seen as worthy only of disdain can be looked upon with awe.

Cultural appropriation of the Other assuages feelings of deprivation and lack that assault the psyches of radical white youth who choose to be disloyal to western civilization. Concurrently, marginalized groups, deemed Other, who have been ignored, rendered invisible, can be seduced by the emphasis on Otherness, by its commodification, because it offers the promise of recognition and reconciliation. When the dominant culture demands that the Other be offered as sign that progressive political change is taking place, that the American Dream can indeed be inclusive of difference, it invites a resurgence of essentialist cultural nationalism. The acknowledged Other must assume recognizable forms. Hence, it is not African American culture formed in resistance to contemporary situations that surfaces, but nostalgic evocation of a "glorious" past. And even though the focus is often on the ways that this past was "superior" to the present, this cultural narrative relies on stereotypes of the "primitive," even as it eschews the term, to evoke a world where black people were in harmony with nature and with one another. This narrative is linked to white western conceptions of the dark Other, not to a radical questioning of those representations.

Should youth of any other color not know how to move closer to the Other, or how to get in touch with the "primitive," consumer culture promises to show the way. It is within the commercial realm of advertising that the drama of Otherness finds expression. Encounters with Otherness are clearly marked as more exciting, more intense, and more threatening. The lure is the combination of pleasure and danger. In the cultural marketplace the Other is coded as having the capacity to be more alive, as holding the secret that will allow those who venture and dare to break with the cultural anhedonia (defined in Sam Keen's *The Passionate Life* as "the insensitivity to pleasure, the incapacity for experiencing happiness") and experience sensual and spiritual renewal. Before his untimely death, Michel Foucault, the quintessential transgressive thinker in the west, confessed that he had real difficulties experiencing pleasure:

> I think that pleasure is a very difficult behavior. It's not as simple as that to enjoy one's self. And I must say that's my dream. I would like and I hope I die of an overdose of pleasure of any kind. Because I think it's really difficult and I always have the feeling that I do not feel *the* pleasure, the complete total pleasure and, for me, it's related to death. Because I think that the kind of pleasure

I would consider as *the* real pleasure, would be so deep, so intense, so overwhelming that I couldn't survive it. I would die.

Though speaking from the standpoint of his individual experience, Foucault voices a dilemma felt by many in the west. It is precisely that longing for *the* pleasure that has led the white west to sustain a romantic fantasy of the "primitive" and the concrete search for a real primitive paradise, whether that location be a country or a body, a dark continent or dark flesh, perceived as the perfect embodiment of that possibility.

Within this fantasy of Otherness, the longing for pleasure is projected as a force that can disrupt and subvert the will to dominate. It acts to both mediate and challenge. In Lorraine Hansberry's play *Les Blancs,* it is the desire to experience closeness and community that leads the white American journalist Charles to make contact and attempt to establish a friendship with Tshembe, the black revolutionary. Charles struggles to divest himself of white supremacist privilege, eschews the role of colonizer, and refuses racist exoticization of blacks. Yet he continues to assume that he alone can decide the nature of his relationship to a black person. Evoking the idea of a universal transcendent subject, he appeals to Tshembe by repudiating the role of oppressor, declaring, "I am a man who feels like talking." When Tshembe refuses to accept the familiar relationship offered him, refuses to satisfy Charles' longing for camaraderie and contact, he is accused of hating white men. Calling attention to situations where white people have oppressed other white people, Tshembe challenges Charles, declaring that "race is a device—no more, no less," that "it explains nothing at all." Pleased with this disavowal of the importance of race, Charles agrees, stating "race hasn't a thing to do with it." Tshembe then deconstructs the category "race" without minimizing or ignoring the impact of racism, telling him:

> I believe in the recognition of devices as *devices*—but I also believe in the reality of those devices. In one century men choose to hide their conquests under religion, in another under race. So you and I may recognize the fraudulence of the device in both cases, but the fact remains that a man who has a sword run through him because he will not become a Moslem or a Christian—or who is lynched in Mississippi or Zatembe because he is black—is suffering the utter reality of that device of conquest. And it is pointless to pretend that it doesn't *exist*—merely because it is a lie…

Again and again Tshembe must make it clear to Charles that subject to subject contact between white and black which signals the absence of domination, of an oppressor/oppressed relationship, must emerge through mutual choice and negotiation. That simply by expressing their desire for "intimate" contact with black people, white people do not eradicate the politics of racial domination as they are made manifest in personal interaction.

Mutual recognition of racism, its impact both on those who are dominated and those who dominate, is the only standpoint that makes possible an encounter between races that is not based on denial and fantasy. For it is the ever present reality of racist domination, of white supremacy, that renders problematic the desire of white people to have contact with the Other. Often it is this reality that is most masked when representations of contact between white and non-white, white and black, appear in mass culture. One area where the politics of diversity and its concomitant insistence on inclusive representation have had serious impact is advertising. Now that sophisticated market surveys reveal the extent to which poor and materially underprivileged people of all races/ethnicities consume products, sometimes in a quantity disproportionate to income, it has become more evident that these markets can be appealed to with advertising. Market surveys revealed that black people buy more Pepsi than other soft drinks and suddenly we see more Pepsi commercials with black people in them.

The world of fashion has also come to understand that selling products is heightened by the exploitation of Otherness. The success of Benneton ads, which with their racially diverse images have become a model for various advertising strategies, epitomize this trend. Many ads that focus on Otherness make no explicit comments, or rely solely on visual messages, but the recent fall *Tweeds* catalogue provides an excellent example of the way contemporary culture exploits notions of Otherness with both visual images and text. The catalogue cover shows a map of Egypt. Inserted into the heart of the country, so to speak, is a photo of a white male (an *Out of Africa* type) holding an Egyptian child in his arms. Behind them is not the scenery of Egypt as modern city, but rather shadowy silhouettes resembling huts and palm trees. Inside, the copy quotes Gustave Flaubert's comments from *Flaubert in Egypt*. For seventy-five pages Egypt becomes a landscape of dreams, and its darker-skinned people background, scenery to highlight whiteness, and the longing of whites to inhabit, if only for a time, the world of the Other. The front page copy declares:

> We did not want our journey to be filled with snapshots of an
> antique land. Instead, we wanted to rediscover our clothing in
> the context of a different culture. Was it possible, we won-
> dered, to express our style in an unaccustomed way, sur-
> rounded by Egyptian colors, Egyptian textures, even bathed in
> an ancient Egyptian light?

Is this not imperialist nostalgia at its best—potent expression of
longing for the "primitive"? One desires "a bit of the Other" to
enhance the blank landscape of whiteness. Nothing is said in the
text about Egyptian people, yet their images are spread throughout
its pages. Often their faces are blurred by the camera, a strategy
which ensures that readers will not become more enthralled by the
images of Otherness than those of whiteness. The point of this
photographic attempt at defamiliarization is to distance us from
whiteness, so that we will return to it more intently.

In most of the "snapshots," all carefully selected and posed, there
is no mutual looking. One desires contact with the Other even as one
wishes boundaries to remain intact. When bodies contact one another,
touch, it almost always a white hand doing the touching, white hands
that rest on the bodies of colored people, unless the Other is a child.
One snapshot of "intimate" contact shows two women with their arms
linked, the way close friends might link arms. One is an Egyptian
woman identified by a caption that reads "with her husband and baby,
Ahmedio A'bass, 22, leads a gypsy's life"; the second woman is a
white-skinned model. The linked hands suggest that these two women
share something, have a basis of contact and indeed they do, they
resemble one another, look more alike than different. The message
again is that "primitivism," though more apparent in the Other, also
resides in the white self. It is not the world of Egypt, of "gypsy" life, that
is affirmed by this snapshot, but the ability of white people to roam the
world, making contact. Wearing pants while standing next to her dark
"sister" who wears a traditional skirt, the white woman appears to be
cross-dressing (an ongoing theme in *Tweeds*). Visually the image suggests that she and first world white women like her are liberated, have
greater freedom to roam than darker women who live peripatetic
lifestyles.

Significantly, the catalogue that followed this one focused on
Norway. There the people of Norway are not represented, only the
scenery. Are we to assume that white folks from this country are as at
"home" in Norway as they are here so there is no need for captions and

explanations? In this visual text, whiteness is the unifying feature—not culture. Of course, for *Tweeds* to exploit Otherness to dramatize "whiteness" while in Egypt, it cannot include darker-skinned models since the play on contrasts that is meant to highlight "whiteness" could not happen nor could the exploitation that urges consumption of the Other whet the appetite in quite the same way; just as inclusion of darker-skinned models in the Norway issue might suggest that the west is not as unified by whiteness as this visual text suggests. Essentially speaking, both catalogues evoke a sense that white people are homogeneous and share "white bread culture."

Those progressive white intellectuals who are particularly critical of "essentialist" notions of identity when writing about mass culture, race, and gender have not focused their critiques on white identity and the way essentialism informs representations of whiteness. It is always the non-white, or in some cases the non-heterosexual Other, who is guilty of essentialism. Few white intellectuals call attention to the way in which the contemporary obsession with white consumption of the dark Other has served as a catalyst for the resurgence of essentialist based racial and ethnic nationalism. Black nationalism, with its emphasis on black separatism, is resurging as a response to the assumption that white cultural imperialism and white yearning to possess the Other are invading black life, appropriating and violating black culture. As a survival strategy, black nationalism surfaces most strongly when white cultural appropriation of black culture threatens to decontextualize and thereby erase knowledge of the specific historical and social context of black experience from which cultural productions and distinct black styles emerge. Yet most white intellectuals writing critically about black culture do not see these constructive dimensions of black nationalism and tend to see it instead as naive essentialism, rooted in notions of ethnic purity that resemble white racist assumptions.

In the essay "Hip, and the Long Front of Color," white critic Andrew Ross interprets Langston Hughes' declaration ("You've taken my blues and gone—You sing 'em on Broadway—And you sing 'em in Hollywood Bowl—And you mixed 'em up with symphonies—And you fixed 'em—So they don't sound like me. Yep, you done taken my blues and gone.") as a "complaint" that "celebrates...folk purism." Yet Hughes' declaration can be heard as a critical comment on appropriation (not a complaint). A distinction must be made between the longing for ongoing cultural recognition of the creative source of particular African American cultural productions that emerge from distinct black experience, and essentialist investments in notions of ethnic purity that undergird crude versions of black nationalism.

Currently, the commodification of difference promotes paradigms of consumption wherein whatever difference the Other inhabits is eradicated, *via* exchange, by a consumer cannibalism that not only displaces the Other but denies the significance of that Other's history through a process of decontextualization. Like the "primitivism" Hal Foster maintains "absorbs the primitive, in part *via* the concept of affinity" contemporary notions of "crossover" expand the parameters of cultural production to enable the voice of the non-white Other to be heard by a larger audience even as it denies the specificity of that voice, or as it recoups it for its own use.

This scenario is played out in the film *Heart Condition* when Mooney, a white racist cop, has a heart transplant and receives a heart from Stone, a black man he has been trying to destroy because Stone has seduced Chris, the white call girl that Mooney loves. Transformed by his new "black heart," Mooney learns how to be more seductive, changes his attitudes towards race, and, in perfect Hollywood style, wins the girl in the end. Unabashedly dramatizing a process of "eating the Other" (in ancient religious practices among so called "primitive" people, the heart of a person may be ripped out and eaten so that one can embody that person's spirit or special characteristics), a film like *Heart Condition* addresses the fantasies of a white audience. At the end of the film, Mooney, reunited with Chris through marriage and surrounded by Stone's caring black kin, has become the "father" of Chris and Stone's bi-racial baby who is dark-skinned, the color of his father. Stone, whose ghost has haunted Mooney, is suddenly "history"—gone. Interestingly, this mainstream film suggests that patriarchal struggle over "ownership" (i.e., sexual possession of white women's bodies) is the linchpin of racism. Once Mooney can accept and bond with Stone on the phallocentric basis of their mutual possession and "desire" for Chris, their homosocial bonding makes brotherhood possible and eradicates the racism that has kept them apart. Significantly, patriarchal bonding mediates and becomes the basis for the eradication of racism.

In part, this film offers a version of racial pluralism that challenges racism by suggesting that the white male's life will be richer, more pleasurable, if he accepts diversity. Yet it also offers a model of change that still leaves a white supremacist capitalist patriarchy intact, though no longer based on coercive domination of black people. It insists that white male desire must be sustained by the "labor" (in this case the heart) of a dark Other. The fantasy, of course, is that this labor will no longer be exacted *via* domination, but will be given willingly. Not surprisingly, most black folks talked about this film as "racist." The young desirable handsome intelligent black male (who we are told *via* his own self-portrait is "hung like a shetland pony") must die so that the aging white male can both restore his potency (he awakens from the transplant to find a replica of a huge black penis standing between his legs) and be more sensitive and loving. Torgovnick reminds readers in *Gone Primitive* that a central element in the western fascination with primitivism is its focus on "overcoming alienation from the body, restoring the body, and hence the self, to a relation of full and easy harmony with nature or the cosmos." It is this conceptualization of the "primitive" and the black male as quintessential representative that is dramatized in *Heart Condition*. One weakness in Torgovnick's work is her refusal to recognize how deeply the idea of the "primitive" is entrenched in the psyches of everyday people, shaping contemporary racist stereotypes, perpetuating racism. When she suggests, "our own culture by and large rejects the association of blackness with rampant sexuality and irrationality, with decadence and corruption, with disease and death," one can only wonder what culture she is claiming as her own.

Films like *Heart Condition* make black culture and black life backdrop, scenery for narratives that essentially focus on white people. Nationalist black voices critique this cultural crossover, its decentering of black experience as it relates to black people, and its insistence that it is acceptable for whites to explore blackness as long as their ultimate agenda is appropriation. Politically "on the case" when they critique white cultural appropriation of black experience that reinscribes it within a "cool" narrative of white supremacy, these voices can not be dismissed as naive. They are misguided when they suggest that white cultural imperialism is best critiqued and resisted by black separatism, or when they evoke outmoded notions of ethnic purity that deny the way in which black people exist in the west, are western, and are at times positively influenced by aspects of white culture.

Steve Perry's essay "The Politics of Crossover" deconstructs no-tions of racial purity by outlining the diverse inter-cultural exchanges between black and white musicians, yet he seems unable to ac-knowledge that this reality does not alter the fact that white cultural imperialist appropriation of black culture maintains white supremacy and is a constant threat to black liberation. Even though Perry can admit that successful black crossover artists, such as Prince, carry the "cross-over impulse" to the point where it "begins to be a denial of blackness," he is unable to see this as threatening to black people who are daily resisting racism, advocating ongoing decolonization, and in need of an effective black liberation struggle.

Underlying Perry's condescension, and at times contemptuous attitude towards all expressions of black nationalism, is a traditional leftist insistence on the primacy of class over race. This standpoint inhibits his capacity to understand the specific political needs of black people that are addressed, however inadequately, by essentialist-based black separatism. As Howard Winant clarifies in "Postmodern Racial Politics in the United States: Difference and Inequality," one must understand race to understand class because "in the postmodern political framework of the contemporary United States, hegemony is determined by the articulation of race and class." And most importantly it is the "ability of the right to represent class issues in racial terms" that is "central to the current pattern of conservative hegemony." Certainly an essentialist-based black nationalism imbued with and perpetuating many racial stereotypes is an inadequate and ineffective response to the urgent demand that there be renewed and viable revolutionary black liberation struggle that would take radical politicization of black people, strategies of decolonization, critiques of capitalism, and ongoing resistance to racist domination as its central goals.

Resurgence of black nationalism as an expression of black people's desire to guard against white cultural appropriation indicates the extent to which the commodification of blackness (including the nationalist agenda) has been reinscribed and marketed with an atavistic narrative, a fantasy of Otherness that reduces protest to spectacle and stimulates even greater longing for the "primitive." Given this cultural context, black nationalism is more a gesture of powerlessness than a sign of critical resistance. Who can take seriously Public Enemy's insistence that the dominated and their allies "fight the power" when that declaration is in no way linked to a collective organized struggle. When young black people mouth 1960s' black nationalist rhetoric, don Kente cloth, gold medallions, dread their hair, and diss the white folks they hang out with, they expose the way meaningless commodification strips these signs of political integrity and meaning, denying the possibility that they can serve as a catalyst for concrete political action. As signs, their power to ignite critical consciousness is diffused when they are commodified. Communities of resistance are replaced by communities of consumption. As Stuart and Elizabeth Ewen emphasize in *Channels of Desire:*

> The politics of consumption must be understood as something more than what to buy, or even what to boycott. Consumption is a social relationship, the dominant relationship in our society—

one that makes it harder and harder for people to hold together, to create community. At a time when for many of us the possibility of meaningful change seems to elude our grasp, it is a question of immense social and political proportions. To establish popular initiative, consumerism must be transcended—a difficult but central task facing all people who still seek a better way of life.

Work by black artists that is overtly political and radical is rarely linked to an oppositional political culture. When commodified it is easy for consumers to ignore political messages. And even though a product like rap articulates narratives of coming to critical political consciousness, it also exploits stereotypes and essentialist notions of blackness (like black people have natural rhythm and are more sexual). The television show *In Living Color* is introduced by lyrics that tell listeners "do what you wanna do." Positively, this show advocates transgression, yet it negatively promotes racist stereotypes, sexism, and homophobia. Black youth culture comes to stand for the outer limits of "outness." The commercial nexus exploits the culture's desire (expressed by whites and blacks) to inscribe blackness as "primitive" sign, as wildness, and with it the suggestion that black people have secret access to intense pleasure, particularly pleasures of the body. It is the young black male body that is seen as epitomizing this promise of wildness, of unlimited physical prowess and unbridled eroticism. It was this black body that was most "desired" for its labor in slavery, and it is this body that is most represented in contemporary popular culture as the body to be watched, imitated, desired, possessed. Rather than a sign of pleasure in daily life outside the realm of consumption, the young black male body is represented most graphically as the body in pain.

Regarded fetishisticly in the psycho-sexual racial imagination of youth culture, the real bodies of young black men are daily viciously assaulted by white racist violence, black on black violence, the violence of overwork, and the violence of addiction and disease. In her introduction to *The Body in Pain,* Elaine Scarry states that "there is ordinarily no language for pain," that "physical pain is difficult to express; and that this inexpressibility has political consequences." This is certainly true of black male pain. Black males are unable to fully articulate and acknowledge the pain in their lives. They do not have a public discourse or audience within racist society that enables them to give their pain a hearing. Sadly, black men often evoke racist rhetoric that identifies the black male as animal, speaking of themselves as "endangered species," as "primitive," in their bid to gain recognition of their suffering.

When young black men acquire a powerful public voice and presence *via* cultural production, as has happened with the explosion of rap music, it does not mean that they have a vehicle that will enable them to articulate that pain. Providing narratives that are mainly about power and pleasure, that advocate resistance to racism yet support phallocentrism, rap denies this pain. True, it was conditions of suffering and survival, of poverty, deprivation, and lack that characterized the marginal locations from which breakdancing and rap emerged. Described as "rituals" by participants in the poor urban non-white communities where they first took place, these practices offered individuals a means to gain public recognition and voice. Much of the psychic pain that black people experience daily in a white supremacist context is caused by dehumanizing oppressive forces, forces that render us invisible and deny us recognition. Michael H. (commenting on style in Stuart Ewen's book *All Consuming Images*) also talks about this desire for attention, stating that breakdancing and rap are a way to say "listen to my story, about myself, life, and romance." Rap music provides a public voice for young black men who are usually silenced and overlooked. It emerged in the streets—outside the confines of a domesticity shaped and informed by poverty, outside enclosed spaces where young males body had to be contained and controlled.

In its earliest stages, rap was "a male thing." Young black and brown males could not breakdance and rap in cramped living spaces. Male creativity, expressed in rap and dancing, required wide-open spaces, symbolic frontiers where the body could do its thing, expand, grow, and move, surrounded by a watching crowd. Domestic space, equated with repression and containment, as well as with the "feminine" was resisted and rejected so that an assertive patriarchal paradigm of competitive masculinity and its concomitant emphasis on physical prowess could emerge. As a result, much rap music is riddled with sexism and misogyny. The public story of black male lives narrated by rap music speaks directly to and against white racist domination, but only indirectly hints at the enormity of black male pain. Constructing the black male body as site of pleasure and power, rap and the dances associated with it suggest vibrancy, intensity, and an unsurpassed joy in living. It may very well be that living on the edge, so close to the possibility of being "exterminated" (which is how many young black males feel) heightens one's ability to risk and make one's pleasure more intense. It is this charge, generated by the tension between pleasure and danger, death and desire, that Foucault evokes when he speaks of that *complete total pleasure* that is related to death. Though Foucault is speaking as an individual, his words resonate in a culture affected by anhedonia—the inability to feel pleasure. In the United States, where our senses are daily assaulted and bombarded to such an extent that an emotional numbness sets in, it may take being "on the edge" for individuals to feel intensely. Hence the overall tendency in the culture is to see young black men as both dangerous and desirable.

Certainly the relationship between the experience of Otherness, of pleasure and death, is explored in the film *The Cook, the Thief, His Wife and Her Lover,* which critiques white male imperialist domination even though this dimension of the movie was rarely mentioned when it was discussed in this country. Reviewers of the film did not talk about the representation of black characters, one would have assumed from such writing that the cast was all white and British. Yet black males are a part of the community of subordinates who are dominated by one controlling white man. After he has killed her lover, his blonde white wife speaks to the dark-skinned cook, who clearly represents non-white immigrants, about the links between death and pleasure. It is he who explains to her the way blackness is viewed in the white imagination. The cook tells her that black foods are desired because they remind those who eat them of death, and that this is why they cost so much. When they are eaten (in the film, always and only by white people), the cook as native informant tells us it is a way to flirt with death, to flaunt one's power. He says that to eat black food is a way to say "death, I am eating you" and thereby conquering fear and acknowledging power. White racism, imperialism, and sexist domination prevail by courageous consumption. It is by eating the Other (in this case, death) that one asserts power and privilege.

A similar confrontation may be taking place within popular culture in this society as young white people seek contact with dark Others. They may long to conquer their fear of darkness and death. On the reactionary right, white youth may be simply seeking to affirm "white power" when they flirt with having contact with the Other. Yet there are many white youths who desire to move beyond whiteness. Critical of white imperialism and "into" difference, they desire cultural spaces where boundaries can be transgressed, where new and alternative relations can be formed. These desires are dramatized by two contemporary films, John Waters' *Hairspray* and the more recent film by Jim Jarmusch, *Mystery Train.* In *Hairspray,* the "cool" white people, working-class Traci and her middle-class boyfriend, transgress class and race boundaries to dance with black folks. She says to him as they stand in a rat-infested alley with winos walking about, "I wish I was dark-skinned." And he replies, "Traci, our souls are black even though our skin is white." Blackness—the culture, the music, the people—is once again associated with pleasure as well as death and decay. Yet their recognition of the particular pleasures and sorrows black folks experience does not lead to cultural appropriation but to an appreciation that extends into the realm of the political—Traci dares to support racial integration. In this film, the longing and desire whites express for contact with black culture is coupled with the recognition of the culture's value. One does not transgress boundaries to stay the same, to reassert white domination. *Hairspray* is nearly unique in its attempt to construct a fictive universe where white working class "undesirables" are in solidarity with black people. When Traci says she wants to be black, blackness becomes a metaphor for freedom, an end to boundaries. Blackness is vital not because it represents the "primitive" but because it invites engagement in a revolutionary ethos that dares to challenge and disrupt the *status quo*. Like white rappers MC Search and Prime Minister Pete Nice who state that they "want to bring forth some sort of positive message to black people, that there are white people out there who understand what this is all about, who understand we have to get past all the hatred," Traci shifts her positionality to stand in solidarity with black people. She is concerned about her freedom and sees her liberation linked to black liberation and an effort to end racist domination.

Expressing a similar solidarity with the agenda of "liberation," which includes freedom to transgress, Sandra Bernhard, in her new film *Without You I'm Nothing,* also associates blackness with this struggle. In the March issue of *Interview* she says that the movie has "this whole black theme, which is like a personal metaphor for being on the outside." This statement shows that Bernhard's sense of blackness is both problematic and complex. The film opens with her pretending she is black. Dressed in African clothing, she renders problematic the question of race and identity, for this representation suggests that racial identity can be socially constructed even as it implies that cultural appropriation falls short because it is always imitation, fake. Conversely, she contrasts her attempt to be a black woman in drag with the black female's attempt to imitate a white female look. Bernhard's film suggests that alternative white culture derives its standpoint, its impetus from black culture. Identifying herself with marginalized Others, Bernhard's Jewish heritage as well as her sexually ambiguous erotic practices are experiences that already place her outside the mainstream. Yet the film does not clarify the nature of her identification with black culture. Throughout the film, she places herself in a relationship of comparison and competition with black women, seemingly exposing white female envy of black women and their desire to "be" imitation black women; yet she also pokes fun at black females. The unidentified black woman who appears in the film, like a phantom, looking at herself in the mirror has no name and no voice. Yet her image is always contrasted with that of Bernhard. Is she the fantasy Other Bernhard desires to become? Is she the fantasy Other Bernhard desires? The last scene of the film seems to confirm that black womanhood is the yardstick Bernhard uses to measure herself. Though she playfully suggests in the film that the work of black women singers like Nina Simone and Diana Ross is derivative, "stolen" from her work, this inversion of reality ironically calls attention to the way white women have "borrowed" from black women without acknowledging the debt they owe. In many ways, the film critiques white cultural appropriation of "blackness" that leaves no trace. Indeed, Bernhard identifies that she had her artistic beginnings working in black clubs, among black people. Though acknowledging where she is coming from, the film shows Bernhard clearly defining an artistic performance space that only she as a white woman can inhabit. Black women have no public, paying audience for our funny imitations of white girls. Indeed, it is difficult to imagine any setting other than an all black space where black women could use comedy to critique and ridicule white womanhood in the way Bernhard mocks black womanhood.

Closing the scene shrouded in a cloak that resembles an American flag, Bernhard unveils her nearly nude body. The film ends with the figure of the black woman, who has heretofore only been in the background, foregrounded as the only remaining audience watching this seductive performance. As though she is seeking acknowledgment of her identity, her power, Bernhard stares at the black woman, who returns her look with a contemptuous gaze. As if this look of disinterest and dismissal is not enough to convey her indifference, she removes a tube of red lipstick from her purse and writes on the table "fuck Sandra Bernhard." Her message seems to be: "you may need black culture since without us you are nothing, but black women have no need of you." In the film, all the white women strip, flaunt their sexuality, and appear to be directing their attention to a black male gaze. It is this standpoint that the film suggests may lead them to ignore black women and only notice what black women think of them when we are "right up in their face."

Bernhard's film walks a critical tightrope. On one hand it mocks white appropriation of black culture, white desire for black (as in the scene where Bernhard with a blonde white girl persona is seen being "boned" by a black man whom we later find is mainly concerned about his hair—i.e., his own image) even as the film works as spectacle largely because of the clever ways Bernhard "uses" black culture and standard racial stereotypes. Since so many of the representations of blackness in the film are stereotypes it does not really go against the Hollywood cinematic grain. And like the *Tweeds* catalogue on Egypt, ultimately black people are reduced, as Bernhard declares in *Interview,* to "a personal metaphor." Blackness is the backdrop of Otherness she uses to insist on and clarify her status as Other, as cool, hip, and transgressive. Even though she lets audiences know that as an entertainment "rookie" she had her start working in close association with black people, the point is to name where she begins to highlight how far she has come. When Bernhard "arrives," able to exploit Otherness in a big time way, she arrives alone, not in the company of black associates. They are scenery, backdrop, background. Yet the end of the film problematizes this leave-taking. Is Bernhard leaving black folks or has she been rejected and dismissed? Maybe it's mutual. Like her entertainment cohort Madonna, Bernhard leaves her encounters with the Other richer than she was at the onset. We have no idea how the Other leaves her.

When I began thinking and doing research for this piece, I talked to folks from various locations about whether they thought the focus on race, Otherness, and difference in mass culture was challenging racism. There was overall agreement that the message that acknowledgment and exploration of racial difference can be pleasurable represents a breakthrough, a challenge to white supremacy, to various systems of domination. The over-riding fear is that cultural, ethnic, and racial differences will be continually commodified and offered up as new dishes to enhance the white palate—that the Other will be eaten, consumed, and forgotten. After weeks of debating with one another about the distinction between cultural appropriation and cultural appreciation, students in my introductory course on black literature were convinced that something radical was happening, that these issues were "coming out in the open." Within a context where desire for contact with those who are different or deemed Other is not considered bad, politically incorrect, or wrong-minded, we can begin to conceptualize and identify ways that desire informs our political choices and affiliations. Acknowledging ways the desire for pleasure, and that includes erotic longings, informs our politics, our understanding of difference, we may know better how desire disrupts, subverts, and makes resistance possible. We cannot, however, accept these new images uncritically.

Chapter 3

Revolutionary Black Women
Making Ourselves Subject

Sitting in a circle with several black women and one black man, children running in and out, on a hot Saturday evening at the office of the Council on Battered Women, after working all day, my spirits are renewed sharing with this group aspects of my development as a feminist thinker and writer. I listen intently as a sister comrade talks about her responses to my work. Initially she was disturbed by it. "I didn't want to hear it," she says. "I resented it." The talk in the group is about black women and violence, not just the violence inflicted by black men, but the violence black women do to children, and the violence we do to one another. Particularly challenged by the essay in *Talking Back,* "Violence in Intimate Relationships: A Feminist Perspective," because of its focus on a continuum of dominating violence that begins not with male violence against women but with the violence parents do to children, individual black women in the group felt they had to interrogate their parental practice.

There is little feminist work focusing on violence against children from a black perspective. Sharing our stories, we talked about the ways styles of parenting in diverse black communities support and perpetuate the use of violence as a means of domestic social control. We connected common acceptance of violence against children with community acceptance of male violence against women. Indeed, I suggested many of us were raised in families where we completely accepted the notion that violence was an appropriate response to crisis.

In such settings it was not rare for black women to be verbally abusive and physically violent with one another. Our most vivid memories (in the group) of black women fighting one another took place in public settings where folks struggled over men or over gossip. There was no one in the group who had not witnessed an incident of black women doing violence to one another.

I shared with the group the declaration from Nikki Giovanni's "Woman Poem": "I ain't shit. You must be lower than that to care." This quote speaks directly to the rage and hostility oppressed/exploited people can turn inward on themselves and outward towards those who care about them. This has often been the case in black female encounters with one another. A vast majority of black women in this society receive sustained care only from other black women. That care does not always mediate or alter rage, or the desire to inflict pain; it may provoke it. Hostile responses to care echo the truth of Giovanni's words. When I first puzzled over them, I could hear voices in the background questioning, "How can you be worth anything if you care about me, who is worth nothing?" Among black women, such deeply internalized pain and self-rejection informs the aggression inflicted on the mirror image—other black women. It is this reality Audre Lorde courageously describes in her essay "Eye to Eye: Black Women, Hatred, and Anger." Critically interrogating, Lorde asks:

> ...why does that anger unleash itself most tellingly against another Black woman at the least excuse? Why do I judge her in a more critical light than any other, becoming enraged when she does not measure up? And if behind the object of my attack should lie the face of my own self, unaccepted, then what could possibly quench a fire fueled by such reciprocating passions?

I was reminded of Lorde's essay while seated among black women, listening to them talk about the intensity of their initial "anger" at my work. Retrospectively, that anger was vividly evoked so that I would know that individual black women present had grappled with it, moved beyond it, and come to a place of political awareness that allowed us to openly acknowledge it as part of their process of coming to consciousness and go on to critically affirm one another. They wanted me to understand the process of transformation, the movement of their passions from rage to care and recognition. It is this empowering process that enables us to meet face to face, to greet one another with solidarity, sisterhood, and love. In this space we talk about our different experiences of black womanhood, informed by class, geographical location, religious backgrounds, etc. We do not assume that all black women are violent or have internalized rage and hostility.

In contrast, Lorde writes in "Eye to Eye":

> We do not love ourselves, therefore we cannot love each other. Because we see in each other's face our own face, the face we never stopped wanting. Because we survived and survival breeds desire for more self. A face we never stopped wanting at the same time as we try to obliterate it. Why don't we meet each other's eyes? Do we expect betrayal in each other's gaze, or recognition.

Lorde's essay chronicles an understanding of ways "wounded" black women, who are not in recovery, interact with one another, helping us to see the way in which sexism and racism as systems of domination can shape and determine how we regard one another. Deeply moved by her portrait of the way internalized racism and sexism informs the formation of black female social identity, the way it can and often does affect us, I was simultaneously disturbed by the presumption, expressed by her continual use of a collective "we," that she was speaking to an experience all black women share. The experience her essay suggests black women share is one of passively receiving and absorbing messages of self-hate, then directing rage and hostility most intensely at one another. While I wholeheartedly agree with Lorde that many black women feel and act as she describes, I am interested in the reality of those black women, however few, who even if they have been the targets of black female rage do not direct hostility or rage toward other black women.

Throughout "Eye to Eye," Lorde constructs a monolithic paradigm of black female experience that does not engage our differences. Even as her essay urges black women to openly examine the harshness and cruelty that may be present in black female interaction so that we can regard one another differently, an expression of that regard would be recognition, without hatred or envy, that not all black women share the experience she describes. To some extent Lorde's essay acts to shut down, close off, erase, and deny those black female experiences that do not fit the norm she constructs from the location of her experience. Never in Lorde's essay does she address the issue of whether or not black women from different cultural backgrounds (Caribbean, Latina, etc.) construct diverse identities. Do we all feel the same about black womanhood? What about regional differences? What about those black women who have had the good fortune to be raised in a politicized context where their identities were constructed by resistance and not passive acceptance? By evoking this negative experience of black womanhood as "commonly" shared, Lorde presents it in a way that suggests it represents "authentic" black female reality. To not share the critique she posits is to be made an "outsider" yet again. In Donna Haraway's essay "A Manifesto for Cyborgs," she warns feminist thinkers against assuming positions that "appear to be the telos of the whole," so that we do not "produce epistemologies to police deviation from official women's experience." Though Haraway is speaking about mainstream feminist practice, her warning is applicable to marginalized groups who are in the process of making and remaking critical texts that name our politics and experience.

Years ago I attended a small gathering of black women who were meeting to plan a national conference on black feminism. As we sat in a circle talking about our experiences, those individuals who were most listened to all told stories of how brutally they had been treated by "the" black community. Speaking against the construction of a monolithic experience, I talked about the way my experience of black community differed, sharing that I had been raised in a segregated rural black community that was very supportive. Our segregated church and schools were places where we were affirmed. I was continually told that I was "special" in those settings, that I would be "somebody" someday and do important work to "uplift" the race. I felt loved and cared about in the segregated black community of my growing up. It gave me the grounding in a positive experience of "blackness" that sustained me when I left that community to enter racially integrated settings, where racism informed most social interactions. Before I could finish speaking, I was interrupted by one of the "famous" black women present, who chastised me for trying to erase another black woman's pain by bringing up a different experience. Her voice was hostile and angry. She began by saying she was "sick of people like me." I felt both silenced and misunderstood. It seemed that the cathartic expression of collective pain wiped out any chance that my insistence on the diversity of black experience would be heard.

My story was reduced to a competing narrative, one that was seen as trying to divert attention from the "true" telling of black female experience. In this gathering, black female identity was made synonymous again and again with "victimization." The black female voice that was deemed "authentic" was the voice in pain; only the sound of hurting could be heard. No narrative of resistance was voiced and respected in this setting. I came away wondering why it was these black women could only feel bonded to each other if our narratives echoed, only if we were telling the same story of shared pain and victimization. Why was it impossible to speak an identity emerging from a different location?

A particular brand of black feminist "essentialism" had been constructed in that place. It would not allow for difference. Any individual present who was seen as having inappropriate thoughts or lingering traces of politically incorrect ideas was the target for unmediated hostility. Not surprisingly, those who had the most to say about victimization were also the ones who judged others harshly, who silenced others. Individual black women who were not a part of that inner circle learned that if they did not know the "right" thing to say, it was best to be silent. To speak against the grain was to risk punishment. One's speech might be interrupted or one might be subjected to humiliating verbal abuse.

At the close of this gathering, many black women gave testimony about how this had been a wonderful experience of sisterhood and black woman-bonding. There was no space for those individuals whose spirits had been assaulted and attacked to name their experience. Ironically, they were leaving this gathering with a sense of estrangement, carrying with them remembered pain. Some of them felt that this was the first time in their lives that they had been so cruelly treated by other black women. The oldest black woman present, an academic intellectual who had often been the target for verbal assault, who often wept in her room at night, vowed never again to attend such a gathering. The memory of her pain has lingered in my mind. I have not forgotten this collective black female "rage" in the face of difference, the anger directed at individual black women who dared to speak as though we were more than our pain, more than the collective pain black females have historically experienced.

Sitting at the offices of the Council on Battered Women was different. After many years of feminist movement, it seems to me that black women can now come together in ways that allow for difference. At the Council, women could speak openly and honestly about their experience, describe their negative and positive responses to my work without fear of rebuke. They could name their rage, annoyance, frustration, and simultaneously critique it. In a similar setting where black women had talked openly about the way my work "enraged" them, I had asked a sister if she would talk about the roots of her hostility. She responded by telling me that I was "daring to be different, to have a different response to the shit black women were faced with everyday." She said, "It's like you were saying, this is what the real deal is and this what we can do about it. When most of us have just been going along with the program and telling ourselves that's all we could do. You were saying that it don't have to be that way." The rage she articulated was in response to the demand that black women acknowledge the impact of sexism on our lives and engage in feminist movement. That was a demand for transformation. At the offices of the Council, I was among black comrades who were engaged in a process of transformation. Collectively, we were working to problematize our notions of black female subjectivity. None of us assumed a fixed essential identity. It was so evident that we did not all share a common understanding of being black and female, even though some of our experiences were similar. We did share the understanding that it is difficult for black women to construct radical subjectivity within white supremacist capitalist patriarchy, that our struggle to be "subject," though similar, also differs from that of black men, and that the politics of gender create that difference.

Much creative writing by contemporary black women authors highlights gender politics, specifically black male sexism, poverty, black female labor, and the struggle for creativity. Celebrating the "power" of black women's writing in her essay "Women Warriors: Black Women Writers Load the Canon" in the *Voice Literary Supplement,* dated May 1990, Michelle Cliff asserts:

> There is continuity in the written work of many African-American women, whether writer is their primary identity or not. You can draw a line from the slave narrative of Linda Brent to Elizabeth Keckley's life to *Their Eyes Were Watching God* to *Coming of Age in Mississippi* to *Sula* to *The Salteaters* to *Praisesong for the Widow.* All of these define a response to power. All structure that response as a quest, a journey to complete, to realize the self; all involve the attempt to break out of expectations imposed on black and female identity. All work against the odds to claim the *I.*

Passionate declarations like this one, though seductive, lump all black female writing together in a manner that suggests there is indeed a totalizing *telos* that determines black female subjectivity. This narrative constructs a homogenous black female subject whose subjectivity is most radically defined by those experiences she shares with other black women. In this declaration, as in the entire essay, Cliff glorifies black women writers even though she warns against the kind of glorification (particularly that accorded a writer that is expressed by sustained academic literary critique of their work) that has the potential to repress and contain.

Cliff's piece also contains. Defining black women's collective work as a critical project that problematizes the quest for "identity," she subsumes that quest solely by focusing on rites of passages wherein black women journey to find themselves. She does not talk about whether that journeying is fruitful. By focusing attention primarily on the journey, she offers paradigms for reading and understanding black women writers that invite readers (critics included) to stop there, to romanticize the journey without questioning the location of that journey's end. Sadly, in much of the fiction by contemporary black women writers, the struggle by black female characters for subjectivity, though forged in radical resistance to the *status quo* (opposition to racist oppression, less frequently to class and gender) usually takes the form of black women breaking free from boundaries imposed by others, only to practice their newfound "freedom" by setting limits and boundaries for themselves. Hence though black women may make themselves "subject" they do not become radical subjects. Often they simply conform to existing norms, even ones they once resisted.

Despite all the "radical" shifts in thought, location, class position, etc., that Celie undergoes in Alice Walker's novel *The Color Purple,* from her movement from object to subject to her success as a capitalist entrepreneur, Celie is reinscribed within the context of family and domestic relations by the novel's end. The primary change is that those relations are no longer abusive. Celie has not become a "feminist," a civil rights activist, or a political being in any way. Breaking free from the patriarchal prison that is her "home" when the novel begins, she creates her own household, yet radical politics of collective struggle against racism or sexism do not inform her struggle for self-actualization.

Earlier writing by black women, Linda Brent's slave narrative for example, records resistance struggles where black women confront and overcome incredible barriers in the quest to be self-defining. Often after those barriers have been passed, the heroines settle down into conventional gender roles. No tale of woman's struggle to be self-defining is as powerful as the Brent narrative. She is ever conscious of the way in which being female makes slavery "far more grievous." Her narrative creates powerful groundwork for the construction of radical black female subjectivity. She engages in a process of critical thinking that enables her to rebel against the notion that her body can be sold and insists on placing the sanctity of black ontological being outside modes of exchange. Yet this radical, visionary "take" on subjectivity does not inform who she becomes once she makes her way to freedom. After breaking the bonds of slavery, Harriet Jacobs takes on the pseudonym Linda Brent when she writes about the past and falls into the clutches of conventional notions of womanhood. Does the radical invented self "Linda Brent" have no place in the life of Harriet Jacobs? Freed, descriptions of her life indicate no use of the incredible oppositional imagination that has been a major resource enabling her to transgress boundaries, to take risks, and dare to survive. Does Jacobs' suppression of the radical self chart the journey that black women will follow, both in real life and in their fictions?

More than any other novel by a contemporary black woman writer, Toni Morrison's *Sula* chronicles the attempt by a black female to constitute radical black female subjectivity. Sula challenges every restriction imposed upon her, transgressing all boundaries. Defying conventional notions of passive female sexuality, she asserts herself as desiring subject. Rebelling against enforced domesticity, she chooses to roam the world, to remain childless and unmarried. Refusing standard sexist notions of the exchange of female bodies, she engages in the exchange of male bodies as part of a defiant effort to displace their importance. Asserting the primacy of female friendship, she attempts to break with patriarchal male identification and loses the friendship of her "conservative" buddy Nel, who has indeed capitulated to convention.

Even though readers of *Sula* witness her self-assertion and celebration of autonomy, which Sula revels in even as she is dying, we also know that she is not self-actualized enough to stay alive. Her awareness of what it means to be a radical subject does not cross the boundaries of public and private; hers is a privatized self-discovery. Sula's death at an early age does not leave the reader with a sense of her "power," instead she seems powerless to assert agency in a world that has no interest in radical black female subjectivity, one that seeks to repress, contain, and annihilate it. Sula is annihilated. The reader never knows what force is killing her, eating her from the inside out. Since her journey has been about the struggle to invent herself, the narrative implies that it is the longing for "selfhood" that leads to destruction. Those black women who survive, who live to tell the tale, so to speak, are the "good girls," the ones who have been self-sacrificing, hardworking black women. Sula's fate suggests that charting the journey of radical black female subjectivity is too dangerous, too risky. And while Sula is glad to have broken the rules, she is not a triumphant figure. Sula, like so many other black female characters in contemporary fiction, has no conscious politics, never links her struggle to be self-defining with the collective plight of black women. Yet this novel was written at the peak of contemporary feminist movement. Given the "power" of Sula's black female author/creator, Toni Morrison, why does she appear on the page as an "artist without an art form"? Is it too much like "treason"—like disloyalty to black womanhood—to question this portrait of (dare I say it) "victimization," to refuse to be seduced by Sula's exploits or ignore their outcome?

There are black female characters in contemporary fictions who are engaged in political work. Velma, the radical activist in Toni Cade Bambara's *The Salteaters,* has grounded her struggle for meaning within activist work for black liberation. Overwhelmed by responsibility, by the sense of having to bear too much, too great a weight, she attempts suicide. This novel begins with older radical black women problematizing the question of black female subjectivity. Confronting Velma's attempt at self-destruction and self-erasure, they want to know, "are you sure, sweetheart, that you want to be well?" Wellness here is synonymous with radical subjectivity. Indeed, the elders will go on to emphasize that Velma's plight, and that of other black women like her, reflects the loss of "maps" that will chart the journey for black females. They suggest that it is the younger generation's attempt to assimilate, to follow alien maps, that leads to the loss of perspective. Velma only came back to life (for though she fails to kill herself, she is spiritually dead) when she testifies to herself that she indeed will choose wellness, will claim herself and nurture that radical subjectivity. Like Paule Marshall's *Praisesong for the Widow* and Gloria Naylor's *Mama Day,* the "radical" black women elders with fresh memories of slavery holocaust, of the anguish of reconstruction, who sustain their courage in resistance, live fruitfully outside conventional gender roles. They either do not conform or they acknowledge the way conformity rarely enables black female self-actualization.

Representing a new generation of "modern" black women, Velma, even as she is in the process of recovery, critiques her desire to make a self against the grain, and questions "what good did wild do you, since there was always some low-life gruesome gang-bang raping lawless careless petty last straw nasty thing ready to pounce—put your shit under total arrest and crack your back?" Wild is the metaphoric expression of that inner will to rebel, to move against the grain, to be out of one's place. It is the expression of radical black female subjectivity. Law professor Regina Austin calls black women to cultivate this "wildness" as a survival strategy in her piece "Sapphire Bound." Significantly, she begins the essay by calling attention to the fact that folks seem to be more eager to read about wild black women in fictions than to make way for us in real life. Reclaiming that wildness, she declares:

> Well, I think the time has come for us to get truly hysterical, to
> take on the role of "professional Sapphires" in a forthright way, to
> declare that we are serious about ourselves, and to capture some
> of the intellectual power and resources that are necessary to
> combat the systematic denigration of minority women. It is time
> for Sapphire to testify on her own behalf, *in writing,* complete
> with footnotes. ·

If the writers of black women's fiction are not able to express the wilder,
more radical dimensions of themselves, in sustained and fruitful ways,
it is unlikely that they will create characters who "act up" and flourish.
They may doubt that there is an audience for fictions where black
women are not first portrayed as victims. Though fictions portray black
women being wild in resistance, confronting barriers that impede
self-actualization, rarely is the new "self" defined. Though Bambara
includes passages that let the reader know Velma lives, there are no
clues that indicate how her radical subjectivity will emerge in the
context of "wildness."

Consistently, contemporary black women writers link the struggle to become subject with a concern with emotional and spiritual
well-being. Most often the narcissistic-based individual pursuit of self
and identity subsumes the possibility of sustained commitment to
radical politics. This tension is played out again and again in Alice
Walker's *The Third Life of Grange Copeland.* While the heroine, Ruth,
is schooled by her grandfather to think critically, to develop radical
political consciousness, in the end he fights against whites alone. It is
not clear what path Ruth will take in the future. Will she be a militant
warrior for the revolution or be kept in her place by "strong" black male
lovers/patriarchs who, like her grandfather, will be convinced that they
can best determine what conditions are conducive to producing black
female well-being? Ironically, *Meridian* takes up where Ruth's story
ends, yet the older black woman activist, like Ruth, remains confined
and contained by a self-imposed domesticity. Is Meridian in hiding
because there is no place where her radical black subjectivity can be
expressed without punishment? Is the non-patriarchal home the only
safe place?

Contemporary fiction by black women focusing on the construction of self and identity breaks new ground in that it clearly names the
ways structures of domination, racism, sexism, and class exploitation,
oppress and make it practically impossible for black women to survive
if they do not engage in meaningful resistance on some level. Defiantly

naming the condition of oppression and personal strategies of opposition, such writing enables the individual black woman reader who has not yet done so to question, and/or critically affirms the efforts of those readers who are already involved in resistance. Yet these writings often fail to depict any location for the construction of new identities. It is this textual gap that leads critic Sondra O'Neale to ask in her essay "Inhibiting Midwives, Usurping Creators: The Struggling Emergence of Black Women in American Fiction":

> For instance, where are the Angela Davises, Ida B. Wellses, and Daisy Bateses of black feminist literature? Where are the portraits of those women who fostered their own action to liberate themselves, other black women, and black men as well? We see a sketch of such a character in *Meridian,* but she is never developed to a social and political success.

In an earlier essay, "The Politics of Radical Black Subjectivity," I emphasized that opposition and resistance cannot be made synonymous with self-actualization on an individual or collective level: "Opposition is not enough. In that vacant space after one has resisted there is still the necessity to become—to make oneself anew." While contemporary writing by black women has brought into sharp focus the idea that black females must "invent" selves, the question—what kind of self?—usually remains unanswered. The vision of selfhood that does emerge now and then is one that is in complete concordance with conventional western notions of a "unitary" self. Again it's worth restating Donna Haraway's challenge to feminist thinkers to resist making "one's own political tendencies to be the telos of the whole" so we can accept different accounts of female experience and also face ourselves as complex subjects who embody multiple locations. In "A Manifesto for Cyborgs," she urges us to remember that, "The issue is dispersion. The task is to survive in diaspora."

Certainly, collective black female experience has been about the struggle to survive in diaspora. It is the intensity of that struggle, the fear of failure (as we face daily the reality that many black people do not and are not surviving) that has led many black women thinkers, especially within feminist movement, to wrongly assume that strength in unity can only exist if difference is suppressed and shared experience is highlighted. Though feminist writing by black women is usually critical of the racism that has shaped and defined the parameters of much contemporary feminist movement, it usually reiterates, in an uncritical manner, major tenets of dominant feminist thought. Admonishing black women for wasting time critiquing white female racism, Sheila Radford-Hill, in "Considering Feminism as a Model for Social Change," urges black feminists:

> ...to build an agenda that meets the needs of black women by helping black women to mobilize around issues that they perceive to have a direct impact on the overall quality of their lives. Such is the challenge that defined our struggle and constitutes our legacy...Thus, black women need to develop their own leadership and their own agenda based on the needs of their primary constituent base; that is, based around black women, their families, and their communities. This task cannot be furthered by dialoging with white women about their inherent racism.

While I strongly agree with Radford-Hill's insistence that black critical thinkers engaged in feminist movement develop strategies that directly address the concerns of our diverse black communities, she constructs an either/or proposition that obscures the diversity of our experiences and locations. For those black women who live and work in predominantly white settings (and of course the reality is that most black women work jobs where their supervisors are white women and men), it is an appropriate and necessary political project for them to work at critical interrogations and interventions that address white racism. Such efforts do not preclude simultaneous work in black communities. Evocations of an "essentialist" notion of black identity seek to deny the extent to which all black folk must engage with whites as well as exclude individuals from "blackness" whose perspectives, values, or lifestyles may differ from a totalizing notion of black experience that sees only those folk who live in segregated communities or have little contact with whites as "authentically" black.

Radford-Hill's essay is most insightful when she addresses "the crisis of black womanhood," stating that "the extent to which black feminists can articulate and solve the crisis of black womanhood is the extent to which black women will undergo a feminist transformation." The crisis Radford-Hill describes is a crisis of identity and subjectivity. When the major struggle black women addressed was opposition to racism and the goal of that struggle was equality in the existing social structures, when most black folks were poor and lived in racially segregated neighborhoods, gender roles for black women were more clearly defined. We had a place in the "struggle" as well as a place in the social institutions of our communities. It was easier for black women to chart the journey of selfhood. With few job options in the segregated labor force, most black women knew that they would be engaged in service work or become teachers. Today's black woman has more options even though most of the barriers that would keep her from exercising those options are still in place. Racial integration, economic changes in black class relations, the impact of consumer capitalism, as well as a male-centered contemporary black liberation struggle (which devalued the contributions of black females) and a feminist movement which called into question idealized notions of womanhood have radically altered black female reality. For many black women, especially the underclass, the dream of racial equality was intimately linked with the fantasy that once the struggle was over, black women would be able to assume conventional sexist gender roles. To some extent there is a crisis in black womanhood because most black women have not responded to these changes by radically reinventing themselves, by developing new maps to chart future journeys. And more crucially, most black women have not responded to this crisis by developing critical consciousness, by becoming engaged in radical movements for social change.

When we examine the lives of individual black women who did indeed respond to contemporary changes, we see just how difficult it is for black women to construct radical subjectivity. Two powerful autobiographies of radical black women were published in the early 1970s. In 1970, Shirley Chisholm published *Unbought and Unbossed,* chronicling the events that led to her becoming the first black congress-woman. In 1974, *Angela Davis: An Autobiography* was published. Both accounts demonstrate that the construction of radical black female subjectivity is rooted in a willingness to go against the grain. Though many folks may not see Chisholm as "radical," she was one of the first black female leaders to speak against sexism, stressing in the introduction to her book: "Of my two 'handicaps,' being female put many more obstacles in my path than being black." An outspoken advocate of reproductive and abortion rights for women, Chisholm responded to black males who were not opposed to compulsory pregnancy for black women by arguing: "Which is more like genocide, I have asked some of my black brothers—this, the way things are, or the conditions I am fighting for in which the full range of family planning service is fully available to women of all classes and colors; starting with effective contraception and extending to safe, legal termination of undesired pregnancies, at a price they can afford?"

Militant in her response to racism, Chisholm also stressed the need for education for critical consciousness to help eradicate internalized racism:

It is necessary for our generation to repudiate Carver and all the
lesser-known black leaders who cooperated with the white design
to keep their people down. We need none of their kind today.
Someday, when, God willing, the struggle is over and its bitterness
has faded, those men and woman may be rediscovered and given
their just due for working as best they could see to do in their time
and place, for their brothers and sisters. But at present their
influence is pernicious, and where they still control education in
the North or the South, they must be replaced with educators who
are ready to demand full equality for the oppressed races and fight
for it at any cost.

As a radical black female subject who would not allow herself to
be the puppet of any group, Chisholm was often harassed, mocked,
and ridiculed by colleagues. Psychological terrorism was often the
weapon used to try and coerce her into silence, to convince her she
knew nothing about politics, or worse yet that she was "crazy." Often
her colleagues described her as mad if she took positions they could
not understand or would not have taken. Radical black female subjects
are constantly labeled crazy by those who hope to undermine our
personal power and our ability to influence others. Fear of being seen
as insane may be a major factor keeping black women from expressing
their most radical selves. Just recently, when I spoke against the
omnipresent racism and sexism at a conference, calling it terroristic, the
organizers told folks I was "crazy." While this hurt and angered, it would
have wounded me more had I not understood the ways this appellation
is used by those in power to keep the powerless in their place.
Remembering Chisholm's experience, I knew that I was not alone in
confronting racist, sexist attacks that are meant to silence. Knowing that
Chisholm claimed her right to subjectivity without apology inspires me
to maintain courage.

Recently rereading the autobiography of Angela Davis, I was
awed by her courage. I could appreciate the obstacles she confronted
and her capacity to endure and persevere in a new way. Reading this
work in my teens, her courage seemed like "no big deal." At the
beginning of the work, Davis eschews any attempt to see herself as
exceptional. Framing the narrative in this way, it is easy for readers to
ignore the specificity of her experience. In fact, very few black females
at the time had gone to radical high schools where they learned about
socialism or traveled to Europe and studied at the Sorbonne. Yet Davis
insists that her situation is like that of all black people. This gesture of
solidarity, though important, at times obscures the reality that Davis'

radical understanding of politics was learned as was her critical consciousness. Had she voiced her solidarity with underclass black people, while simultaneously stressing the importance of learning, of broadening one's perspective, she would have shared with black females tools that enable one to be a radical subject.

Like Chisholm, Davis confronted sexism when she fully committed herself to working for political change:

> I became acquainted very early with the widespread presence of an unfortunate syndrome among some Black male activists—namely to confuse their political activity with an assertion of their maleness. They saw—and some continue to see—Black manhood as something separate from Black womanhood. These men view Black women as a threat to their attainment of manhood—especially those Black women who take initiative and work to become leaders in their own right.

Working in the radical black liberation movement, Davis constantly confronted and challenged sexism even as she critiqued the pervasive racism in mainstream feminist movement. Reading her autobiography, it is clear that reading and studying played a tremendous role in shaping her radical political consciousness. Yet Davis understood that one needed to go beyond books and work collectively with comrades for social change. She critiqued self-focused work to emphasize the value of working in solidarity:

> Floating from activity to activity was no revolutionary anything. Individual activity—sporadic and disconnected—is not revolutionary work. Serious revolutionary work consists of persistent and methodical efforts through a collective of other revolutionaries to organize the masses for action. Since I had long considered myself a Marxist, the alternatives open to me were very limited.

Despite limited options, Davis' decision to advocate communism was an uncommon and radical choice.

When the Davis autobiography was written, she was thirty years old; her most militant expression of subjectivity erupted in her twenties. Made into a cultural icon, a gesture that was not in line with her insistence on the importance of collectivity and fellowship, she came to be represented in mass media as an "exceptional" black woman. Her experience was not seen as a model young black women could learn from. Many parents pointed to the prison sentence she served as reason enough for black women not to follow in her footsteps. Black males who wanted the movement to be male-centered were not trying to encourage other black women to be on the Left, to fully commit themselves to a revolutionary black liberation struggle. At public appearances, Angela Davis was not and is not flanked by other black women on the Left. Constantly projected as an "isolated" figure, her presence, her continued commitment to critical thinking and critical pedagogy, has not had the galvanizing impact on black females that it could have. Black women "worship" Davis from a distance, see her as exceptional. Though young black women adore Davis, they do not often read her work nor seek to follow her example. Yet learning about those black women who have dared to assert radical subjectivity, is a necessary part of black female self-actualization. Coming to power, to selfhood, to radical subjectivity cannot happen in isolation. Black women need to study the writings, both critical and autobiographical, of those women who have developed their potential and chosen to be radical subjects.

Critical pedagogy, the sharing of information and knowledge by black women with black women, is crucial for the development of radical black female subjectivity (not because black women can only learn from one another, but because the circumstances of racism, sexism, and class exploitation ensure that other groups will not necessarily seek to further our self-determination). This process requires of us a greater honesty about how we live. Black females (especially students) who are searching for answers about the social formation of identity want to know how radical black women think but they also want to know about our habits of being. Willingness to share openly one's personal experience ensures that one will not be made into a deified icon. When black females learn about my life, they also learn about the mistakes I make, the contradictions. They come to know my limitations as well as my strengths. They cannot dehumanize me by placing me on a pedestal. Sharing the contradictions of our lives, we help each other learn how to grapple with contradictions as part of the process of becoming a critical thinker, a radical subject.

The lives of Ella Baker, Fannie Lou Hamer, Septima Clark, Lucy Parson, Ruby Doris Smith Robinson, Angela Davis, Bernice Reagon, Alice Walker, Audre Lorde, and countless others bear witness to the difficulty of developing radical black female subjectivity even as they attest to the joy and triumph of living with a decolonized mind and participating in ongoing resistance struggle. The narratives of black women who have militantly engaged in radical struggles for change offer insights. They let us know the conditions that enable the construction of radical black female subjectivity as well as the obstacles that impede its development. In most cases, radical black female subjects have willingly challenged the *status quo* and gone against the grain. Despite the popularity of Angela Davis as a cultural icon, most black women are "punished" and "suffer" when they make choices that go against the prevailing societal sense of what a black woman should be and do. Most radical black female subjects are not caught up in consumer capitalism. Living simply is often the price one pays for choosing to be different. It was no accident that Zora Neale Hurston died poor. Radical black female subjects have had to educate ourselves for critical consciousness, reading, studying, engaging in critical pedagogy, transgressing boundaries to acquire the knowledge we need. Those rare radical black women who have started organizations and groups are attempting to build a collective base that will support and enable their work. Many of these black women create sites of resistance that are far removed from conservatizing institutions in order to sustain their radical commitments. Those of us who remain in institutions that do not support our efforts to be radical subjects are daily assaulted. We persevere because we believe our presence is needed, is important.

Developing a feminist consciousness is a crucial part of the process by which one asserts radical black female subjectivity. Whether she has called herself a feminist or not, there is no radical black woman subject who has not been forced to confront and challenge sexism. If, however, that individual struggle is not connected to a larger feminist movement, then every black woman finds herself reinventing strategies to cope when we should be leaving a legacy of feminist resistance that can nourish, sustain, and guide other black women and men. Those black women who valiantly advocate feminism often bear the brunt of severe critique from other black folks. As radical subject, the young Michele Wallace wrote one of the first book length, polemical works on feminism that focused on black folks. She did not become a cultural icon; to a great extent she was made a pariah. Writing about her experience in "The Politics of Location: Cinema/ Theory/ Literature/ Ethnicity/ Sexuality/ Me," she remembers the pain:

> I still ponder the book I wrote, *Black Macho and The Myth of the Superwoman,* and the disturbance it caused: how black women are not allowed to establish their own intellectual terrain, to make their own mistakes, to invent their own birthplace in writing. I still ponder my book's rightness and wrongness, and how its reception almost destroyed me so that I vowed never to write political and/or theoretical statements about feminism again.

Wallace suffered in isolation, with no group of radical black women rallying to her defense, or creating a context where critique would not lead to trashing.

Without a context of critical affirmation, radical black female subjectivity cannot sustain itself. Often black women turn away from the radicalism of their younger days as they age because the isolation, the sense of estrangement from community, becomes too difficult to bear. Critical affirmation is a concept that embraces both the need to affirm one another and to have a space for critique. Significantly, that critique is not rooted in negative desire to compete, to wound, to trash. Though I began this piece with critical statements about Audre Lorde's essay, I affirm the value of her work. The "Eye to Eye" essay remains one of the most insightful discussions of black female interaction. Throughout the essay, Lorde emphasizes the importance of affirmation, encouraging black women to be gentle and affectionate with one another. Tenderness should not simply be a form of care extended to those black women who think as we do. Many of us have been in situations where black females are sweet to the folks in their clique and completely hostile to anyone deemed an outsider.

In "Eye to Eye," Lorde names this problem. Offering strategies black women might use to promote greater regard and respect, she says that "black women must love ourselves." Loving ourselves begins with understanding the forces that have produced whatever hostility toward blackness and femaleness that is felt, but it also means learning new ways to think about ourselves. Often the black women who speak the most about love and sisterhood are deeply attached to essentialist notions of black female identity that promote a "policing" of anyone who does not conform. Ironically, of course, the only way black women can construct radical subjectivity is by resisting set norms and challenging the politics of domination based on race, class, and sex. Essentialist perspectives on black womanhood often perpetuate the false assumption that black females, simply by living in white supremacist/capitalist/patriarchy, are radicalized. They do not encourage black women to develop their critical thinking. Individual black women on the Left often find their desire to read or write "theory," to be engaged in critical dialogues with diverse groups, mocked and ridiculed. Often, I am criticized for studying feminist theory, especially writing by white women. And I am seen as especially "naive" when I suggest that even though a white woman theorist may be "racist," she may also have valuable information that I can learn from. Until black women fully recognize that we must collectively examine and study our experience from a feminist standpoint, there will always be lags and gaps in the structure of our epistemologies. Where are our feminist books on mothering, on sexuality, on feminist film criticism? Where are our autobiographies that do not falsely represent our reality in the interest of promoting monolithic notions of black female experience or celebrating how wonderfully we have managed to overcome oppression?

Though autobiography or any type of confessional narrative is often devalued in North American letters, this genre has always had a privileged place in African American literary history. As a literature of resistance, confessional narratives by black folks were didactic. More than any other genre of writing, the production of honest confessional narratives by black women who are struggling to be self-actualized and to become radical subjects are needed as guides, as texts that affirm our fellowship with one another. (I need not feel isolated if I know that there are other comrades with similar experiences. I learn from their strategies of resistance and from their recording of mistakes.) Even as the number of novels published by black women increase, this writing cannot be either a substitute for theory or for autobiographical narrative. Radical black women need to tell our stories; we cannot document our experience enough. Works like *Lemon Swamp, Balm in Gilead, Ready From Within,* and *Every Goodbye Ain't Gone,* though very different, and certainly not all narratives of radical black female subjectivity, enable readers to understand the complexity and diversity of black female experience.

There are few contemporary autobiographies by black women on the Left. We need to hear more from courageous black women who have gone against the grain to assert nonconformist politics and habits of being, folks like Toni Cade Bambara, Gloria Joseph, Faye Harrison, June Jordan, and so many others. These voices can give testimony and share the process of transformation black women undergo to emerge as radical subjects. Black females need to know who our revolutionary comrades are. Speaking about her commitment to revolution, Angela Davis notes:

> For me revolution was never an interim "thing-to-do" before settling down: it was no fashionable club with newly minted jargon, or a new kind of social life—made thrilling by risk and confrontation, made glamorous by costume. Revolution is a serious thing, the most serious thing about a revolutionary's life. When one commits oneself to the struggle, it must be for a lifetime.

The crisis of black womanhood can only be addressed by the development of resistance struggles that emphasize the importance of decolonizing our minds, developing critical consciousness. Feminist politics can be an integral part of a renewed black liberation struggle. Black women, particularly those of us who have chosen radical subjectivity, can move toward revolutionary social change that will address the diversity of our experiences and our needs. Collectively bringing our knowledge, resources, skills, and wisdom to one another, we make the site where radical black female subjectivity can be nurtured and sustained.

Chapter 4

Selling Hot Pussy

Representations of Black Female Sexuality in the Cultural Marketplace

Friday night in a small midwestern town—I go with a group of artists and professors to a late night dessert place. As we walk past a group of white men standing in the entry way to the place, we overhear them talking about us, saying that my companions, who are all white, must be liberals from the college, not regular "townies," to be hanging out with a "nigger." Everyone in my group acts as though they did not hear a word of this conversation. Even when I call attention to the comments, no one responds. It's like I am not only not talking, but suddenly, to them, I am not there. I am invisible. For my colleagues, racism expressed in everyday encounters—this is our second such experience together—is only an unpleasantness to be avoided, not something to be confronted or challenged. It is just something negative disrupting the good time, better to not notice and pretend it's not there.

As we enter the dessert place they all burst into laughter and point to a row of gigantic chocolate breasts complete with nipples—huge edible tits. They think this is a delicious idea—seeing no connection between this racialized image and the racism expressed in the entry way. Living in a world where white folks are no longer nursed and nurtured primarily by black female caretakers, they do not look at these symbolic breasts and consciously think about "mammies." They do not see this representation of chocolate breasts as a sign of displaced

longing for a racist past when the bodies of black women were
commodity, available to anyone white who could pay the price. I look
at these dark breasts and think about the representation of black female
bodies in popular culture. Seeing them, I think about the connection
between contemporary representations and the types of images popularized from slavery on. I remember Harriet Jacobs' powerful *exposé* of
the psycho-sexual dynamics of slavery in *Incidents in the Life of a Slave
Girl*. I remember the way she described that "peculiar" institution of
domination and the white people who constructed it as "a cage of
obscene birds."

Representations of black female bodies in contemporary popular
culture rarely subvert or critique images of black female sexuality which
were part of the cultural apparatus of 19th-century racism and which
still shape perceptions today. Sander Gilman's essay, "Black Bodies,
White Bodies: Toward an Iconography of Female Sexuality in Late
Nineteenth-Century Art, Medicine, and Literature," calls attention to the
way black presence in early North American society allowed whites to
sexualize their world by projecting onto black bodies a narrative of
sexualization disassociated from whiteness. Gilman documents the
development of this image, commenting that "by the eighteenth century, the sexuality of the black, male and female, becomes an icon for
deviant sexuality." He emphasizes that it is the black female body that
is forced to serve as "an icon for black sexuality in general."

Most often attention was not focused on the complete black
female on display at a fancy ball in the "civilized" heart of European
culture, Paris. She is there to entertain guests with the naked image of
Otherness. They are not to look at her as a whole human being. They
are to notice only certain parts. Objectified in a manner similar to that
of black female slaves who stood on auction blocks while owners and
overseers described their important, salable parts, the black women
whose naked bodies were displayed for whites at social functions had
no presence. They were reduced to mere spectacle. Little is known of
their lives, their motivations. Their body parts were offered as evidence
to support racist notions that black people were more akin to animals
than other humans. When Sarah Bartmann's body was exhibited in
1810, she was ironically and perversely dubbed "the Hottentot Venus."
Her naked body was displayed on numerous occasions for five years.
When she died, the mutilated parts were still subject to scrutiny. Gilman
stressed that: "The audience which had paid to see her buttocks and
had fantasized about the uniqueness of her genitalia when she was alive
could, after her death and dissection, examine both." Much of the

racialized fascination with Bartmann's body concentrated attention on her buttocks.

A similar white European fascination with the bodies of black people, particularly black female bodies, was manifest during the career of Josephine Baker. Content to "exploit" white eroticization of black bodies, Baker called attention to the "butt" in her dance routines. Phyllis Rose, though often condescending in her recent biography, *Jazz Cleopatra: Josephine Baker In Her Time,* perceptively explores Baker's concentration on her ass:

> She handled it as though it were an instrument, a rattle, something apart from herself that she could shake. One can hardly overemphasize the importance of the rear end. Baker herself declared that people had been hiding their asses too long. "The rear end exists. I see no reason to be ashamed of it. It's true there are rear ends so stupid, so pretentious, so insignificant that they're good only for sitting on." With Baker's triumph, the erotic gaze of a nation moved downward: she had uncovered a new region for desire.

Many of Baker's dance moves highlighting the "butt" prefigure movements popular in contemporary black dance.

Although contemporary thinking about black female bodies does not attempt to read the body as a sign of "natural" racial inferiority, the fascination with black "butts" continues. In the sexual iconography of the traditional black pornographic imagination, the protruding butt is seen as an indication of a heightened sexuality. Contemporary popular music is one of the primary cultural locations for discussions of black sexuality. In song lyrics, "the butt" is talked about in ways that attempt to challenge racist assumptions that suggest it is an ugly sign of inferiority, even as it remains a sexualized sign. The popular song, "Doin' the Butt," fostered the promotion of a hot new dance favoring those who could most protrude their buttocks with pride and glee. A scene in Spike Lee's film *School Daze* depicts an all black party where everyone is attired in swimsuits dancing—doing the butt. It is one of the most compelling moments in the film. The black "butts" on display are unruly and outrageous. They are not the still bodies of the female slave made to appear as mannequin. They are not a silenced body. Displayed as playful cultural nationalist resistance, they challenge assumptions that the black body, its skin color and shape, is a mark of shame. Undoubtedly the most transgressive and provocative moment in *School Daze,* this celebration of buttocks either initiated or coincided with an emphasis on butts, especially the buttocks of women, in fashion magazines. Its potential to disrupt and challenge notions of black bodies, specifically female bodies, was undercut by the overall sexual humiliation and abuse of black females in the film. Many people did not see the film so it was really the song "Doin' the Butt" that challenged dominant ways of thinking about the body which encourage us to ignore asses because they are associated with undesirable and unclean acts. Unmasked, the "butt" could be once again worshiped as an erotic seat of pleasure and excitement.

When calling attention to the body in a manner inviting the gaze to mutilate black female bodies yet again, to focus solely on the "butt," contemporary celebrations of this part of the anatomy do not successfully subvert sexist/racist representations. Just as 19th-century representations of black female bodies were constructed to emphasize that these bodies were expendable, contemporary images (even those created in black cultural production) give a similar message. When Richard Wright's protest novel *Native Son* was made into a film in the 1980s, the film did not show the murder of Bigger's black girlfriend Bessie. This was doubly ironic. She is murdered in the novel and then systematically eliminated in the film. Painters exploring race as artistic subject matter in the 19th century often created images contrasting white female bodies with black ones in ways that reinforced the greater value of the white female icon. Gilman's essay colludes in this critical project: he is really most concerned with exploring white female sexuality.

A similar strategy is employed in the Wright novel and in the film version. In the novel, Bessie is expendable because Bigger has already committed the more heinous crime of killing a white woman. The first and more important murder subsumes the second. Everyone cares about the fate of Mary Dalton, the ruling class white female daughter; no one cares about the fate of Bessie. Ironically, just at the moment when Bigger decides that Bessie's body is expendable, that he will kill her, he continues to demand that she help him, that she "do the right thing." Bigger intends to use her then throw her away, a gesture reinforcing that hers is an expendable body. While he must transgress dangerous boundaries to destroy the body of a white female, he can invade and violate a black female body with no fear of retribution and retaliation.

Black and female, sexual outside the context of marriage, Bessie represents "fallen womanhood." She has no protectors, no legal system will defend her rights. Pleading her cause to Bigger, she asks for recognition and compassion for her specific condition.

> Bigger, please! Don't do this to me! Please! All I do is work, work like a dog! From morning till night. I ain't got no happiness. I ain't never had none. I ain't got nothing and you do this to me...

Poignantly describing the lot of working-class poor black women in the 1940s, her words echo those of poet Nikki Giovanni describing the status of black women in the late 1960s. The opening lines to "Woman Poem" reads: "You see my whole life is tied up to unhappiness." There is a radical difference, however. In the 1960s, the black female is naming her unhappiness to demand a hearing, an acknowledgment of her reality, and change her status. This poem speaks to the desire of black women to construct a sexuality apart from that imposed upon us by a racist/sexist culture, calling attention to the ways we are trapped by conventional notions of sexuality and desirability:

> ...it's a sex object if you're pretty and no love or love and no sex if you're fat get back fat black woman be a mother grandmother strong thing but not woman gameswoman romantic woman love needer man seeker dick eater sweat getter fuck needing love seeking woman

"Woman Poem" is a cry of resistance urging those who exploit and oppress black women, who objectify and dehumanize, to confront the consequences of their actions. Facing herself, the black female realizes all that she must struggle against to achieve self-actualization. She must counter the representation of herself, her body, her being as expendable.

Bombarded with images representing black female bodies as expendable, black women have either passively absorbed this thinking or vehemently resisted it. Popular culture provides countless examples of black female appropriation and exploitation of "negative stereotypes" to either assert control over the representation or at least reap the benefits of it. Since black female sexuality has been represented in racist/sexist iconography as more free and liberated, many black women singers, irrespective of the quality of their voices, have cultivated an image which suggests they are sexually available and licentious. Undesirable in the conventional sense, which defines beauty and sexuality as desirable only to the extent that it is idealized and unattainable, the black female body gains attention only when it is synonymous with accessibility, availability, when it is sexually deviant.

Tina Turner's construction of a public sexual persona most conforms to this idea of black female sexuality. In her recent autobiography *I, Tina* she presents a sexualized portrait of herself—providing a narrative that is centrally "sexual confession." Even though she begins by calling attention to the fact that she was raised with puritanical notions of innocence and virtuous womanhood which made her reticent and fearful of sexual experience, all that follows contradicts this portrait. Since the image that has been cultivated and commodified in popular culture is of her as "hot" and highly sexed—the sexually ready and free black woman—a tension exists in the autobiography between the reality she presents and the image she must uphold. Describing her first sexual experience, Turner recalls:

> Naturally, I lost my virginity in the backseat of a car. This was the fifties, right? I think he had planned it, the little devil—he knew by then that he could get into my pants, because there's already been a lot of kissing and touching inside the blouse, and then under the skirt and so forth. The next step was obvious. And me, as brazen as I was, when it came down to finally doing the real thing, it was like: "Uh-oh, it's time." I mean, I was scared. And then it happened.
>
> Well, it hurt so bad—I think my earlobes were hurting. I was just dying, God. And he wanted to do it two or three times! It was like poking an open wound. I could hardly walk afterwards.
>
> But I did it for love. The pain was excruciating; but I loved him and he loved me, and that made the pain less—Everything was right. So it was beautiful.

Only there is nothing beautiful about the scenario Turner describes. A tension exists between the "cool" way she describes this experience, playing it off to suggest she was in control of the situation, and the reality she recounts where she succumbs to male lust and suffers sex. After describing a painful rite of sexual initiation, Turner undermines the confession by telling the reader that she felt good. Through retrospective memory, Turner is able to retell this experience in a manner that suggests she was comfortable with sexual experience at an early age, yet cavalier language does not completely mask the suffering evoked by the details she gives. However, this cavalier attitude accords best with how her fans "see" her. Throughout the biography she will describe situations of extreme sexual victimization and then undermine the impact of her words by evoking the image of herself and other black women as sexually free, suggesting that we assert sexual agency in ways that are never confirmed by the evidence she provides.

Tina Turner's singing career has been based on the construction of an image of black female sexuality that is made synonymous with wild animalistic lust. Raped and exploited by Ike Turner, the man who made this image and imposed it on her, Turner describes the way her public persona as singer was shaped by his pornographic misogynist imagination:

> Ike explained: As a kid back in Clarksdale, he'd become fixated on the white jungle goddess who romped through Saturday matinee movie serials—revealing rag-clad women with long flowing hair and names like Sheena, Queen of the Jungle, and Nyoka—particularly Nyoka. He still remembered *The Perils of Nyoka*, a fifteen-part Republic Picture serial from 1941, starring Kay Alridge in the title role and featuring a villainess named Vultura, an ape named Satan, and Clayton Moore (later to be TV's Lone Ranger) as love interest. Nyoka, Sheena—Tina! Tina Turner—Ike's own personal Wild Woman. He loved it.

Turner makes no comment about her thoughts about this image. How can she? It is part of the representation which makes and maintains her stardom.

Ike's pornographic fantasy of the black female as wild sexual savage emerged from the impact of a white patriarchal controlled media shaping his perceptions of reality. His decision to create the wild black woman was perfectly compatible with prevailing representations of black female sexuality in a white supremacist society. Of course the Tina Turner story reveals that she was anything but a wild woman; she was fearful of sexuality, abused, humiliated, fucked, and fucked over. Turner's friends and colleagues document the myriad ways she suffered about the experience of being brutally physically beaten prior to appearing on stage to perform, yet there is no account of how she coped with the contradiction (this story is told by witnesses in *I, Tina*). She was on one hand in excruciating pain inflicted by a misogynist man who dominated her life and her sexuality, and on the other hand projecting in every performance the image of a wild tough sexually liberated woman. Not unlike the lead character in the novel *Story of O* by Pauline Reage, Turner must act as though she glories in her submission, that she delights in being a slave of love. Leaving Ike, after many years of forced marital rape and physical abuse, because his violence is utterly uncontrollable, Turner takes with her the "image" he created.

Despite her experience of abuse rooted in sexist and racist objectification, Turner appropriated the "wild woman" image, using it for career advancement. Always fascinated with wigs and long hair, she created the blonde lioness mane to appear all the more savage and animalistic. Blondeness links her to jungle imagery even as it serves as an endorsement of a racist aesthetics which sees blonde hair as the epitome of beauty. Without Ike, Turner's career has soared to new heights, particularly as she works harder to exploit the visual representation of woman (and particularly black woman) as sexual savage. No longer caught in the sadomasochistic sexual iconography of black female in erotic war with her mate that was the subtext of the Ike and Tina Turner show, she is now portrayed as the autonomous black woman whose sexuality is solely a way to exert power. Inverting old imagery, she places herself in the role of dominator.

Playing the role of Aunty Entity in the film *Mad Max: Beyond the Thunderdome,* released in 1985, Turner's character evokes two racist/sexist stereotypes, that of the black "mammy" turned power hungry and the sexual savage who uses her body to seduce and conquer men. Portrayed as lusting after the white male hero who will both conquer and reject her, Aunty Entity is the contemporary reenactment of that mythic black female in slavery who supposedly "vamped" and seduced virtuous white male slave owners. Of course the contemporary white male hero of *Mad Max* is stronger than his colonial forefathers. He does not succumb to the dangerous lure of the deadly black seductress who rules over a mini-nation whose power is based on the use of shit. Turner is the bad black woman in this film, an image she will continue to exploit.

Turner's video "What's Love Got To Do With It" also highlights the convergence of sexuality and power. Here, the black woman's body is represented as potential weapon. In the video, she walks down rough city streets, strutting her stuff, in a way that declares desirability, allure, while denying access. It is not that she is no longer represented as available; she is "open" only to those whom she chooses. Assuming the role of hunter, she is the sexualized woman who makes men and women her prey (in the alluring gaze of the video, the body moves in the direction of both sexes). This tough black woman has no time for woman bonding, she is out to "catch." Turner's fictive model of black female sexual agency remains rooted in misogynist notions. Rather than being a pleasure-based eroticism, it is ruthless, violent; it is about women using sexual power to do violence to the male Other.

Appropriating the wild woman pornographic myth of black female sexuality created by men in a white supremacist patriarchy, Turner exploits it for her own ends to achieve economic self-sufficiency. When she left Ike, she was broke and in serious debt. The new Turner image conveys the message that happiness and power come to women who learn to beat men at their own game, to throw off any investment in romance and get down to the real dog-eat-dog thing. "What's Love Got To Do With It" sung by Turner evokes images of the strong bitchified black woman who is on the make. Subordinating the idea of romantic love and praising the use of sex for pleasure as commodity to exchange, the song had great appeal for contemporary postmodern culture. It equates pleasure with materiality, making it an object to be sought after, taken, acquired by any means necessary. When sung by black women singers, "What's Love Got To Do With It" called to mind old stereotypes which make the assertion of black female sexuality and prostitution synonymous. Just as black female prostitutes in the 1940s and 1950s actively sought clients in the streets to make money to survive, thereby publicly linking prostitution with black female sexuality, contemporary black female sexuality is fictively constructed in popular rap and R&B songs solely as commodity—sexual service for money and power, pleasure is secondary.

Contrasted with the representation of wild animalistic sexuality, black female singers like Aretha Franklin and younger contemporaries like Anita Baker fundamentally link romance and sexual pleasure. Aretha, though seen as a victim of no-good men, the classic "woman who loves too much" and leaves the lyrics to prove it, also sang songs of resistance. "Respect" was heard by many black folks, especially black women, as a song challenging black male sexism and female victimization while evoking notions of mutual care and support. In a recent PBS special highlighting individual musicians, Aretha Franklin was featured. Much space was given in the documentary to white male producers who shaped her public image. In the documentary, she describes the fun of adding the words "sock it to me" to "Respect" as a powerful refrain. One of the white male producers, Jerry Wexler, offers his interpretation of its meaning, claiming that it was a call for "sexual attention of the highest order." His sexualized interpretations of the song seemed far removed from the way it was heard and celebrated in black communities. Looking at this documentary, which was supposedly a tribute to Aretha Franklin's power, it was impossible not to have one's attention deflected away from the music by the subtext of the film, which can be seen as a visual narrative documenting her obsessive concern with the body and achieving a look suggesting desirability. To achieve this end, Franklin constantly struggles with her weight, and the images in the film chronicle her various shifts in body size and shape. As though mocking this concern with her body, throughout most of the documentary Aretha appears in what seems to be a household setting, a living room maybe, wearing a strapless evening dress, much too small for her breast size, so her breasts appear like two balloons filled with water about to burst. With no idea who shaped and controlled this image, I can only reiterate that it undermined the insistence in the film that she has overcome sexual victimization and remained a powerful singer; the latter seemed more likely than the former.

Black female singers who project a sexualized persona are as obsessed with hair as they are with body size and body parts. As with 19th-century sexual iconography, specific parts of the anatomy are designated more sexual and worthy of attention than others. Today much of the sexualized imagery for black female stars seems to be fixated on hair; it and not buttocks signifies animalistic sexuality. This is quintessentially so for Tina Turner and Diana Ross. It is ironically appropriate that much of this hair is synthetic and man-made, artificially constructed as is the sexualized image it is meant to evoke. Within a patriarchal culture where women over forty are not represented as sexually desirable, it is understandable that singers exploiting sexualized representations who are near the age of fifty place less emphasis on body parts that may reflect aging while focusing on hair.

In a course I teach on "The Politics of Sexuality," where we often examine connections between race and sex, we once critically analyzed a *Vanity Fair* cover depicting Diana Ross. Posed on a white background, apparently naked with the exception of white cloth draped loosely around her body, the most striking element in the portrait was the long mane of jet black hair cascading down. There was so much hair that it seemed to be consuming her body (which looked frail and anorexic), negating the possibility that this naked flesh could represent active female sexual agency. The white diaper-like cloth reinforced the idea that this was a portrait of an adult female who wanted to be seen as childlike and innocent. Symbolically, the hair that is almost a covering hearkens back to early pictorial images of Eve in the garden. It evokes wildness, a sense of the "natural" world, even as it shrouds the body, repressing it, keeping it from the gaze of a culture that does not invite women to be sexual subjects. Concurrently, this cover contrasts whiteness and blackness. Whiteness dominates the page, obscuring and erasing the possibility of any assertion of black power. The longing that is most visible in this cover is that of the black woman to embody and be encircled by whiteness, personified by the possession of long straight hair. Since the hair is produced as commodity and purchased, it affirms contemporary notions of female beauty and desirability as that which can be acquired.

According to postmodern analyses of fashion, this is a time when commodities produce bodies, as this image of Ross suggests. In her essay "Fashion and the Cultural Logic of Postmodernity," Gail Faurshou explains that beauty is no longer seen as a sustained "category of precapitalist culture." Instead, "the colonization and the appropriation of the body as its own production/consumption machine in late capitalism is a fundamental theme of contemporary socialization." This cultural shift enables the bodies of black women to be represented in certain domains of the "beautiful" where they were once denied entry, i.e., high fashion magazines. Reinscribed as spectacle, once again on display, the bodies of black women appearing in these magazines are not there to document the beauty of black skin, of black bodies, but rather to call attention to other concerns. They are represented so readers will notice that the magazine is racially inclusive even though their features are often distorted, their bodies contorted into strange and bizarre postures that make the images appear monstrous or grotesque. They seem to represent an anti-aesthetic, one that mocks the very notion of beauty.

Often black female models appear in portraits that make them look less like humans and more like mannequins or robots. Currently, black models whose hair is not straightened are often photographed wearing straight wigs; this seems to be especially the case if the models' features are unconventional, i.e., if she has large lips or particularly dark skin, which is not often featured in the magazine. The October 1989 issue of *Elle* presented a short profile of designer Azzedine Alaia. He stands at a distance from a black female body holding the sleeves of her dress. Wearing a ridiculous straight hair-do, she appears naked holding the dress in front of her body. The caption reads, "THEY ARE BEAUTIFUL AREN'T THEY!" His critical gaze is on the model and not the dress. As commentary it suggests that even black women can look beautiful in the right outfit. Of course when you read the piece, this statement is not referring to the model, but is a statement Alaia makes about his clothes. In contemporary postmodern fashion sense, the black female is the best medium for the showing of clothes because her image does not detract from the outfit; it is subordinated.

Years ago, when much fuss was made about the reluctance of fashion magazines to include images of black women, it was assumed that the presence of such representations would in and of themselves challenge racist stereotypes that imply black women are not beautiful. Nowadays, black women are included in magazines in a manner that tends to reinscribe prevailing stereotypes. Darker-skinned models are most likely to appear in photographs where their features are distorted. Bi-racial women tend to appear in sexualized images. Trendy catalogues like *Tweeds* and *J. Crew* make use of a racialized subtext in their layout and advertisements. Usually they are emphasizing the connection between a white European and American style. When they began to include darker-skinned models, they chose bi-racial or fair-skinned black women, particularly with blonde or light brown long hair. The non-white models appearing in these catalogues must resemble as closely as possible their white counterparts so as not to detract from the racialized subtext. A recent cover of *Tweeds* carried this statement:

> Color is, perhaps, one of the most important barometers of character and self-assurance. It is as much a part of the international language of clothes as silhouette. The message colors convey, however, should never overwhelm. They should speak as eloquently and intelligently as the wearer. Whenever colors have that intelligence, subtlety, and nuance we tend to call them European...

Given the racialized terminology evoked in this copy, it follows that when flesh is exposed in attire that is meant to evoke sexual desirability it is worn by a non-white model. As sexist/racist sexual mythology would have it, she is the embodiment of the best of the black female savage tempered by those elements of whiteness that soften this image, giving it an aura of virtue and innocence. In the racialized pornographic imagination, she is the perfect combination of virgin and whore, the ultimate vamp. The impact of this image is so intense that Iman, a highly paid black fashion model who once received worldwide acclaim because she was the perfect black clone of a white ice goddess beauty, has had to change. Postmodern notions that black female beauty is constructed, not innate or inherent, are personified by the career of Iman. Noted in the past for features this culture sees as "Caucasian"—thin nose, lips, and limbs—Iman appears in the October 1989 issue of *Vogue* "made over." Her lips and breasts are suddenly full.

Having once had her "look" destroyed by a car accident and then remade, Iman now goes a step further. Displayed as the embodiment of a heightened sexuality, she now looks like the racial/sexual stereotype. In one full-page shot, she is naked, wearing only a pair of brocade boots, looking as though she is ready to stand on any street corner and turn a trick, or worse yet, as though she just walked off one of the pages of *Players* (a porn magazine for blacks). Iman's new image appeals to a culture that is eager to reinscribe the image of black woman as sexual primitive. This new representation is a response to contemporary fascination with an ethnic look, with the exotic Other who promises to fulfill racial and sexual stereotypes, to satisfy longings. This image is but an extension of the edible black tit.

Currently, in the fashion world the new black female icon who is also gaining greater notoriety, as she assumes both the persona of sexually hot "savage" and white-identified black girl, is the Caribbean-born model Naomi Campbell. Imported beauty, she, like Iman, is almost constantly visually portrayed nearly nude against a sexualized background. Abandoning her "natural" hair for blonde wigs or ever-lengthening weaves, she has great crossover appeal. Labeled by fashion critics as the black Briget Bardot, she embodies an aesthetic that suggests black women, while appealingly "different," must resemble white women to be considered really beautiful.

Within literature and early film, this sanitized ethnic image was defined as that of the "tragic mulatto." Appearing in film, she was the vamp that white men feared. As Julie Burchill puts it outrageously in *Girls On Film:*

> In the mature Forties, Hollywood decided to get to grips with the meaty and messy topic of multiracial romance, but it was a morbid business. Even when the girls were gorgeous white girls—multi-racial romance brought tears, traumas, and suicide. The message was clear: you intelligent white men suffer enough guilt because of what your grandaddy did—you want to suffer some more! Keep away from those girls...

Contemporary films portraying bi-racial stars convey this same message. The warning for women is different from that given men—we are given messages about the danger of asserting sexual desire. Clearly the message from *Imitation of Life* was that attempting to define oneself as sexual subject would lead to rejection and abandonment. In the film *Choose Me,* Rae Dawn Chong plays the role of the highly sexual black woman chasing and seducing the white man who does not desire her (as was first implied in *Imitation of Life*) but instead uses her sexually, beats her, then discards her. The bi-racial black woman is constantly "gaslighted" in contemporary film. The message her sexualized image conveys does not change even as she continues to chase the white man as if only he had the power to affirm that she is truly desirable.

European films like *Mephisto* and the more recent *Mona Lisa* also portray the almost white, black woman as tragically sexual. The women in the films can only respond to constructions of their reality created by the more powerful. They are trapped. Mona Lisa's struggle to be sexually self-defining leads her to choose lesbianism, even though she is desired by the white male hero. Yet her choice of a female partner does not mean sexual fulfillment as the object of her lust is a drug-addicted young white woman who is always too messed up to be sexual. Mona Lisa nurses and protects her. Rather than asserting sexual agency, she is once again in the role of mammy.

In a more recent film, *The Virgin Machine*, a white German woman obsessed by the longing to understand desire goes to California where she hopes to find a "paradise of black Amazons." However, when she arrives and checks out the lesbian scene, the black women she encounters are portrayed as mean fat grotesques, lewd and licentious. Contemporary films continue to place black women in two categories, mammy or slut, and occasionally a combination of the two. In *Mona Lisa,* one scene serves as powerful commentary on the way black sexuality is perceived in a racist and imperialist social context. The white male who desires the black prostitute Mona Lisa is depicted as a victim of romantic love who wishes to rescue her from a life of ruin. Yet he is also the conqueror, the colonizer, and this is most evident in the scene where he watches a video wherein she engages in fellatio with the black male pimp who torments her. Both the black man and the black woman are presented as available for the white male's sexual consumption. In the context of postmodern sexual practice, the masturbatory voyeuristic technologically-based fulfillment of desire is more exciting than actually possessing any real Other.

There are few films or television shows that attempt to challenge assumptions that sexual relationships between black women and white men are not based solely on power relationships which mirror master/slave paradigms. Years ago, when soap operas first tried to portray romantic/sexual involvement between a black woman and a white man, the station received so many letters of protest from outraged viewers that they dropped this plot. Today many viewers are glued to the television screen watching the soap opera *All My Children* primarily to see if the black woman played by Debbie Morgan will win the white man she so desperately loves. These two lovers are never portrayed in bedroom scenes so common now in daytime soaps. Morgan's character is competing not just with an old white woman flame to get her white man, she is competing with a notion of family. And the story poses the question of whether white male desire for black flesh will prevail over commitments to blood and family loyalty.

Despite this plot of interracial sexual romance on the soaps, there is little public discussion of the connections between race and sexuality. In real life, it was the Miss America pageant where a black woman was chosen to represent beauty and therefore desirability which forced a public discussion of race and sex. When it was revealed that Vanessa Williams, the fair-skinned straightened-hair "beauty," had violated the representation of the Miss America girl as pure and virtuous by having posed nude in a series of photographs showing her engaged in sexual play with a white woman, she lost her crown but gained a different status. After her public "disgrace," she was able to remain in the limelight by appropriating the image of sexualized vamp and playing sexy roles in films. Unmasked by a virtuous white public, she assumed (according to their standards) the rightful erotic place set aside for black women in the popular imagination. The American public that had so brutally critiqued Williams and rejected her had no difficulty accepting and applauding her when she accepted the image of fallen woman. Again, as in the case of Tina Turner, Williams bid for continued success necessitated her acceptance of conventional racist/sexist representations of black female sexuality.

The contemporary film that has most attempted to address the issue of black female sexual agency is Spike Lee's *She's Gotta Have It*. Sad to say, the black woman does not get "it." By the end of the film, she is still unable to answer the critical question, posed by one of her lovers as he rapes her, "whose pussy is this?" Reworded the question might be: How and when will black females assert sexual agency in ways that liberate us from the confines of colonized desire, of racist/sexist imagery and practice? Had Nola Darling been able to claim her sexuality and name its power, the film would have had a very different impact.

There are few films that explore issues of black female sexuality in ways that intervene and disrupt conventional representations. The short film *Dreaming Rivers*, by the British black film collective Sankofa, juxtaposes the idealized representation of black woman as mother with that of sexual subject, showing adult children facing their narrow notions of black female identity. The film highlights the autonomous sexual identity of a mature black woman which exists apart from her role as mother and caregiver. *Passion of Remembrance,* another film by Sankofa, offers exciting new representations of the black female body and black female sexuality. In one playfully erotic scene, two young black women, a lesbian couple, get dressed to go out. As part of their celebratory preparations they dance together, painting their lips, looking at their images in the mirror, exulting in their black female bodies. They shake to a song that repeats the refrain "let's get loose" without conjuring images of a rotgut colonized sexuality on display for the racist/sexist imagination. Their pleasure, the film suggests, emerges in a decolonized erotic context rooted in commitments to feminist and anti-racist politics. When they look in the mirror and focus on specific body parts (their full thick lips and buttocks), the gaze is one of recognition. We see their pleasure and delight in themselves.

Films by African American women filmmakers also offer the most oppositional images of black female sexuality. Seeing for a second time Kathleen Collin's film *Losing Ground,* I was impressed by her daring, the way she portrays black female sexuality in a way that is fresh and exciting. Like *Passion of Remembrance* it is in a domestic setting, where black women face one another (in Collin's film—as mother and daughter), that erotic images of black female sexuality surface outside a context of domination and exploitation. When daughter and mother share a meal, the audience watches as a radical sexual aesthetics emerges as the camera moves from woman to woman, focusing on the shades and textures of their skin, the shapes of their bodies, and the way their delight and pleasure in themselves is evident in their environment. Both black women discreetly flaunt a rich sensual erotic energy that is not directed outward, it is not there to allure or entrap; it is a powerful declaration of black female sexual subjectivity.

When black women relate to our bodies, our sexuality, in ways that place erotic recognition, desire, pleasure, and fulfillment at the center of our efforts to create radical black female subjectivity, we can make new and different representations of ourselves as sexual subjects. To do so we must be willing to transgress traditional boundaries. We must no longer shy away from the critical project of openly interrogating and exploring representations of black female sexuality as they appear everywhere, especially in popular culture. In *The Power of the Image: Essays on Representation and Sexuality,* Annette Kuhn offers a critical manifesto for feminist thinkers who long to explore gender and representation:

...in order to challenge dominant representations, it is necessary first of all to understand how they work, and thus where to seek points of possible productive transformation. From such understanding flow various politics and practices of oppositional cultural production, among which may be counted feminist interventions...there is another justification for a feminist analysis of mainstream images of women: may it not teach us to recognize inconsistencies and contradictions within dominant traditions of representation, to identify points of leverage for our own intervention: cracks and fissures through which may be captured glimpses of what in other circumstance might be possible, visions of "a world outside the order not normally seen or thought about?"

This is certainly the challenge facing black women, who must confront the old painful representations of our sexuality as a burden we must suffer, representations still haunting the present. We must make the oppositional space where our sexuality can be named and represented, where we are sexual subjects—no longer bound and trapped.

Chapter 5

A Feminist Challenge
Must We Call Every Woman Sister?

Watching the Clarence Thomas hearings was disempowering for masses of individuals, many of us female. While viewers admired Anita Hill's courage, daring to name publicly that she had been sexually harassed by Thomas, it was never clear what Hill intended by her disclosure. She never really stated an agenda. Did she feel that Thomas' willingness to use power coercively, to dominate via sexual harassment meant that he was an unworthy candidate for the Supreme Court? Did she speak out to protest because female subordinates working "under" Thomas might suffer the same fate were he to gain even more power? Did she believe that the nation would suffer having a person on the Supreme Court who lies, manipulates, and deceives? And having decided to participate in public hearings, why didn't it occur to Hill (or her advisors) that she would need to explain, even justify in a compelling and convincing way, why, at her own initiative, she continued working relations with Thomas. Though many women viewers felt we understood Hill's actions, for any woman to make such charges within the context of white supremacist capitalist patriarchy, especially a black woman, if indeed she expected to be taken seriously, there should have been full recognition that she would need to do more than simply state her case.

Anita Hill stated her case. She did not appear to have a strategy that was based on considering the needs, desires, and expectations of her audience, both that of the Senate committee or the millions of viewers watching her. While I have talked with many women of various races and ethnicities who admired Hill's calmness, her steadfast mono-tone as she gave rational testimony, such admiration need not obscure the reality that Hill's performance suggests that she brought to the hearings misguided faith in a system that has rarely worked for women seeking justice in cases of sexual harassment. Needless to say, this faith led her to enter the lion's den without necessary protection. This is not admirable. Had Anita Hill been an advocate of feminism, mild or militant, she would have brought to the hearings the kind of feminist thinking and awareness that would have enabled her to face the reality that white supremacist patriarchy had already chosen Thomas. It would have given her the wisdom to understand that to challenge that choice, either by creating powerful opposition or by exposing his true character, she would need to subvert the system. Subversion requires strategy. Simply stating the case was not enough. Hill has stated: "I am hopeful that others who may have suffered sexual harassment will not become discouraged by my experience but instead will find the strength to speak." Yet the Thomas hearings made it abundantly clear that coming to voice around sexual harassment is only one stage of a process for any individual female seeking justice.

While it is crucial that women come to voice in a patriarchal society that socializes us to repress and contain, it is also crucial what we say, how we say it, and what our politics are. To see the Thomas hearings as solely an issue of a female coming to voice in a case of sexual harassment, as many folks chose to do, is to reduce the com-plexity of both the issue of Thomas' appointment to the Supreme Court and of Hill's relationship to the political system that chose to support and affirm that appointment. Watching these hearings, we were not just seeing a black man and a black woman at odds with one another about sexual harassment. We were watching two conservative black folks who have shown by their political allegiances that they identify with mainstream white conservative culture and politics. Both parties sug-gested by their willingness to participate in the public spectacle of these hearings that they believed it was indeed possible for them to gain recognition, voice, a fair and just hearing within a white supremacist patriarchal state that has historically, stubbornly refused to hear the voices of oppressed and marginalized black people seeking justice.

Ironically, Clarence Thomas, whose advisors were evidently far more astute than the folks working with Anita Hill, did not act as though he could simply state his case. He clearly strategized. A major moment of victory occurred when Thomas dropped the mask of rational cool and expressed anger and rage at the process. His declaration that he was a victim of a "high-tech lynching" was a shrewd move which not only deflected away from the victimization of Anita Hill; it shifted the nature of the public discourse. Prior to these comments, race had not been seen as a primary factor shaping the contents of the interrogations. By raising the historical specter of lynching, Thomas evoked images that are both racial and sexual in nature. Practically all the visual images that remain of lynchings of black males by white mobs show blacks to be sexually mutilated, usually castrated. Lynching, then, must be seen as both a racial and sexual crime. In effect, Thomas covertly suggested that he was being subjected to a form of sexual harassment more gruesome and brutal than any verbal harassment could ever be. To use the vernacular, he was saying, "y'all trying to punish me for using nasty talk to harass when you trying to cut off my dick." And it is not surprising that the specter of castration which haunts white America's racial imagination should in the context of patriarchy appear to be the more heinous crime. The white patriarchal members of the Senate committee could empathize with the idea of an endangered phallus. They could not and did not empathize with the suffering of Anita Hill. Hence, Thomas' "pain" at being the object of what he strategically implied was the continuation of white male rape and castration of black males was seen as far more brutal than any pain Hill could possibly have suffered. Displacing the narrative of male domination and sexual harassment of females, Thomas placed himself outside the borders of the white phallocentric culture he had previously been so intimately allied with.

Having refused to acknowledge the importance of racial differ-ence and white victimization of black folks in the past, he chose to identify himself with the black men (and women) who were the victims of one of the cruelest expressions of white supremacy. His evocation of lynching echoed the work of Eldridge Cleaver, a self-confessed sexual harasser and rapist, who, in *Soul On Ice,* attempted to justify this perverse aggressive sexist behavior as a necessary response to racialized sexual victimization at the hands of white men. Millions of white and black readers responded with compassion to Cleaver's insistence that it was white racism that had forced him to become a rapist. Suggesting that white men were obsessed by their desire to control black men's bodies, Cleaver wrote in the persona of a white male speaker:

> ...the Brain must control the Body. To prove my omnipotence I must cuckold you and fetter your bull balls. I will fetter the range of your rod and limit its reach. My prick will excel your rod. I have

made a calculation. I will have sexual freedom. But I will bind
your rod with my omnipotent will, and place a limitation on its
aspiration which you will violate on pain of death...By subjecting
your manhood to the control of my will, I shall control you. The
stem of the Body, the penis, must submit to the will of the Brain.

Clarence Thomas evoked this image of white males controlling
black manhood, and it was most effective. In the popular imagination
of white and black folks alike, he represented the black male standing
up for his right to participate fully in patriarchy, in the culture of the
phallus. He became a heroic symbol of sexist black male resistance to
being controlled by the white man. As one white male cabdriver said
to me: "So what if he's a harasser and a pornographer. Aren't they all?
Why should he be punished?" After all, Thomas, even in the act of
attempting to sexually coerce a black female, was only acting as white
men have acted with impunity in white racist society. And in choosing
to marry a white female (whose image was always behind his during
the hearing), he was also expressing his allegiance to white supremacist
patriarchy. Hence, Thomas, who had no qualms about publicly naming
his objectification of black females, his preference for light-skinned
women, could join the culture in presenting Anita Hill as just another
"black bitch" scorned and seeking revenge.

In such a context, it is not surprising that Anita Hill became the
object of fierce, sexist interrogation. To many viewers, her calm
demeanor was a sign of her integrity, that she had chosen the high
moral ground. Yet to some of us, it was yet another example of black
female stoicism in the face of sexist/racist abuse. While it may not have
changed the outcome of the hearings in any way, had Hill been more
strategic and passionate, and dare I say it, even angry at the assault on
her character, it would have made the hearings less an assault on the
psyches of black females watching and on women viewers in general.

Contrary to those who wish to claim that the hearings were in
some way a feminist victory, it was precisely the absence of either a
feminist analysis on Hill's part or a feminist response that made this
spectacle more an example of female martyrdom and victimization than
of a constructive confrontation with patriarchal male domination. Black
women have always held an honored place in the hall of female
martyrdom. As Anita Hill's friend Ellen Wells declared in a passionate
defense of Hill not initiating a case against Thomas when the harassment first occurred, "Being a black woman, you know you have to put
up with a lot so you grit your teeth and do it." With this comment, Wells
evoked a tradition of female martyrdom and masochism. There is no

suggestion on the part of these conservative black women that there is a place for feminist rebellion and resistance. Indeed, they seemed to be strong advocates for a position that suggests women have no choice but to be "dutiful daughters." And certainly, from this standpoint, Hill's actions appear heroic. Commenting on the hearings, Michele Wallace suggests that it was "gratifying to see such a display of courage and dignity on the part of any woman participating in the dominant discourse." While this may be true, it should not lead to uncritical acceptance of Hill's or any woman's allegiance to white supremacist patriarchy. Advocates of feminism should be among those adamantly stressing that Hill had other options and did not have to act only in the role of dutiful daughter. Perhaps, it is her allegiance to that role that not only made her reluctant to speak in the first place but finally unable to speak in a manner that would make her case convincing. Unable to step outside the boundaries of patriarchal discourse, Hill was never disloyal to patriarchy or, for that matter, to the institution of white supremacy. Instead she expressed her loyalty consistently by the manner in which she appealed to the system for justice. By appropriating her as feminist hero, women, and white women in particular, show that they are more interested in positioning Hill in support of a feminism that she never espoused.

Anita Hill had every right to justice in her case against Clarence Thomas. Let's be clear about that fact. That she deserves justice as a victim of sexual harassment does not preclude the possibility that she may have chosen to remain silent about this abuse for reasons other than victimization. It is possible that both career opportunism and allegiance to being a dutiful daughter led Hill to feel that she could not confront Thomas early on. Neither possibility justifies Thomas' actions. However, the decision to publicly name him as a sexual harasser does not necessarily indicate that Hill is in rebellion against patriarchy and male domination.

Ultimately, the nature of the hearings suggest that there is still no place within white supremacist capitalist patriarchy for a discussion of black gender relations that would enable black women and men to confront questions of power and domination, of black male sexism and black female resistance. For, to a grave extent, the spectacle of the Thomas hearings had little to do with any desire on the part of the American public to determine whether or not Thomas was a worthy candidate for the Supreme Court or to truthfully examine his coercive relations with black female subordinates. These issues were completely displaced and subsumed as the hearings became a public occasion for an assault on feminism, a place where those with a right-wing agenda around sexuality and censorship could press their points. That Anita Hill's personal political reality was obscured by those who positioned her as feminist symbol cannot be denied. And it is this positioning that allowed many people to see the hearings as the death of feminism. The hearings were an attack on feminism (defined here as a movement to end sexism and sexist oppression) and an attack on feminist principles.

As Orlando Patterson stated in his misogynist rant, "Race, Gender and Liberal Fallacies," published in the op-ed section of the *New York Times:*

> Thanks to this drama, we have entered an important new phase in the nation's discourse on gender relations, and it goes well beyond the enhanced realization by men that the complaints of women must be taken seriously. Implicit in these hearings was an overdue questioning of the legalistic, neo-Puritan and elitist model of gender relations promoted by the dominant school of American feminists.

Contrary to Patterson's assertion that the hearings were a "ritual of inclusion," indicating public affirmation that blacks belong in the system, that "the culture of slavery is dead," we were witnessing yet another plantation drama where the labor and bodies of black folks were made to serve the interests of a system that has no intention of fostering and promoting the social and political growth of black people or eradicating racism and white supremacy.

Visually, what millions of Americans saw as they watched the hearings was the representation of white supremacist capitalist patriarchy as it truly is. There was no racial or sexual diversity on the committee, none of that "inclusion" that would indicate shared positions of equality within the existing social structure, which Patterson alludes to in his commentary. And it was more than evident, both visually and in terms of their demeanor, that bonds of white supremacy and maleness transcended differences of political position among the white male Senate committee members. Those bonds could extend to and include Clarence Thomas because he so fundamentally allied himself with the interests of white supremacist capitalist patriarchy.

Recently, white controlled and dominated mass media has constructed and promoted the fiction that black conservatism is something new, fostering as well the concomitant assumption that it is not tolerated in black life. Hence, understanding white folks, both liberal and conservative alike, must "protect" the "dissident" voices of black conservatives from those more commonly radical black voices that would "censor and silence" them. In reality, black folks have always known that many of us were conservative and all too often conservative political viewpoints have determined the nature of black rebellion and reform. It's white folks who have just recently discovered the militant black conservative and recognized that he or she can be a powerful spokesperson for agendas that serve the interest of mainstream white culture. When journalists suggest, as one did in the October issue of *New York* magazine, that one of the important victories of the hearing was that "the nation was treated to a parade of blacks who—for once—weren't crack dealers, athletes, welfare mothers, or any of the other stereotypes but solid citizens, fine friends, and excellent character witnesses for the two principals," it is obvious that the audience that comprises this "nation" is white. This comment confirms that ultimately the Thomas hearings were not only a public political spectacle orchestrated by whites but that whites were, indeed, the intended audience. The rest of us were merely voyeurs.

Many black folks can testify that the Thomas hearings seemed to have a profound impact on many white Americans. Often fearful of black people and issues concerning race, the Thomas hearings provided many white folks with an issue that they could talk to black people about. It was a safe way for them to talk about race and gender. Before the Thomas hearings, no strange white man had ever attempted to talk with me about his desire for attractive black women. Yet, several white men initiated conversations with me on airplanes, in lines at the bank, in taxicabs where they could share that they identified with Thomas, that they too found Anita Hill attractive and could see why Thomas would approach her. As one young white man put it, "He was only doing what a man does."

A number of black females I know have said they have been the objects of unprecedented assaults both verbal and physical by white males since the Thomas hearings. Concurrently, the Thomas hearings exacerbated overall social bashing of black females, and professional black females in particular. Recently, about to give a lecture at the University of Arizona, I spotted a young black female sitting in the audience and greeted her with warmth and sisterly regard. At the end of my lecture she came up and stated that she had not read my work, that a class assignment had compelled her attendance at the talk but that she was glad she had come because my recognition of her had, as she put it, "done a lot to restore her faith in black women, a faith that the Thomas hearings had shaken." She was referring to the many black women, especially those who were seen on television opposing and denouncing Hill while supporting Thomas. While the hearings did not signal the death of feminism, they did dramatize the triumph of sexist justice.

The hearings were a brutal reminder to advocates of feminism— to all of us who are concerned with progressive agendas—that conservative politics will rule the day if there is not sufficient protest, subversion, and rebellion. Many groups, including feminists, have been galvanized to action by the hearings. Progressives can only hope that the spirit of rebellion and resistance will not be transitory but will serve to foster a climate of critical vigilance and radical action that will once again make the transformation of this culture into a truly democratic and just society a meaningful agenda, a cause worth struggling for.

Chapter 6

Reconstructing Black Masculinity

Black and white snapshots of my childhood always show me in the company of my brother. Less than a year older than me, we looked like twins and for a time in life we did everything together. We were inseparable. As young children, we were brother and sister, comrades, in it together. As adolescents, he was forced to become a boy and I was forced to become a girl. In our southern black Baptist patriarchal home, being a boy meant learning to be tough, to mask one's feelings, to stand one's ground and fight—being a girl meant learning to obey, to be quiet, to clean, to recognize that you had no ground to stand on. I was tough, he was not. I was strong willed, he was easygoing. We were both a disappointment. Affectionate, full of good humor, loving, my brother was not at all interested in becoming a patriarchal boy. This lack of interest generated a fierce anger in our father.

We grew up staring at black and white photos of our father in a boxing ring, playing basketball, with the black infantry he was part of in World War II. He was a man in uniform, a man's man, able to hold his own. Despising his one son for not wanting to become the strong silent type (my brother loved to talk, tell jokes, and make us happy), our father let him know early on that he was no son to him, real sons wanted to be like their fathers. Made to feel inadequate, less than male in his childhood, one boy in a house full of six sisters, he became forever haunted by the idea of patriarchal masculinity. All that he had questioned in his childhood was sought after in his early adult life in order to become a man's man—phallocentric, patriarchal, and masculine. In traditional black communities when one tells a grown male to "be a man," one is urging him to aspire to a masculine identity rooted in the patriarchal ideal. Throughout black male history in the United States there have been black men who were not at all interested in the patriarchal ideal. In the black community of my childhood, there was no monolithic standard of black masculinity. Though the patriarchal ideal was the most esteemed version of manhood, it was not the only version. No one in our house talked about black men being no good, shiftless, trifling. Head of the household, our father was a "much man," a provider, lover, disciplinarian, reader, and thinker. He was introverted, quiet, and slow to anger, yet fierce when aroused. We respected him. We were in awe of him. We were afraid of his power, his physical prowess, his deep voice, and his rare unpredictable but intense rage. We were never allowed to forget that, unlike other black men, our father was the fulfillment of the patriarchal masculine ideal.

Though I admired my father, I was more fascinated and charmed by black men who were not obsessed with being patriarchs: by Felix, a hobo who jumped trains, never worked a regular job, and had a missing thumb; by Kid, who lived out in the country and hunted the rabbits and coons that came to our table; by Daddy Gus, who spoke in hushed tones, sharing his sense of spiritual mysticism. These were the men who touched my heart. The list could go on. I remember them because they loved folks, especially women and children. They were caring and giving. They were black men who chose alternative life-styles, who questioned the *status quo,* who shunned a ready made patriarchal identity and invented themselves. By knowing them, I have never been tempted to ignore the complexity of black male experience and identity. The generosity of spirit that characterized who they were and how they lived in the world lingers in my memory. I write this piece to honor them, knowing as I do now that it was no simple matter for them to choose against patriarchy, to choose themselves, their lives. And I write this piece for my brother in hopes that he will recover one day, come back to himself, know again the way to love, the peace of an unviolated free spirit. It was this peace that the quest for an unattainable life-threatening patriarchal masculine ideal took from him.

When I left our segregated southern black community and went to a predominately white college, the teachers and students I met knew nothing about the lives of black men. Learning about the matriarchy myth and white culture's notion that black men were emasculated, I was shocked. These theories did not speak to the world I had most intimately known, did not address the complex gender roles that were so familiar to me. Much of the scholarly work on black masculinity that was presented in the classroom then was based on material gleaned from studies of urban black life. This work conveyed the message that black masculinity was homogenous. It suggested that all black men were tormented by their inability to fulfill the phallocentric masculine ideal as it has been articulated in white supremacist capitalist patriarchy. Erasing the realities of black men who have diverse understandings of masculinity, scholarship on the black family (traditionally the framework for academic discussion of black masculinity) puts in place of this lived complexity a flat, one-dimensional representation.

The portrait of black masculinity that emerges in this work perpetually constructs black men as "failures" who are psychologically "fucked up," dangerous, violent, sex maniacs whose insanity is informed by their inability to fulfill their phallocentric masculine destiny in a racist context. Much of this literature is written by white people, and some of it by a few academic black men. It does not interrogate the conventional construction of patriarchal masculinity or question the extent to which black men have historically internalized this norm. It never assumes the existence of black men whose creative agency has enabled them to subvert norms and develop ways of thinking about masculinity that challenge patriarchy. Yet, there has never been a time in the history of the United States when black folks, particularly black men, have not been enraged by the dominant culture's stereotypical, fantastical representations of black masculinity. Unfortunately, black people have not systematically challenged these narrow visions, insisting on a more accurate "reading" of black male reality. Acting in complicity with the *status quo,* many black people have passively absorbed narrow representations of black masculinity, perpetuated stereotypes, myths, and offered one-dimensional accounts. Contemporary black men have been shaped by these representations.

No one has yet endeavored to chart the journey of black men from Africa to the so called "new world" with the intent to reconstruct how they saw themselves. Surely the black men who came to the American continent before Columbus, saw themselves differently from those who were brought on slave ships, or from those few who freely immigrated to a world where the majority of their brethren were enslaved. Given all that we know of the slave context, it is unlikely that enslaved black men spoke the same language, or that they bonded on the basis of shared "male" identity. Even if they had come from cultures where gender difference was clearly articulated in relation to specific roles that was all disrupted in the "new world" context. Transplanted African men, even those who were coming from cultures where sex roles shaped the division of labor, where the status of men was different and most often higher than that of females, had imposed on them the white colonizer's notions of manhood and masculinity. Black men did not respond to this imposition passively. Yet it is evident in black male slave narratives that black men engaged in racial uplift were often most likely to accept the norms of masculinity set by white culture.

Although the gendered politics of slavery denied black men the freedom to act as "men" within the definition set by white norms, this notion of manhood did become a standard used to measure black male progress. Slave narratives document ways black men thought about manhood. The narratives of Henry "Box" Brown, Josiah Henson, Frederick Douglass, and a host of other black men reveal that they saw "freedom" as that change in status that would enable them to fulfill the role of chivalric benevolent patriarch. Free, they would be men able to provide for and take care of their families. Describing how he wept as he watched a white slave overseer beat his mother, William Wells Brown lamented, "Experience has taught me that nothing can be more heart-rending than for one to see a dear and beloved mother or sister tortured, and to hear their cries and not be able to render them assistance. But such is the position which an American slave occupies." Frederick Douglass did not feel his manhood affirmed by intellectual progress. It was affirmed when he fought man to man with the slave overseer. This struggle was a "turning point" in Douglass' life: "It rekindled in my breast the smoldering embers of liberty. It brought up my Baltimore dreams and revived a sense of my own manhood. I was a changed being after that fight. I was nothing before—I was a man now." The image of black masculinity that emerges from slave narratives is one of hardworking men who longed to assume full patriarchal responsibility for families and kin.

Given this aspiration and the ongoing brute physical labor of black men that was the backbone of slave economy (there were more male slaves than black female slaves, particularly before breeding became a common practice), it is really amazing that stereotypes of black men as lazy and shiftless so quickly became common in public imagination. In these 19th and early 20th-century representations, black men were cartoon-like creatures only interested in drinking and having a good time. Such stereotypes were an effective way for white racists to erase the significance of black male labor from public consciousness. Later on, these same stereotypes were evoked as reasons to deny black men jobs. They are still evoked today.

Male "idleness" did not have the same significance in African and Native American cultures that it had in the white mindset. Many 19th-century Christians saw all forms of idle activity as evil, or at least a breeding ground for wrong-doing. For Native Americans and Africans, idle time was space for reverie and contemplation. When slavery ended, black men could once again experience that sense of space. There are no studies which explore the way Native American cultures altered notions of black masculinity, especially for those black men who lived as Indians or who married Indian wives. Since we know there were many tribes who conceived of masculine roles in ways that were quite different from those of whites, black men may well have found African ideas about gender roles affirmed in Native traditions.

There are also few confessional narratives by black men that chronicle how they felt as a group when freedom did not bring with it the opportunity for them to assume a "patriarchal" role. Those black men who worked as farmers were often better able to assume this role than those who worked as servants or who moved to cities. Certainly, in the mass migration from the rural south to the urban north, black men lost status. In southern black communities there were many avenues for obtaining communal respect. A man was not respected solely because he could work, make money, and provide. The extent to which a given black man absorbed white society's notion of man-hood likely determined the extent of his bitterness and despair that white supremacy continually blocked his access to the patriarchal ideal.

Nineteenth century black leaders were concerned about gender roles. While they believed that men should assume leadership positions in the home and public life, they were also concerned about the role of black women in racial uplift. Whether they were merely paying lip-service to the cause of women's rights or were true believers, exceptional individual black men advocated equal rights for black women. In his work, Martin Delaney continually stressed that both genders needed to work in the interest of racial uplift. To him, gender equality was more a way to have greater involvement in racial uplift than a way for black women to be autonomous and independent. Black male leaders like Martin Delaney and Frederick Douglass were patri-archs, but as benevolent dictators they were willing to share power with women, especially if it meant they did not have to surrender any male privilege. As co-editors of the *North Star,* Douglass and Delaney had a masthead in 1847 which read "right is of no sex—truth is of no color..." The 1848 meeting of the National Negro Convention included a pro-posal by Delaney stating: "Whereas we fully believe in the equality of the sexes, therefore, resolved that we hereby invite females hereafter to take part in our deliberation." In Delaney's 1852 treatise *The Condition, Elevation, Emigration, and Destiny of the Colored People of the United States, Politically Considered,* he argued that black women should have full access to education so that they could be better mothers, asserting:

> The potency and respectability of a nation or people, depends entirely upon the position of their women; therefore, it is essential to our elevation that the female portion of our children be instructed in all the arts and sciences pertaining to the highest civilization.

In Delaney's mind, equal rights for black women in certain public spheres such as education did not mean that he was advocating a change in domestic relations whereby black men and women would have co-equal status in the home.

Most 19th-century black men were not advocating equal rights for women. On one hand, most black men recognized the powerful and necessary role black women had played as freedom fighters in the movement to abolish slavery and other civil rights efforts, yet on the other hand they continued to believe that women should be subordinate to men. They wanted black women to conform to the gender norms set by white society. They wanted to be recognized as "men," as patriarchs, by other men, including white men. Yet they could not assume this position if black women were not willing to conform to prevailing sexist gender norms. Many black women who had endured white supremacist patriarchal domination during slavery did not want to be dominated by black men after manumission. Like black men, they had contradictory positions on gender. On one hand they did not want to be "dominated," but on the other hand they wanted black men to be protectors and providers. After slavery ended, enormous tension and conflict emerged between black women and men as folks struggled to be self-determining. As they worked to create standards for community and family life, gender roles continued to be problematic.

Black men and women who wanted to conform to gender role norms found that this was nearly impossible in a white racist economy that wanted to continue its exploitation of black labor. Much is made, by social critics who want to further the notion that black men are symbolically castrated, of the fact that black women often found work in service jobs while black men were unemployed. The reality, however, was that in some homes it was problematic when a black woman worked and the man did not, or when she earned more than he, yet, in other homes, black men were quite content to construct alternative roles. Critics who look at black life from a sexist standpoint advance the assumption that black men were psychologically devastated because they did not have the opportunity to slave away in low paying jobs for white racist employers when the truth may very well be that those black men who wanted to work but could not find jobs, as well as those who did not want to find jobs, may simply have felt relieved that they did not have to submit to economic exploitation. Concurrently, there were black women who wanted black men to assume patriarchal roles and there were some who were content to be autonomous, independent. And long before contemporary feminist movement sanctioned the idea that men could remain home and rear children while women worked, black women and men had such arrangements and were happy with them.

Without implying that black women and men lived in gender utopia, I am suggesting that black sex roles, and particularly the role of men, have been more complex and problematized in black life than is believed. This was especially the case when all black people lived in segregated neighborhoods. Racial integration has had a profound impact on black gender roles. It has helped to promote a climate wherein most black women and men accept sexist notions of gender roles. Unfortunately, many changes have occurred in the way black people think about gender, yet the shift from one standpoint to another has not been fully documented. For example: To what extent did the civil rights movement, with its definition of freedom as having equal opportunity with whites, sanction looking at white gender roles as a norm black people should imitate? Why has there been so little positive interest shown in the alternative lifestyles of black men? In every segregated black community in the United States there are adult black men married, unmarried, gay, straight, living in households where they do not assert patriarchal domination and yet live fulfilled lives, where they are not sitting around worried about castration. Again it must be emphasized that the black men who are most worried about castration and emasculation are those who have completely absorbed white supremacist patriarchal definitions of masculinity.

Advanced capitalism further changed the nature of gender roles for all men in the United States. The image of the patriarchal head of the household, ruler of this mini-state called the "family," faded in the 20th century. More men than ever before worked for someone else. The state began to interfere more in domestic matters. A man's time was not his own; it belonged to his employer, and the terms of his rule in the family were altered. In the old days, a man who had no money could still assert tyrannic rule over family and kin, by virtue of his patriarchal status, usually affirmed by Christian belief systems. Within a burgeoning capitalist economy, it was wage-earning power that determined the extent to which a man would rule over a household, and even that rule was limited by the power of the state. In *White Hero, Black Beast,* Paul Hoch describes the way in which advanced capitalism altered representations of masculinity:

> The concept of masculinity is dependent at its very root on the concepts of sexual repression and private property. Ironically, it is sexual repression and economic scarcity that give masculinity its main significance as a symbol of economic status and sexual opportunity. The shrinkage of the concept of man into the narrowed and hierarchical conceptions of masculinity of the various work and consumption ethics also goes hand in hand with an increasing social division of labor, and an increasing shrinkage of the body's erogenous potentials culminating in a narrow genital sexuality. As we move from the simpler food-gathering societies to the agricultural society to the urbanized work and warfare society, we notice that it is a narrower and narrower range of activities that yield masculine status.

In feminist terms, this can be described as a shift from emphasis on patriarchal status (determined by one's capacity to assert power over others in a number of spheres based on maleness) to a phallocentric model, where what the male does with his penis becomes a greater and certainly a more accessible way to assert masculine status. It is easy to see how this served the interests of a capitalist state which was indeed depriving men of their rights, exploiting their labor in such a way that they only indirectly received the benefits, to deflect away from a patriarchal power based on ruling others and to emphasize a masculine status that would depend solely on the penis.

With the emergence of a fierce phallocentrism, a man was no longer a man because he provided care for his family, he was a man simply because he had a penis. Furthermore, his ability to use that penis in the arena of sexual conquest could bring him as much status as being a wage earner and provider. A sexually defined masculine ideal rooted in physical domination and sexual possession of women could be accessible to all men. Hence, even unemployed black men could gain status, could be seen as the embodiment of masculinity, within a phallocentric framework. Barbara Ehrenreich's *The Hearts of Men* chronicles white male repudiation of a masculine ideal rooted in a notion of patriarchal rule requiring a man to marry and care for the material well-being of women and children and an increasing embrace of a phallocentric "playboy" ideal. At the end of the chapter "Early Rebels," Ehrenreich describes rites of passage in the 1950s which led white men away from traditional nonconformity into a rethinking of masculine status:

> ...not every would-be male rebel had the intellectual reserves to gray gracefully with the passage of the decade. They drank beyond excess, titrating gin with coffee in their lunch hours, gin with Alka-Seltzer on the weekends. They had stealthy affairs with secretaries, and tried to feel up their neighbors' wives at parties. They escaped into Mickey Spillane mysteries, where naked blondes were routinely perforated in a hail of bullets, or into Westerns, where there were no women at all and no visible sources of white-collar employment. And some of them began to discover an alternative, or at least an entirely new style of male rebel who hinted, seductively, that there was an alternative. The new rebel was the playboy.

Even in the restricted social relations of slavery black men had found a way to practice the fine art of phallocentric seduction. Long before white men stumbled upon the "playboy" alternative, black vernacular culture told stories about that non-working man with time on his hands who might be seducing somebody else's woman. Blues songs narrate the "playboy" role. Ehrenreich's book acknowledges that the presence of black men in segregated black culture and their engagement in varied expressions of masculinity influenced white men:

> The Beat hero, the male rebel who actually walks away from responsibility in any form, was not a product of middle-class angst. The possibility of walking out, without money or guilt, and without ambition other than to see and do everything, was not even imminent in the middle-class culture of the early fifties... The new bohemianism of the Beats came from somewhere else entirely, from an underworld and an underclass invisible from the corporate "crystal palace" or suburban dream houses.

Alternative male lifestyles that opposed the *status quo* were to be found in black culture.

White men seeking alternatives to a patriarchal masculinity turned to black men, particularly black musicians. Norman Podhoretz's 1963 essay "My Negro Problem—And Ours" names white male fascination with blackness, and black masculinity:

> Just as in childhood I envied Negroes for what seemed to me their superior masculinity, so I envy them today for what seems to be their superior physical grace and beauty. I have come to value physical grace very highly and I am now capable of aching with all my being when I watch a Negro couple on the dance floor, or a Negro playing baseball or basketball. They are on the kind of terms with their own bodies that I should like to be on with mine, and for that precious quality they seem blessed to me.

Black masculinity, as fantasized in the racist white imagination, is the quintessential embodiment of man as "outsider" and "rebel." They were the ultimate "traveling men" drifting from place to place, town to town, job to job.

Within segregated black communities, the "traveling" black man was admired even as he was seen as an indictment of the failure of black men to achieve the patriarchal masculine ideal. Extolling the virtues of traveling black men in her novels, Toni Morrison sees them as "truly masculine in the sense of going out so far where you're not supposed to go and running toward confrontations rather than away from them." This is a man who takes risks, what Morrison calls a "free man":

> This is a man who is stretching, you know, he's stretching, he's going all the way within his own mind and within whatever his outline might be. Now that's the tremendous possibility for masculinity among black men. And you see it a lot...They may end up in sort of twentieth-century, contemporary terms being also unemployed. They may be in prison. They may be doing all sorts of things. But they are adventuresome in that regard.

Within white supremacist capitalist patriarchy, rebel black masculinity has been idolized and punished, romanticized yet vilified. Though the traveling man repudiates being a patriarchal provider, he does not necessarily repudiate male domination.

Collectively, black men have never critiqued the dominant culture's norms of masculine identity, even though they have reworked those norms to suit their social situation. Black male sociologist Robert Staples argues that the black male is "in conflict with the normative definition of masculinity," yet this conflict has never assumed the form of complete rebellion. Assuming that black men are "crippled emotionally" when they cannot fully achieve the patriarchal ideal, Staples asserts: "This is a status which few, if any, black males have been able to achieve. Masculinity, as defined in this culture, has always implied a certain autonomy and mastery of one's environment." Though Staples suggests, "the black male has always had to confront the contradiction between the normative expectation attached to being male in this society and proscriptions on his behavior and achievement of goals," implicit in his analysis is the assumption that black men could only internalize this norm and be victimized by it. Like many black men, he assumes that patriarchy and male domination is not a socially constructed social order but a "natural" fact of life. He therefore cannot acknowledge that black men could have asserted meaningful agency by repudiating the norms white culture was imposing.

These norms could not be repudiated by black men who saw nothing problematic or wrong minded about them. Staples, like most black male scholars writing about black masculinity, does not attempt to deconstruct normative thinking, he laments that black men have not had full access to patriarchal phallocentrism. Embracing the phallocentric ideal, he explains black male rape of women by seeing it as a reaction against their inability to be "real men" (i.e., assert legitimate domination over women). Explaining rape, Staples argues:

> In the case of black men, it is asserted that they grow up feeling emasculated and powerless before reaching manhood. They often encounter women as authority figures and teachers or as the head of their household. These men consequently act out their feelings of powerlessness against black women in the form of sexual aggression. Hence, rape by black men should be viewed as both an aggressive and political act because it occurs in the context of racial discrimination which denies most black men a satisfying manhood.

Staples does not question why black women are the targets of black male aggression if it is white men and a white racist system which prevents them from assuming the "patriarchal" role. Given that many white men who fully achieve normal masculinity rape, his implied argument that black men would not rape if they could be patriarchs seems ludicrous. And his suggestion that they would not rape if they could achieve a "satisfying manhood" is pure fantasy. Given the context of this paragraph, it is safe to assume that the "satisfying manhood" he evokes carries with it the phallocentric right of men to dominate women, however benevolently. Ultimately, he is suggesting that if black men could legitimately dominate women more effectively they would not need to coerce them outside the law. Growing up in a black community where there were individual black men who critiqued normative masculinity, who repudiated patriarchy and its concomitant support of sexism, I fully appreciate that it is a tremendous loss that there is little known of their ideas about black masculinity. Without documentation of their presence, it has been easier for black men who embrace patriarchal masculinity, phallocentrism, and sexism to act as though they speak for all black men. Since their representations of black masculinity are in complete agreement with white culture's assessment, they do not threaten or challenge white domination, they reinscribe it.

Contemporary black power movement made synonymous black liberation and the effort to create a social structure wherein black men could assert themselves as patriarchs, controlling community, family, and kin. On one hand, black men expressed contempt for white men yet they also envied them their access to patriarchal power. Using a "phallocentric" stick to beat white men, Amiri Baraka asserted in his 1960s essay "american sexual reference: black male":

> Most American white men are trained to be fags. For this reason it is no wonder that their faces are weak and blank, left without the hurt that reality makes—anytime. That red flush, those silk blue faggot eyes…They are the 'masters' of the world, and their children are taught this as God's fingerprint, so they can devote most of their energies to the nonrealistic, having no use for the real. They devote their energies to the nonphysical, the nonrealistic, and become estranged from them. Even their wars move to the stage where whole populations can be destroyed by pushing a button…can you, for a second imagine the average middle class white man able to do somebody harm? Alone? Without the technology that at this moment still has him rule the world: Do you understand the softness of the white man, the weakness…

This attack on white masculinity, and others like it, did not mean that black men were attacking normative masculinity, they were simply pointing out that white men had not fulfilled the ideal. It was a case of "will the real man please stand up." And when he stood up, he was, in the eyes of black power movement, a black male.

This phallocentric idealization of masculinity is most powerfully expressed in the writings of George Jackson. Throughout *Soledad Brother,* he announces his uncritical acceptance of patriarchal norms, especially the use of violence as a means of social control. Critical of nonviolence as a stance that would un-man black males, he insisted:

The symbol of the male here in North American has always been the gun, the knife, the club. Violence is extolled at every exchange: the TV, the motion pictures, the best-seller lists. The newspapers that sell best are those that carry the boldest, bloodiest headlines and most sports coverage. To die for king and country is to die a hero.

Jackson felt black males would need to embrace this use of violence if they hoped to defeat white adversaries. And he is particularly critical of black women for not embracing these notions of masculinity:

I am reasonably certain that I draw from every black male in this country some comments to substantiate that his mother, the black female, attempted to aid his survival by discouraging his violence or by turning it inward. The blacks of slave society, U.S.A., have always been a matriarchal subsociety. The implication is clear, black mama is going to have to put a sword in that brother's hand and stop that "be a good boy" shit.

A frighteningly fierce misogyny informs Jackson's rage at black women, particularly his mother. Even though he was compelled by black women activists and comrades to reconsider his position on gender, particularly by Angela Davis, his later work, *Blood In My Eye,* continues to see black liberation as a "male thing," to see revolution as a task for men:

At the end of this massive collective struggle, we will uncover a new man, the unpredictable culmination of the revolutionary process. He will be better equipped to wage the real struggle, the permanent struggle after the revolution—the one for new relationships between men.

Although the attitudes expressed by Baraka and Jackson appear dated, they have retained their ideological currency among black men through time. Black female critiques of black male phallocentrism and sexism have had little impact on black male consciousness. Michele Wallace's *Black Macho and the Myth of the SuperWoman* was the first major attempt by a black woman to speak from a feminist standpoint about black male sexism. Her analysis of black masculinity was based primarily on her experience in the urban northern cities, yet she wrote as if she were speaking comprehensively about collective black experience. Even so, her critique was daring and courageous. However, like other critics she evoked a monolithic homogenous representation of black masculinity. Discussing the way black male sexism took precedence over racial solidarity during Shirley Chisolm's presidential campaign, Wallace wrote:

> The black political forces in existence at the time—in other words, the black male political forces—did not support her. In fact, they actively opposed her nomination. The black man in the street seemed either outraged that she dared to run or simply indifferent.
>
> Ever since then it has really baffled me to hear black men say that black women have no time for feminism because being black comes first. For them, when it came to Shirley Chisholm, being black no longer came first at all. It turned out that what they really meant all along was that the black man came before the black woman.

Chisholm documented in her autobiography that sexism stood in her way more than racism. Yet she also talks about the support she received from her father and her husband for her political work. Commenting on the way individuals tried to denigrate this support by hinting that there was something wrong with her husband, Chisholm wrote: "Thoughtless people have suggested that my husband would have to be a weak man who enjoys having me dominate him. They are wrong on both counts." Though fiercely critical of sexism in general and black male sexism in particular, Chisholm acknowledged the support she had received from black men who were not advancing patriarchy. Any critique of "black macho," of black male sexism, that does not acknowledge the actions of black men who subvert and challenge the *status quo* can not be an effective critical intervention. If feminist critics ignore the efforts of individual black men to oppose sexism, our critiques seem to be self-serving, appear to be anti-male rather than anti-sexist. Absolutist portraits that imply that all black men are irredeemably sexist, inherently supportive of male domination, make it appear that there is no way to change this, no alternative, no other way to be. When attention is focused on those black men who oppose sexism, who are disloyal to patriarchy, even if they are exceptions, the possibility for change, for resistance is affirmed. Those representations of black gender relationships that perpetually pit black women and men against one another deny the complexity of our experiences and intensify mutually destructive internecine gender conflict. More than ten years have passed since Michele Wallace encouraged black folks to take gender conflict as a force that was undermining our solidarity and creating tension. Without biting her tongue, Wallace emphatically stated:

> I am saying, among other things, that for perhaps the last fifty years there has been a growing distrust, even hatred, between black men and black women. It has been nursed along not only by racism on the part of whites but also by an almost deliberate ignorance on the part of blacks about the sexual politics of their experience in this country.

The tensions Wallace describes between black women and men have not abated, if anything they have worsened. In more recent years they have taken the public form of black women and men competing for the attention of a white audience. Whether it be the realm of job hunting or book publishing, there is a prevailing sense within white supremacist capitalist patriarchy that black men and women cannot both be in the dominant culture's limelight. While it obviously serves the interests of white supremacy for black women and men to be divided from one another, perpetually in conflict, there is no overall gain for black men and women. Sadly, black people collectively refuse to take seriously issues of gender that would undermine the support for male domination in black communities.

Since the 1960s black power movement had worked over-time to let sisters know that they should assume a subordinate role to lay the groundwork for an emergent black patriarchy that would elevate the status of black males, women's liberation movement has been seen as a threat. Consequently, black women were and are encouraged to think that any involvement with feminism was/is tantamount to betraying the race. Such thinking has not really altered over time. It has become more entrenched. Black people responded with rage and anger to Wallace's book, charging that she was a puppet of white feminists who were motivated by vengeful hatred of black men, but they never argued that her assessment of black male sexism was false. They critiqued her harshly because they sincerely believed that sexism was not a problem in black life and that black female support of black patriarchy and phallocentrism might heal the wounds inflicted by racist domination. As long as black people foolishly cling to the rather politically naive and dangerous assumption that it is in the interests of black liberation to support sexism and male domination, all our efforts to decolonize our minds and transform society will fail.

Perhaps black folks cling to the fantasy that phallocentrism and patriarchy will provide a way out of the havoc and wreckage wreaked by racist genocidal assault because it is an analysis of our current political situation that places a large measure of the blame on the black community, the black family, and, most specifically, black women. This way of thinking means that black people do not have to envision creative strategies for confronting and resisting white supremacy and internalized racism. Tragically, internecine gender conflict between black women and men strengthens white supremacist capitalist patriarchy. Politically behind the times where gender is concerned, many black people lack the skills to function in a changed and changing world. They remain unable to grapple with a contemporary reality where male' domination is consistently challenged and under siege. Primarily it is white male advocates of feminist politics who do the scholarly work that shows the crippling impact of contemporary patriarchy on men, particularly those groups of men who do not receive maximum benefit from this system. Writing about the way patriarchal masculinity undermines the ability of males to construct self and identity with their well-being in mind, creating a life-threatening masculinist sensibility, these works rarely discuss black men.

Most black men remain in a state of denial, refusing to acknowledge the pain in their lives that is caused by sexist thinking and patriarchal, phallocentric violence that is not only expressed by male domination over women but also by internecine conflict among black men. Black people must question why it is that, as white culture has responded to changing gender roles and feminist movement, they have turned to black culture and particularly to black men for articulations of misogyny, sexism, and phallocentrism. In popular culture, representations of black masculinity equate it with brute phallocentrism, woman-hating, a pugilistic "rapist" sexuality, and flagrant disregard for individual rights. Unlike the young George Jackson who, however wrong-minded, cultivated a patriarchal masculinist ethic in the interest of providing black males with a revolutionary political consciousness and a will to resist race and class domination, contemporary young black males espousing a masculinist ethic are not radicalized or insightful about the collective future of black people. Public figures such as Eddie Murphy, Arsenio Hall, Chuck D., Spike Lee, and a host of other black males blindly exploit the commodification of blackness and the concomitant exotification of phallocentric black masculinity.

When Eddie Murphy's film *Raw* (which remains one of the most graphic spectacles of black male phallocentrism) was first shown in urban cities, young black men in the audience gave black power salutes. This film not only did not address the struggle of black people to resist racism, Murphy's evocation of homosocial bonding with rich white men against "threatening" women who want to take their money conveyed his conservative politics. *Raw* celebrates a pugilistic eroticism, the logic of which tells young men that women do not want to hear declarations of love but want to be "fucked to death." Women are represented strictly in misogynist terms—they are evil; they are all prostitutes who see their sexuality solely as a commodity to be exchanged for hard cash, and after the man has delivered the goods they betray him. Is this the "satisfying masculinity" black men desire or does it expose a warped and limited vision of sexuality, one that could not possibly offer fulfillment or sexual healing? As phallocentric spectacle, *Raw* announces that black men are controlled by their penises ("it's a dick thing") and asserts a sexual politic that is fundamentally anti-body.

If the black male cannot "trust" his body not to be the agent of his victimization, how can he trust a female body? Indeed, the female body, along with the female person, is constructed in *Raw* as threatening to the male who seeks autonomous self-hood since it is her presence that awakens phallocentric response. Hence her personhood must be erased; she must be like the phallus, a "thing." Commenting on the self-deception that takes place when men convince themselves and one another that women are not persons, in her essay on patriarchal phallocentrism "The Problem That Has No Name," Marilyn Frye asserts:

> The rejection of females by phallists is both morally and conceptually profound. The refusal to perceive females as persons is conceptually profound because it excludes females from that community whose conceptions of things one allows to influence one's concepts—it serves as a police lock on a closed mind. Furthermore, the refusal to treat women with the respect due to persons is in itself a violation of a moral principle that seems to many to be the founding principle of all morality. This violation of moral principle is sustained by an active manipulation of circumstances that is systematic and habitual and unacknowledged. The exclusion of women from the conceptual community simultaneously excludes them from the moral community.

Black male phallocentrism constructs a portrait of woman as immoral, simultaneously suggesting that she is irrational and incapable of reason. Therefore, there is no need for black men to listen to women or to assume that women have knowledge to share.

It is this representation of womanhood that is graphically evoked in Murphy's film *Harlem Nights*. A dramatization of black male patriar-

chal fantasies, this film reinvents the history of Harlem so that black
men do not appear as cowards unable to confront racist white males
but are reinscribed as tough, violent; they talk shit and take none. Again,
the George Jackson revolutionary political paradigm is displaced in the
realm of the cultural. In this fantasy, black men are as able and willing
to assert power "by any means necessary" as are white men. They are
shown as having the same desires as white men; they long for wealth,
power to dominate others, freedom to kill with impunity, autonomy,
and the right to sexually possess women. They embrace notions of
hierarchal rule. The most powerful black man in the film, Quick (played
by Murphy), always submits to the will of his father. In this world where
homosocial black male bonding is glorified and celebrated, black
women are sex objects. The only woman who is not a sex object is the
post-menopausal mama/matriarch. She is dethroned so that Quick can
assert his power, even though he later (again submitting to the father's
will) asks her forgiveness. *Harlem Nights* is a sad fantasy, romanticizing
a world of misogynist homosocial bonding where everyone is dysfunc-
tional and no one is truly cared for, loved, or emotionally fulfilled.

Despite all the male bluster, Quick, a quintessential black male
hero, longs to be loved. Choosing to seek the affections of an unavail-
able and unattainable black woman (the mistress of the most powerful
white man), Quick does attempt to share himself, to drop the masculine
mask and be "real" (symbolized by his willingness to share his real
name). Yet the black woman he chooses rejects him, only seeking his
favors when she is ordered to by the white man who possesses her. It
is a tragic vision of black heterosexuality. Both black woman and black
man are unable to respond fully to one another because they are so
preoccupied with the white power structure, with the white man. The
most valued black woman "belongs" to a white man who willingly
exchanges her sexual favors in the interest of business. Desired by black
and white men alike (it is their joint lust that renders her more valuable,
black men desire her because white men desire her and *vice versa),* her
internalized racism and her longing for material wealth and power drive
her to act in complicity with white men against black men. Before she
can carry out her mission to kill him, Quick shoots her after they have
had sexual intercourse. Not knowing that he has taken the bullets from
her gun, she points it, telling him that her attack is not personal but
"business." Yet when he kills her he makes a point of saying that it is
"personal." This was a very sad moment in the film, in that he destroys
her because she rejects his authentic need for love and care.

Contrary to the phallocentric representation of black masculinity that has been on display throughout the film, the woman-hating black men are really shown to be in need of love from females. Orphaned, Quick, who is "much man" seeking love, demonstrates his willingness to be emotionally vulnerable, to share only to be rejected, humiliated. This drama of internecine conflict between black women and men follows the conventional sexist line that sees black women as betraying black men by acting in complicity with white patriarchy. This notion of black female complicity and betrayal is so fixed in the minds of many black men they are unable to perceive any flaws in its logic. It certainly gives credence to Michele Wallace's assertion that black people do not have a clear understanding of black sexual politics. Black men who advance the notion that black women are complicit with white men make this assessment without ever invoking historical documentation. Indeed, annals of history abound that document the opposite assumption, showing that black women have typically acted in solidarity with black men. While it may be accurate to argue that sexist black women are complicit with white supremacist capitalist patriarchy, so are sexist black men. Yet most black men continue to deny their complicity.

Spike Lee's recent film *Mo' Better Blues* is another tragic vision of contemporary black heterosexuality. Like *Harlem Nights,* it focuses on a world of black male homosocial bonding where black women are seen primarily as sex objects. Even when they have talent, as the black female jazz singer Clarke does, they must still exchange their sexual favors for recognition. Like Quick, Bleek, the black hero, seeks recognition of his value in heterosexual love relations. Yet he is unable to see the "value" of the two black women who care for him. Indeed, scenes where he makes love to Clarke and alternately sees her as Indigo and *vice versa* suggest the dixie cup sexist mentality (i.e., all women are alike). And even after his entire world has fallen apart he never engages in a self-critique that might lead him to understand that phallocentrism (he is constantly explaining himself by saying "it's a dick thing") has blocked his ability to develop a mature adult identity, has rendered him unable to confront pain and move past denial. Spike Lee's use of Murphy's phrase establishes a continuum of homosocial bonding between black men that transcends the cinematic fiction.

Ironically, the film suggests that Bleek's nihilism and despair can only be addressed by a rejection of a playboy, "dick thing" masculinity and the uncritical acceptance of the traditional patriarchal role. His life crisis is resolved by the reinscription of a patriarchal paradigm. Since Clarke is no longer available, he seeks comfort with Indigo, pleads with her to "save his life." Spike Lee, like Murphy to some extent, exposes the essential self-serving narcissism and denial of community that is at the heart of phallocentrism. He does not, however, envision a radical alternative. The film suggests Bleek has no choice and can only reproduce the same family narrative from which he has emerged, effectively affirming the appropriateness of a nuclear family paradigm where women as mothers restrict black masculinity, black male creativity, and fathers hint at the possibility of freedom. Domesticity represents a place where one's life is "safe" even though one's creativity is contained. The nightclub represents a world outside the home where creativity flourishes and with it an uninhibited eroticism, only that world is one of risk. It is threatening.

The "love supreme" (Coltrane's music and image is a motif throughout the film) that exists between Indigo and Bleek appears shallow and superficial. No longer sex object to be "boned" whenever Bleek desires, her body becomes the vessel for the reproduction of himself *via* having a son. Self-effacing, Indigo identifies Bleek's phallocentrism by telling him he is a "dog," but ultimately she rescues the "dog." His willingness to marry her makes up for dishonesty, abuse, and betrayal. The redemptive love Bleek seeks cannot really be found in the model Lee offers and as a consequence this film is yet another masculine fantasy denying black male agency and capacity to assume responsibility for their personal growth and salvation. The achievement of this goal would mean they must give up phallocentrism and envision new ways of thinking about black masculinity.

Even though individual black women adamantly critique black male sexism, most black men continue to act as though sexism is not a problem in black life and refuse to see it as the force motivating oppressive exploitation of women and children by black men. If any culprit is identified, it is racism. Like Staples' suggestion that the explanation of why black men rape is best understood in a context where racism is identified as the problem, any explanation that evokes a critique of black male phallocentrism is avoided. Black men and women who espouse cultural nationalism continue to see the struggle for black liberation largely as a struggle to recover black manhood. In her essay "Africa On My Mind: Gender, Counter Discourse and African-American Nationalism," E. Frances White shows that overall black nationalist perspectives on gender are rarely rooted purely in the Afrocentric logic they seek to advance, but rather reveal their ties to white paradigms:

In making appeals to conservative notions of appropriate gender behavior, African-American nationalists reveal their ideological ties to other nationalist movements, including European and Euro-American bourgeois nationalists over the past 200 years. These parallels exist despite the different class and power base of these movements.

Most black nationalists, men and women, refuse to acknowledge the obvious ways patriarchal phallocentric masculinity is a destructive force in black life, the ways it undermines solidarity between black women and men, or how it is life-threatening to black men. Even though individual black nationalists like Haki Madhubuti speak against sexism, progressive Afrocentric thinking does not have the impact that the old guard message has. Perhaps it provides sexist black men with a sense of power and agency (however illusory) to see black women, and particularly feminist black women, as the enemy that prevents them from fully participating in this society. For such fiction gives them an enemy that can be confronted, attacked, annihilated, an enemy that can be conquered, dominated.

Confronting white supremacist capitalist patriarchy would not provide sexist black men with an immediate sense of agency or victory. Blaming black women, however, makes it possible for black men to negotiate with white people in all areas of their lives without vigilantly interrogating those interactions. A good example of this displacement is evident in Brent Staples' essay "The White Girl Problem." Defending his "politically incorrect taste in women" (i.e., his preference for white female partners), from attacking black women, Staples never interrogates his desire. He does not seek to understand the extent to which white supremacist capitalist patriarchy determines his desire. He does not want desire to be politicized. And of course his article does not address white female racism or discuss the fact that a white person does not have to be anti-racist to desire a black partner. Many inter-racial relationships have their roots in racist constructions of the Other. By focusing in a stereotypical way on black women's anger, Staples can avoid these issues and depoliticize the politics of black and white female interactions. His essay would have been a needed critical intervention had he endeavored to explore the way individuals maintain racial solidarity even as they bond with folks outside their particular group.

Solidarity between black women and men continues to be undermined by sexism and misogyny. As black women increasingly oppose and challenge male domination, internecine tensions abound. Publicly, many of the gender conflicts between black women and men have been exposed in recent years with the increasingly successful commodification of black women's writing. Indeed, gender conflict between sexist black male writers and those black female writers who are seen as feminists has been particularly brutal. Black male critic Stanley Crouch has been one of the leading voices mocking and ridiculing black women. His recently published collection of essays, *Notes of A Hanging Judge,* includes articles that are particularly scathing in their attacks on black women.

His critique of Wallace's *Black Macho* is mockingly titled "Aunt Jemima Don't Like Uncle Ben" (notice that the emphasis is on black women not liking black men, hence the caption already places accountability for tensions on black women). The title deflects attention away from the concrete critique of sexism in *Black Macho* by making it a question of personal taste. Everyone seems eager to forget that it is possible for black women to love black men and yet unequivocally challenge and oppose sexism, male domination, and phallocentrism. Crouch never speaks to the issues of black male sexism in his piece and works instead to make Wallace appear an "unreliable" narrator. His useful critical comments are thus undermined by the apparent refusal to take seriously the broad political issues Wallace raises. His refusal to acknowledge sexism, expressed as "black macho," is a serious problem. It destroys the possibility of genuine solidarity between black women and men, makes it appear that he is really angry at Wallace and other black women because he is fundamentally anti-feminist and unwilling to challenge male domination. Crouch's stance epitomizes the attitude of contemporary black male writers who are either uncertain about their political response to feminism or are adamantly anti-feminist. Much black male anti-feminism is linked to a refusal to acknowledge that the phallocentric power black men wield over black women is "real" power, the assumption being that only the power white men have that black men do not have is real.

If, as Frederick Douglass maintained, "power concedes nothing without a demand," the black women and men who advocate feminism must be ever vigilant, critiquing and resisting all forms of sexism. Some black men may refuse to acknowledge that sexism provides them with forms of male privilege and power, however relative. They do not want to surrender that power in a world where they may feel otherwise quite powerless. Contemporary emergence of a conservative black nationalism which exploits a focus on race to both deny the importance of struggling against sexism and racism simultaneously is both an overt attack on feminism and a force that actively seeks to reinscribe sexist thinking among black people who have been questioning gender. Commodification of blackness that makes phallocentric black masculinity marketable makes the realm of cultural politics a propagandistic site where black people are rewarded materially for reactionary thinking about gender. Should we not be suspicious of the way in which white culture's fascination with black masculinity manifests itself? The very images of phallocentric black masculinity that are glorified and celebrated in rap music, videos, and movies are the representations that are evoked when white supremacists seek to gain public acceptance and support for genocidal assault on black men, particularly youth.

Progressive Afrocentric ideology makes this critique and interrogates sexism. In his latest book, *Black Men: Obsolete, Single, Dangerous,* Haki Madhubuti courageously deplores all forms of sexism, particularly black male violence against women. Like black male political figures of the past, Madhubuti's support of gender equality and his critique of sexism is not linked to an overall questioning of gender roles and a repudiation of all forms of patriarchal domination, however benevolent. Still, he has taken the important step of questioning sexism and calling on black people to explore the way sexism hurts and wounds us. Madhubuti acknowledges black male misogyny:

> The "fear" of women that exists among many Black men runs deep and often goes unspoken. This fear is cultural. Most men are introduced to members of the opposite sex in a superficial manner, and seldom do we seek a more in depth or informed understanding of them...Women have it rough all over the world. Men must become informed listeners.

Woman-hating will only cease to be a norm in black life when black men collectively dare to oppose sexism. Unfortunately, when all black people should be engaged in a feminist movement that addresses the sexual politics of our communities, many of us are tragically investing in old gender norms. At a time when many black people should be reading Madhubuti's *Black Men, Sister Outsider, The Black Women's Health Book, Feminist Theory: From Margin to Center,* and a host of other books that seek to explore black sexual politics with compassion and care, folks are eagerly consuming a conservative tract, *The Blackman's Guide To Understanding The Blackwoman* by Shahrazad Ali. This work actively promotes black male misogyny, coercive domination of females by males, and, as a consequence, feeds the internecine conflict between black women and men. Though many black people have embraced this work there is no indication that it is having a positive impact on black communities, and there is every indication that it is being used to justify male dominance, homophobic assaults on black gay people, and rejection of black styles that emphasize our diasporic connection to Africa and the Caribbean. Ali's book romanticizes black patriarchy, demanding that black women "submit" to black male domination in lieu of changes in society that would make it possible for black men to be more fulfilled.

Calling for a strengthening of black male phallocentric power (to be imposed by force if need be), Ali's book in no way acknowledges sexism. When writing about black men, her book reads like an infantile caricature of the Tarzan fantasy. Urging black men to assert their rightful position as patriarchs, she tells them: "Rise Blackman, and take your rightful place as ruler of the universe and everything in it. Including the black woman." Like *Harlem Nights,* this is the stuff of pure fantasy. That black people, particularly the underclass, are turning to escapist fantasies that can in no way adequately address the collective need of African Americans for renewed black liberation struggle is symptomatic of the crisis we are facing. Desperately clinging to ways of thinking and being that are detrimental to our collective well-being obstructs progressive efforts for change.

More black men have broken their silence to critique Ali's work than have ever offered public support of feminist writing by black women. Yet it does not help educate black people about the ways feminist analysis could be useful in our lives for black male critics to act as though the success of this book represents a failure on the part of feminism. Ali's sexist, homophobic, self-denigrating tirades strike a familiar chord because so many black people who have not de-colonized their minds think as she does. Though black male critic Nelson George critiques Ali's work, stating that it shows "how little Afrocentrism respects the advances of African-American women," he suggests that it is an indication of how "unsuccessful black feminists have been in forging alliance with this ideologically potent community." Statements like this one advance the notion that feminist education is the sole task of black women. It also rather neatly places George outside either one of these potent communities. Why does he not seize the critical moment to bring to public awareness the feminist visions of Afrocentric black women? All too often, black men who are indirectly supportive of feminist movement act as though black women have a personal stake in eradicating sexism that men do not have. Black men benefit from feminist thinking and feminist movement too.

Any examination of the contemporary plight of black men reveals the way phallocentrism is at the root of much black-on-black violence, undermines family relations, informs the lack of preventive health care, and even plays a role in promoting drug addiction. Many of the destructive habits of black men are enacted in the name of "manhood." Asserting their ability to be "tough," to be "cool," black men take grave risks with their lives and the lives of others. Acknowledging this in his essay "Cool Pose: The Proud Signature of Black Survival," Richard Majors argues that "cool" has positive dimensions even though it "is also an aggressive assertion of masculinity." Yet, he never overtly critiques sexism. Black men may be reluctant to critique phallocentrism and sexism, precisely because so much black male "style" has its roots in these positions; they may fear that eradicating patriarchy would leave them without the positive expressive styles that have been life-sustaining. Majors is clear, however, that a "cool pose" linked to aggressive phallocentrism is detrimental to both black men and the people they care about:

> Perhaps black men have become so conditioned to keeping up their guard against oppression from the dominant white society that this particular attitude and behavior represents for them their best safeguard against further mental or physical abuse. However, this same behavior makes it very difficult for these males to let their guard down and show affection...

Elsewhere, he suggests "that the same elements of cool that allow for survival in the larger society may hurt black people by contributing to one of the more complex problems facing black people today—black-on-black crime." Clearly, black men need to employ a feminist analysis that will address the issue of how to construct a life-sustaining black masculinity that does not have its roots in patriarchal phallocentrism.

Addressing the way obsessive concern with the phallus causes black men stress in *No Name in the Street,* James Baldwin explains:

> Every black man walking in this country pays a tremendous price for walking: for men are not women, and a man's balance depends on the weight he carries between his legs. All men, however they may face or fail to face it, however they may handle, or be handled by it, know something about each other, which is simply that a man without balls is not a man...

What might black men do for themselves and for black people if they were not socialized by white supremacist capitalist patriarchy to focus their attention on their penises? Should we not suspect the contemporary commodification of blackness orchestrated by whites that once again tells black men not only to focus on their penis but to make this focus their all consuming passion? Such confused men have little time or insight for resistance struggle. Should we not suspect representations of black men like those that appear in a movie like *Heart Condition,* where the black male describes himself as "hung like a horse" as though the size of his penis defines who he is? And what does it say about the future of black liberation struggles if the phrase "it's a dick thing" is transposed and becomes "its a black thing?" If the "black thing," i.e., black liberation struggle, is really only a "dick thing" in disguise, a phallocentric play for black male power, then black people are in serious trouble.

Challenging black male phallocentrism would also make a space for critical discussion of homosexuality in black communities. Since so much of the quest for phallocentric manhood as it is expressed in black nationalist circles rests on a demand for compulsory heterosexuality, it has always promoted the persecution and hatred of homosexuals. This is yet another stance that has undermined black solidarity. If black men no longer embraced phallocentric masculinity, they would be empowered to explore their fear and hatred of other men, learning new ways to relate. How many black men will have to die before black folks are willing to look at the link between the contemporary plight of black men and their continued allegiance to patriarchy and phallocentrism?

Most black men will acknowledge that black men are in crisis and are suffering. Yet they remain reluctant to engage those progressive movements that might serve as meaningful critical interventions, that might allow them to speak their pain. On the terms set by white supremacist patriarchy, black men can name their pain only by talking about themselves in crude ways that reinscribe them in a context of primitivism. Why should black men have to talk about themselves as an "endangered species" in order to gain public recognition of their plight? And why are the voices of colonized black men, many of whom are in the spotlight, drowning out progressive voices? Why do we not listen to Joseph Beam, one such courageous voice? He had no difficulty sharing the insight that "communism, socialism, feminism and, homosexuality pose far less of a threat to America than racism, sexism, heterosexism, classism, and ageism." Never losing sight of the need for black men to name their realities, to speak their pain and their resistance, Beam concluded his essay "No Cheek To Turn" with these prophetic words:

> I speak to you as a black gay pro-feminist man moving in a world where nobody wants to know my name, or hear my voice. In prison, I'm just a number; in the army, I'm just a rank; on the job and in the hospital, I'm just a statistic; on the street, I'm just a suspect. My head reels. If I didn't have access to print, I, too, would write on walls. I want my life's passage to be acknowledged for at least the length of time it takes pain to fade from brick. With that said I serve my notice: I have no cheek to turn.

Changing representations of black men must be a collective task. Black people committed to renewed black liberation struggle, the de-colonization of black minds, are fully aware that we must oppose male domination and work to eradicate sexism. There are black women and men who are working together to strengthen our solidarity. Black men like Richard Majors, Calvin Hernton, Cornel West, Greg Tate, Essex Hemphill, and others address the issue of sexism and advocate feminism. If black men and women take seriously Malcolm's charge that we must work for our liberation "by any means necessary," then we must be willing to explore the way feminism as a critique of sexism, as a movement to end sexism and sexist oppression, could aid our struggle to be self-determining. Collectively we can break the life-threatening choke-hold patriarchal masculinity imposes on black men and create life sustaining visions of a reconstructed black masculinity that can provide black men ways to save their lives and the lives of their brothers and sisters in struggle.

Chapter 7

The Oppositional Gaze
Black Female Spectators

When thinking about black female spectators, I remember being punished as a child for staring, for those hard intense direct looks children would give grown-ups, looks that were seen as confrontational, as gestures of resistance, challenges to authority. The "gaze" has always been political in my life. Imagine the terror felt by the child who has come to understand through repeated punishments that one's gaze can be dangerous. The child who has learned so well to look the other way when necessary. Yet, when punished, the child is told by parents, "Look at me when I talk to you." Only, the child is afraid to look. Afraid to look, but fascinated by the gaze. There is power in looking.

Amazed the first time I read in history classes that white slave-owners (men, women, and children) punished enslaved black people for looking, I wondered how this traumatic relationship to the gaze had informed black parenting and black spectatorship. The politics of slavery, of racialized power relations, were such that the slaves were denied their right to gaze. Connecting this strategy of domination to that used by grown folks in southern black rural communities where I grew up, I was pained to think that there was no absolute difference between whites who had oppressed black people and ourselves. Years later, reading Michel Foucault, I thought again about these connections, about the ways power as domination reproduces itself in different locations employing similar apparatuses, strategies, and mechanisms of control. Since I knew as a child that the dominating power adults exercised over me and over my gaze was never so absolute that I did not dare to look, to sneak a peep, to stare dangerously, I knew that the slaves had looked. That all attempts to repress our/black peoples' right to gaze had produced in us an overwhelming longing to look, a rebellious desire, an oppositional gaze. By courageously looking, we defiantly declared: "Not only will I stare. I want my look to change reality." Even in the worse circumstances of domination, the ability to manipulate one's gaze in the face of structures of domination that would contain it, opens up the possibility of agency. In much of his work, Michel Foucault insists on describing domination in terms of "relations of power" as part of an effort to challenge the assumption that "power is a system of domination which controls everything and which leaves no room for freedom." Emphatically stating that in all relations of power "there is necessarily the possibility of resistance," he invites the critical thinker to search those margins, gaps, and locations on and through the body where agency can be found.

Stuart Hall calls for recognition of our agency as black spectators in his essay "Cultural Identity and Cinematic Representation." Speaking against the construction of white representations of blackness as total- izing, Hall says of white presence: "The error is not to conceptualize this 'presence' in terms of power, but to locate that power as wholly external to us—as extrinsic force, whose influence can be thrown off like the serpent sheds its skin. What Franz Fanon reminds us, in *Black Skin, White Masks,* is how power is inside as well as outside:

> ...the movements, the attitudes, the glances of the Other fixed me
> there, in the sense in which a chemical solution is fixed by a dye.
> I was indignant; I demanded an explanation. Nothing happened.
> I burst apart. Now the fragments have been put together again by
> another self. This "look," from—so to speak—the place of the
> Other, fixes us, not only in its violence, hostility and aggression,
> but in the ambivalence of its desire.

Spaces of agency exist for black people, wherein we can both interro- gate the gaze of the Other but also look back, and at one another, naming what we see. The "gaze" has been and is a site of resistance for colonized black people globally. Subordinates in relations of power learn experientially that there is a critical gaze, one that "looks" to document, one that is oppositional. In resistance struggle, the power of the dominated to assert agency by claiming and cultivating "aware- ness" politicizes "looking" relations—one learns to look a certain way in order to resist.

When most black people in the United States first had the opportunity to look at film and television, they did so fully aware that mass
media was a system of knowledge and power reproducing and maintaining white supremacy. To stare at the television, or mainstream
movies, to engage its images, was to engage its negation of black
representation. It was the oppositional black gaze that responded to
these looking relations by developing independent black cinema.
Black viewers of mainstream cinema and television could chart the
progress of political movements for racial equality *via* the construction
of images, and did so. Within my family's southern black working-class
home, located in a racially segregated neighborhood, watching television
was one way to develop critical spectatorship. Unless you went to work
in the white world, across the tracks, you learned to look at white
people by staring at them on the screen. Black looks, as they were
constituted in the context of social movements for racial uplift, were
interrogating gazes. We laughed at television shows like *Our Gang* and
Amos 'n' Andy, at these white representations of blackness, but we also
looked at them critically. Before racial integration, black viewers of
movies and television experienced visual pleasure in a context where
looking was also about contestation and confrontation.

Writing about black looking relations in "Black British Cinema:
Spectatorship and Identity Formation in Territories," Manthia Diawara
identifies the power of the spectator: "Every narration places the
spectator in a position of agency; and race, class and sexual relations
influence the way in which this subjecthood is filled by the spectator."
Of particular concern for him are moments of "rupture" when the
spectator resists "complete identification with the film's discourse."
These ruptures define the relation between black spectators and
dominant cinema prior to racial integration. Then, one's enjoyment
of a film wherein representations of blackness were stereotypically
degrading and dehumanizing co-existed with a critical practice that
restored presence where it was negated. Critical discussion of the film
while it was in progress or at its conclusion maintained the distance
between spectator and the image. Black films were also subject to
critical interrogation. Since they came into being in part as a response
to the failure of white-dominated cinema to represent blackness in a
manner that did not reinforce white supremacy, they too were critiqued
to see if images were seen as complicit with dominant cinematic
practices.

Critical, interrogating black looks were mainly concerned with
issues of race and racism, the way racial domination of blacks by whites

overdetermined representation. They were rarely concerned with gender. As spectators, black men could repudiate the reproduction of racism in cinema and television, the negation of black presence, even as they could feel as though they were rebelling against white supremacy by daring to look, by engaging phallocentric politics of spectatorship. Given the real life public circumstances wherein black men were murdered/lynched for looking at white womanhood, where the black male gaze was always subject to control and/or punishment by the powerful white Other, the private realm of television screens or dark theaters could unleash the repressed gaze. There they could "look" at white womanhood without a structure of domination overseeing the gaze, interpreting, and punishing. That white supremacist structure that had murdered Emmet Till after interpreting his look as violation, as "rape" of white womanhood, could not control black male responses to screen images. In their role as spectators, black men could enter an imaginative space of phallocentric power that mediated racial negation. This gendered relation to looking made the experience of the black male spectator radically different from that of the black female spectator. Major early black male independent filmmakers represented black women in their films as objects of male gaze. Whether looking through the camera or as spectators watching films, whether mainstream cinema or "race" movies such as those made by Oscar Micheaux, the black male gaze had a different scope from that of the black female.

Black women have written little about black female spectatorship, about our moviegoing practices. A growing body of film theory and criticism by black women has only begun to emerge. The prolonged silence of black women as spectators and critics was a response to absence, to cinematic negation. In "The Technology of Gender," Teresa de Lauretis, drawing on the work of Monique Wittig, calls attention to "the power of discourses to 'do violence' to people, a violence which is material and physical, although produced by abstract and scientific discourses as well as the discourses of the mass media." With the possible exception of early race movies, black female spectators have had to develop looking relations within a cinematic context that constructs our presence as absence, that denies the "body" of the black female so as to perpetuate white supremacy and with it a phallocentric spectatorship where the woman to be looked at and desired is "white." (Recent movies do not conform to this paradigm but I am turning to the past with the intent to chart the development of black female spectatorship.)

Talking with black women of all ages and classes, in different areas of the United States, about their filmic looking relations, I hear again and again ambivalent responses to cinema. Only a few of the black women I talked with remembered the pleasure of race movies, and even those who did, felt that pleasure interrupted and usurped by Hollywood. Most of the black women I talked with were adamant that they never went to movies expecting to see compelling representations of black femaleness. They were all acutely aware of cinematic racism— its violent erasure of black womanhood. In Anne Friedberg's essay "A Denial of Difference: Theories of Cinematic Identification" she stresses that "identification can only be made through recognition, and all recognition is itself an implicit confirmation of the ideology of the status quo." Even when representations of black women were present in film, our bodies and being were there to serve—to enhance and maintain white womanhood as object of the phallocentric gaze.

Commenting on Hollywood's characterization of black women in *Girls on Film,* Julie Burchill describes this absent presence:

> Black women have been mothers without children (Mammies— who can ever forget the sickening spectacle of Hattie MacDaniels waiting on the simpering Vivien Leigh hand and foot and enquiring like a ninny, "What's ma lamb gonna wear?")...Lena Horne, the first black performer signed to a long term contract with a major (MGM), looked gutless but was actually quite spirited. She seethed when Tallulah Bankhead complimented her on the paleness of her skin and the non-Negroidness of her features.

When black women actresses like Lena Horne appeared in mainstream cinema most white viewers were not aware that they were looking at black females unless the film was specifically coded as being about blacks. Burchill is one of the few white women film critics who has dared to examine the intersection of race and gender in relation to the construction of the category "woman" in film as object of the phallocentric gaze. With characteristic wit she asserts: "What does it say about racial purity that the best blondes have all been brunettes (Harlow, Monroe, Bardot)? I think it says that we are not as white as we think." Burchill could easily have said "we are not as white as we want to be," for clearly the obsession to have white women film stars be ultra-white was a cinematic practice that sought to maintain a distance, a separation between that image and the black female Other; it was a way to perpetuate white supremacy. Politics of race and gender were inscribed into mainstream cinematic narrative from *Birth of A Nation* on. As a seminal work, this film identified what the place and function of white womanhood would be in cinema. There was clearly no place for black women.

Remembering my past in relation to screen images of black womanhood, I wrote a short essay, "Do you remember Sapphire?" which explored both the negation of black female representation in cinema and television and our rejection of these images. Identifying the character of "Sapphire" from *Amos 'n' Andy* as that screen representation of black femaleness I first saw in childhood, I wrote:

> She was even then backdrop, foil. She was bitch—nag. She was there to soften images of black men, to make them seem vulnerable, easygoing, funny, and unthreatening to a white audience. She was there as man in drag, as castrating bitch, as someone to be lied to, someone to be tricked, someone the white and black audience could hate. Scapegoated on all sides. *She was not us.* We laughed with the black men, with the white people. We laughed at this black woman who was not us. And we did not even long to be there on the screen. How could we long to be there when our image, visually constructed, was so ugly. We did not long to be there. We did not long for her. We did not want our construction to be this hated black female thing—foil, backdrop. Her black female image was not the body of desire. There was nothing to see. She was not us.

Grown black women had a different response to Sapphire; they identified with her frustrations and her woes. They resented the way she was mocked. They resented the way these screen images could assault black womanhood, could name us bitches, nags. And in opposition they claimed Sapphire as their own, as the symbol of that angry part of themselves white folks and black men could not even begin to understand.

Conventional representations of black women have done violence to the image. Responding to this assault, many black women spectators shut out the image, looked the other way, accorded cinema no importance in their lives. Then there were those spectators whose gaze was that of desire and complicity. Assuming a posture of subordination, they submitted to cinema's capacity to seduce and betray. They were cinematically "gaslighted." Every black woman I spoke with who was/is an ardent moviegoer, a lover of the Hollywood film, testified that to experience fully the pleasure of that cinema they had to close down critique, analysis; they had to forget racism. And mostly they did not think about sexism. What was the nature then of this adoring black female gaze—this look that could bring pleasure in the midst of negation? In her first novel, *The Bluest Eye,* Toni Morrison constructs a portrait of the black female spectator; her gaze is the masochistic look of victimization. Describing her looking relations, Miss Pauline Breedlove, a poor working woman, maid in the house of a prosperous white family, asserts:

> The onliest time I be happy seem like was when I was in the picture show. Every time I got, I went, I'd go early, before the show started. They's cut off the lights, and everything be black. Then the screen would light up, and I's move right on in them picture. White men taking such good care of they women, and they all dressed up in big clean houses with the bath tubs right in the same room with the toilet. Them pictures gave me a lot of pleasure.

To experience pleasure, Miss Pauline sitting in the dark must imagine herself transformed, turned into the white woman portrayed on the screen. After watching movies, feeling the pleasure, she says, "But it made coming home hard."

We come home to ourselves. Not all black women spectators submitted to that spectacle of regression through identification. Most of the women I talked with felt that they consciously resisted identification with films—that this tension made moviegoing less than pleasurable; at times it caused pain. As one black woman put, "I could always get pleasure from movies as long as I did not look too deep." For black female spectators who have "looked too deep" the encounter with the screen hurt. That some of us chose to stop looking was a gesture of resistance, turning away was one way to protest, to reject negation. My pleasure in the screen ended abruptly when I and my sisters first watched *Imitation of Life.* Writing about this experience in the "Sapphire" piece, I addressed the movie directly, confessing:

> I had until now forgotten you, that screen image seen in adolescence, those images that made me stop looking. It was there in *Imitation of Life,* that comfortable mammy image. There was something familiar about this hard-working black woman who loved her daughter so much, loved her in a way that hurt. Indeed, as young southern black girls watching this film, Peola's mother reminded us of the hardworking, churchgoing, Big Mamas we knew and loved. Consequently, it was not this image that captured our gaze; we were fascinated by Peola.

Addressing her, I wrote:

> You were different. There was something scary in this image of
> young sexual sensual black beauty betrayed—that daughter who
> did not want to be confined by blackness, that "tragic mulatto"
> who did not want to be negated. "Just let me escape this image
> forever," she could have said. I will always remember that image.
> I remembered how we cried for her, for our unrealized desiring
> selves. She was tragic because there was no place in the cinema
> for her, no loving pictures. She too was absent image. It was better
> then, that we were absent, for when we were there it was humil-
> iating, strange, sad. We cried all night for you, for the cinema that
> had no place for you. And like you, we stopped thinking it would
> one day be different.

When I returned to films as a young woman, after a long period
of silence, I had developed an oppositional gaze. Not only would I not
be hurt by the absence of black female presence, or the insertion of
violating representation, I interrogated the work, cultivated a way to
look past race and gender for aspects of content, form, language.
Foreign films and U.S. independent cinema were the primary locations of my filmic looking relations, even though I also watched
Hollywood films.

From "jump," black female spectators have gone to films with
awareness of the way in which race and racism determined the visual
construction of gender. Whether it was *Birth of A Nation* or Shirley
Temple shows, we knew that white womanhood was the racialized
sexual difference occupying the place of stardom in mainstream narrative film. We assumed white women knew it to. Reading Laura Mulvey's
provocative essay, "Visual Pleasure and Narrative Cinema," from a
standpoint that acknowledges race, one sees clearly why black women
spectators not duped by mainstream cinema would develop an
oppositional gaze. Placing ourselves outside that pleasure in looking,
Mulvey argues, was determined by a "split between active/male and
passive/female." Black female spectators actively chose not to identify
with the film's imaginary subject because such identification was dis-
enabling.

Looking at films with an oppositional gaze, black women were
able to critically assess the cinema's construction of white womanhood
as object of phallocentric gaze and choose not to identify with either
the victim or the perpetrator. Black female spectators, who refused to
identify with white womanhood, who would not take on the
phallocentric gaze of desire and possession, created a critical space

where the binary opposition Mulvey posits of "woman as image, man as bearer of the look" was continually deconstructed. As critical spectators, black women looked from a location that disrupted, one akin to that described by Annette Kuhn in *The Power of The Image:*

> ...the acts of analysis, of deconstruction and of reading "against the grain" offer an additional pleasure—the pleasure of resistance, of saying "no": not to "unsophisticated" enjoyment, by ourselves and others, of culturally dominant images, but to the structures of power which ask us to consume them uncritically and in highly circumscribed ways.

Mainstream feminist film criticism in no way acknowledges black female spectatorship. It does not even consider the possibility that women can construct an oppositional gaze via an understanding and awareness of the politics of race and racism. Feminist film theory rooted in an ahistorical psychoanalytic framework that privileges sexual difference actively suppresses recognition of race, reenacting and mirroring the erasure of black womanhood that occurs in films, silencing any discussion of racial difference—of racialized sexual difference. Despite feminist critical interventions aimed at deconstructing the category "woman" which highlight the significance of race, many feminist film critics continue to structure their discourse as though it speaks about "women" when in actuality it speaks only about white women. It seems ironic that the cover of the recent anthology *Feminism and Film Theory* edited by Constance Penley has a graphic that is a reproduction of the photo of white actresses Rosalind Russell and Dorothy Arzner on the 1936 set of the film *Craig's Wife* yet there is no acknowledgment in any essay in this collection that the woman "subject" under discussion is always white. Even though there are photos of black women from films reproduced in the text, there is no acknowledgment of racial difference.

It would be too simplistic to interpret this failure of insight solely as a gesture of racism. Importantly, it also speaks to the problem of structuring feminist film theory around a totalizing narrative of woman as object whose image functions solely to reaffirm and reinscribe patriarchy. Mary Ann Doane addresses this issue in the essay "Remembering Women: Psychical and Historical Construction in Film Theory":

> This attachment to the figure of a degeneralizible Woman as the product of the apparatus indicates why, for many, feminist film theory seems to have reached an impasse, a certain blockage in its theorization...In focusing upon the task of delineating in great

detail the attributes of woman as effect of the apparatus, feminist
film theory participates in the abstraction of women.

The concept "Woman" effaces the difference between women in
specific socio-historical contexts, between women defined precisely as
historical subjects rather than as *a* psychic subject (or non-subject).
Though Doane does not focus on race, her comments speak directly to
the problem of its erasure. For it is only as one imagines "woman" in
the abstract, when woman becomes fiction or fantasy, can race not be
seen as significant. Are we really to imagine that feminist theorists
writing only about images of white women, who subsume this specific
historical subject under the totalizing category "woman," do not "see"
the whiteness of the image? It may very well be that they engage in a
process of denial that eliminates the necessity of revisioning conventional ways of thinking about psychoanalysis as a paradigm of analysis
and the need to rethink a body of feminist film theory that is firmly
rooted in a denial of the reality that sex/sexuality may not be the
primary and/or exclusive signifier of difference. Doane's essay appears in a very recent anthology, *Psychoanalysis and Cinema* edited
by E. Ann Kaplan, where, once again, none of the theory presented
acknowledges or discusses racial difference, with the exception of one
essay, "Not Speaking with Language, Speaking with No Language,"
which problematizes notions of orientalism in its examination of Leslie
Thornton's film *Adynata*. Yet in most of the essays, the theories
espoused are rendered problematic if one includes race as a category
of analysis.
    Constructing feminist film theory along these lines enables the
production of a discursive practice that need never theorize any aspect
of black female representation or spectatorship. Yet the existence of
black women within white supremacist culture problematizes, and
makes complex, the overall issue of female identity, representation, and
spectatorship. If, as Friedberg suggests, "identification is a process
which commands the subject to be displaced by an other; it is a
procedure which breeches the separation between self and other, and,
in this way, replicates the very structure of patriarchy." If identification
"demands sameness, necessitates similarity, disallows difference"—
must we then surmise that many feminist film critics who are "over-
identified" with the mainstream cinematic apparatus produce theories
that replicate its totalizing agenda? Why is it that feminist film criticism,
which has most claimed the terrain of woman's identity, representation,
and subjectivity as its field of analysis, remains aggressively silent on the
subject of blackness and specifically representations of black woman-

hood? Just as mainstream cinema has historically forced aware black female spectators not to look, much feminist film criticism disallows the possibility of a theoretical dialogue that might include black women's voices. It is difficult to talk when you feel no one is listening, when you feel as though a special jargon or narrative has been created that only the chosen can understand. No wonder then that black women have for the most part confined our critical commentary on film to conversations. And it must be reiterated that this gesture is a strategy that protects us from the violence perpetuated and advocated by discourses of mass media. A new focus on issues of race and representation in the field of film theory could critically intervene on the historical repression reproduced in some arenas of contemporary critical practice, making a discursive space for discussion of black female spectatorship possible.

When I asked a black woman in her twenties, an obsessive moviegoer, why she thought we had not written about black female spectatorship, she commented: "We are afraid to talk about ourselves as spectators because we have been so abused by 'the gaze'." An aspect of that abuse was the imposition of the assumption that black female looking relations were not important enough to theorize. Film theory as a critical "turf" in the United States has been and continues to be influenced by and reflective of white racial domination. Since feminist film criticism was initially rooted in a women's liberation movement informed by racist practices, it did not open up the discursive terrain and make it more inclusive. Recently, even those white film theorists who include an analysis of race show no interest in black female spectatorship. In her introduction to the collection of essays *Visual and Other Pleasures,* Laura Mulvey describes her initial romantic absorption in Hollywood cinema, stating:

> Although this great, previously unquestioned and unanalyzed love was put in crisis by the impact of feminism on my thought in the early 1970s, it also had an enormous influence on the development of my critical work and ideas and the debate within film culture with which I became preoccupied over the next fifteen years or so. Watched through eyes that were affected by the changing climate of consciousness, the movies lost their magic.

Watching movies from a feminist perspective, Mulvey arrived at that location of disaffection that is the starting point for many black women approaching cinema within the lived harsh reality of racism. Yet her account of being a part of a film culture whose roots rest on a founding relationship of adoration and love indicates how difficult it would have been to enter that world from "jump" as a critical spectator whose gaze had been formed in opposition.

Given the context of class exploitation, and racist and sexist domination, it has only been through resistance, struggle, reading, and looking "against the grain," that black women have been able to value our process of looking enough to publicly name it. Centrally, those black female spectators who attest to the oppositionality of their gaze deconstruct theories of female spectatorship that have relied heavily on the assumption that, as Doane suggests in her essay, "Woman's Stake: Filming the Female Body," "woman can only mimic man's relation to language, that is assume a position defined by the penis-phallus as the supreme arbiter of lack." Identifying with neither the phallocentric gaze nor the construction of white womanhood as lack, critical black female spectators construct a theory of looking relations where cinematic visual delight is the pleasure of interrogation. Every black woman spectator I talked to, with rare exception, spoke of being "on guard" at the movies. Talking about the way being a critical spectator of Hollywood films influenced her, black woman filmmaker Julie Dash exclaims, "I make films because I was such a spectator!" Looking at Hollywood cinema from a distance, from that critical politicized standpoint that did not want to be seduced by narratives reproducing her negation, Dash watched mainstream movies over and over again for the pleasure of deconstructing them. And of course there is that added delight if one happens, in the process of interrogation, to come across a narrative that invites the black female spectator to engage the text with no threat of violation.

Significantly, I began to write film criticism in response to the first Spike Lee movie, *She's Gotta Have It*, contesting Lee's replication of mainstream patriarchal cinematic practices that explicitly represents woman (in this instance black woman) as the object of a phallocentric gaze. Lee's investment in patriarchal filmic practices that mirror dominant patterns makes him the perfect black candidate for entrance to the Hollywood canon. His work mimics the cinematic construction of white womanhood as object, replacing her body as text on which to write male desire with the black female body. It is transference without transformation. Entering the discourse of film criticism from the politicized location of resistance, of not wanting, as a working-class black woman I interviewed stated, "to see black women in the position white women have occupied in film forever," I began to think critically about black female spectatorship.

For years I went to independent and/or foreign films where I was the only black female present in the theater. I often imagined that in every theater in the United States there was another black woman watching the same film wondering why she was the only visible black female spectator. I remember trying to share with one of my five sisters the cinema I liked so much. She was "enraged" that I brought her to a theater where she would have to read subtitles. To her it was a violation of Hollywood notions of spectatorship, of coming to the movies to be entertained. When I interviewed her to ask what had changed her mind over the years, led her to embrace this cinema, she connected it to coming to critical consciousness, saying, "I learned that there was more to looking than I had been exposed to in ordinary (Hollywood) movies." I shared that though most of the films I loved were all white, I could engage them because they did not have in their deep structure a subtext reproducing the narrative of white supremacy. Her response was to say that these films demystified "whiteness," since the lives they depicted seemed less rooted in fantasies of escape. They were, she suggested, more like "what we knew life to be, the deeper side of life as well." Always more seduced and enchanted with Hollywood cinema than me, she stressed that unaware black female spectators must "break out," no longer be imprisoned by images that enact a drama of our negation. Though she still sees Hollywood films, because "they are a major influence in the culture"—she no longer feels duped or victimized.

Talking with black female spectators, looking at written discussions either in fiction or academic essays about black women, I noted the connection made between the realm of representation in mass media and the capacity of black women to construct ourselves as subjects in daily life. The extent to which black women feel devalued, objectified, dehumanized in this society determines the scope and texture of their looking relations. Those black women whose identities were constructed in resistance, by practices that oppose the dominant order, were most inclined to develop an oppositional gaze. Now that there is a growing interest in films produced by black women and those films have become more accessible to viewers, it is possible to talk about black female spectatorship in relation to that work. So far, most discussions of black spectatorship that I have come across focus on men. In "Black Spectatorship: Problems of Identification and Resistance" Manthia Diawara suggests that "the components of 'difference'" among elements of sex, gender, and sexuality give rise to different readings of the same material, adding that these conditions produce a "resisting" spectator. He focuses his critical discussion on black masculinity.

The recent publication of the anthology *The Female Gaze: Women as Viewers of Popular Culture* excited me, especially as it included an essay, "Black Looks," by Jacqui Roach and Petal Felix that attempts to address black female spectatorship. The essay posed provocative questions that were not answered: Is there a black female gaze? How do black women relate to the gender politics of representation? Concluding, the authors assert that black females have "our own reality, our own history, our own gaze—one which the sees the world rather differently from 'anyone else.' " Yet, they do not name/describe this experience of seeing "rather differently." The absence of definition and explanation suggests they are assuming an essentialist stance wherein it is presumed that black women, as victims of race and gender oppression, have an inherently different field of vision. Many black women do not "see differently" precisely because their perceptions of reality are so profoundly colonized, shaped by dominant ways of knowing. As Trinh T. Minh-ha points out in "Outside In, Inside Out": "Subjectivity does not merely consist of talking about oneself...be this talking indulgent or critical."

Critical black female spectatorship emerges as a site of resistance only when individual black women actively resist the imposition of dominant ways of knowing and looking. While every black woman I talked to was aware of racism, that awareness did not automatically correspond with politicization, the development of an oppositional gaze. When it did, individual black women consciously named the process. Manthia Diawara's "resisting spectatorship" is a term that does not adequately describe the terrain of black female spectatorship. We do more than resist. We create alternative texts that are not solely reactions. As critical spectators, black women participate in a broad range of looking relations, contest, resist, revision, interrogate, and invent on multiple levels. Certainly when I watch the work of black women filmmakers Camille Billops, Kathleen Collins, Julie Dash, Ayoka Chenzira, Zeinabu Davis, I do not need to "resist" the images even as I still choose to watch their work with a critical eye.

Black female critical thinkers concerned with creating space for the construction of radical black female subjectivity, and the way cultural production informs this possibility, fully acknowledge the importance of mass media, film in particular, as a powerful site for critical intervention. Certainly Julie Dash's film *Illusions* identifies the terrain of Hollywood cinema as a space of knowledge production that has enormous power. Yet, she also creates a filmic narrative wherein the black female protagonist subversively claims that space. Inverting the "real-life" power structure, she offers the black female spectator representations that challenge stereotypical notions that place us outside the realm of filmic discursive practices. Within the film she uses the strategy of Hollywood suspense films to undermine those cinematic practices that deny black women a place in this structure. Problematizing the question of "racial" identity by depicting passing, suddenly it is the white male's capacity to gaze, define, and know that is called into question.

When Mary Ann Doane describes in "Woman's Stake: Filming the Female Body" the way in which feminist filmmaking practice can elaborate "a special syntax for a different articulation of the female body," she names a critical process that "undoes the structure of the classical narrative through an insistence upon its repressions." An eloquent description, this precisely names Dash's strategy in *Illusions,* even though the film is not unproblematic and works within certain conventions that are not successfully challenged. For example, the film does not indicate whether the character Mignon will make Hollywood films that subvert and transform the genre or whether she will simply assimilate and perpetuate the norm. Still, subversively, *Illusions* problematizes the issue of race and spectatorship. White people in the film are unable to "see" that race informs their looking relations. Though she is passing to gain access to the machinery of cultural production represented by film, Mignon continually asserts her ties to black community. The bond between her and the young black woman singer Esther Jeeter is affirmed by caring gestures of affirmation, often expressed by eye-to-eye contact, the direct unmediated gaze of recognition. Ironically, it is the desiring objectifying sexualized white male gaze that threatens to penetrate her "secrets" and disrupt her process. Metaphorically, Dash suggests the power of black women to make films will be threatened and undermined by that white male gaze that seeks to reinscribe the black female body in a narrative of voyeuristic pleasure where the only relevant opposition is male/female, and the only location for the female is as a victim. These tensions are not resolved by the narrative. It is not at all evident that Mignon will triumph over the white supremacist capitalist imperialist dominating "gaze."

Throughout *Illusions,* Mignon's power is affirmed by her contact with the younger black woman whom she nurtures and protects. It is this process of mirrored recognition that enables both black women to define their reality, apart from the reality imposed upon them by structures of domination. The shared gaze of the two women reinforces their solidarity. As the younger subject, Esther represents a potential audience for films that Mignon might produce, films wherein black females will be the narrative focus. Julie Dash's recent feature-length film *Daughters of the Dust* dares to place black females at the center of its narrative. This focus caused critics (especially white males) to critique the film negatively or to express many reservations. Clearly, the impact of racism and sexism so over-determine spectatorship—not only what we look at but who we identify with—that viewers who are not black females find it hard to empathize with the central characters in the movie. They are adrift without a white presence in the film.

Another representation of black females nurturing one another *via* recognition of their common struggle for subjectivity is depicted in Sankofa's collective work *Passion of Remembrance*. In the film, two black women friends, Louise and Maggie, are from the onset of the narrative struggling with the issue of subjectivity, of their place in progressive black liberation movements that have been sexist. They challenge old norms and want to replace them with new understandings of the complexity of black identity, and the need for liberation struggles that address that complexity. Dressing to go to a party, Louise and Maggie claim the "gaze." Looking at one another, staring in mirrors, they appear completely focused on their encounter with black femaleness. How they see themselves is most important, not how they will be stared at by others. Dancing to the tune "Let's get Loose," they display their bodies not for a voyeuristic colonizing gaze but for that look of recognition that affirms their subjectivity—that constitutes them as spectators. Mutually empowered they eagerly leave the privatized domain to confront the public. Disrupting conventional racist and sexist stereotypical representations of black female bodies, these scenes invite the audience to look differently. They act to critically intervene and transform conventional filmic practices, changing notions of spectatorship. *Illusions, Daughters of the Dust,* and *A Passion of Remembrance* employ a deconstructive filmic practice to undermine existing grand cinematic narratives even as they retheorize subjectivity in the realm of the visual. Without providing "realistic" positive representations that emerge only as a response to the totalizing nature of existing narratives, they offer points of radical departure. Opening up a space for the assertion of a critical black female spectatorship, they do not simply offer diverse representations, they imagine new transgressive possibilities for the formulation of identity.

In this sense they make explicit a critical practice that provides us with different ways to think about black female subjectivity and black female spectatorship. Cinematically, they provide new points of recognition, embodying Stuart Hall's vision of a critical practice that acknowledges that identity is constituted "not outside but within representation," and invites us to see film "not as a second-order mirror held up to reflect what already exists, but as that form of representation which is able to constitute us as new kinds of subjects, and thereby enable us to discover who we are." It is this critical practice that enables production of feminist film theory that theorizes black female spectatorship. Looking and looking back, black women involve ourselves in a process whereby we see our history as counter-memory, using it as a way to know the present and invent the future.

Chapter 8

Micheaux's Films
Celebrating Blackness

Conceiving of his work in independent filmmaking as counter-hegemonic cultural production, Oscar Micheaux worked doggedly to create screen images that would disrupt and challenge conventional racist representations of blackness. Stating this political agenda in the January 24, 1925 edition of the *Philadelphia Afro-American* newspaper, Micheaux declared:

> I have always tried to make my photoplays present the truth, to lay before the race a cross section of its own life, to view the colored heart from close range. My results might have been narrow at times, due perhaps to certain limited situations, which I endeavored to portray, but in those limited situations, the truth was the predominant characteristic. It is only by presenting those portions of the race portrayed in my pictures, in the light and background of their true state, that we can raise our people to greater heights.

Though Micheaux aimed to produce a counter-hegemonic art that would challenge white supremacist representations of "blackness," he was not concerned with the simple reduction of black representation to a "positive" image. In the spirit of oppositional creativity, he worked to produce images that would convey complexity of experience and feeling, arguing that "before we expect to see ourselves featured on the silver screen as we live, hope, act, and think today, men and women must write original stories of Negro life." Though he did not conceive of his work as documentation, making the camera mirror life, he did want black folks to see images on the screen that were not stereotypes or caricatures. Micheaux endeavored to go beyond the realm of the ordinary—it is this vision that gives his films an element of intrigue and delight that fascinates.

Ironically, his use of melodrama has been misunderstood by contemporary viewers who see this style as undermining cinematic capacity to convey complexity. Micheaux did not suffer from an error of insight. In the essay "Melodrama Inside and Outside the Home," Laura Mulvey explores the subversive possibilities emerging from the location of melodrama, drawing on the *The Melodramatic Imagination* by Peter Brooks:

> Peter Brooks shows how the melodrama's aesthetic strength lies precisely in its displacement of the power of the word. This "low cultural" form could reflect on human struggle with language and expression and thus influence the development of romantic theatre. The aesthetics of the popular melodrama depend on grand gesture, tableaux, broad moral themes, with narratives of coincidence, reverses and sudden happy endings organized around a rigid opposition between good and evil. Characters represent forces rather than people, and fail to control or understand their circumstances so that fate, rather than heroic transcendence, offers a resolution to the drama…While the aesthetics of melodrama evolved for a non-literate audience, the style throws doubt on the adequacy of speech to express the complexities of passion…A whole terrain of the "unspeakable" can thus be depicted.

Micheaux used melodrama in precisely this way. Approaching his work from this standpoint enables the contemporary viewer to see more clearly how his films work to transgress boundaries to offer perspectives, different "takes," on black experience that can be found/seen in no other cinematic practice during his day. Writing about Micheaux's unique vision in her essay "The Changeling: Race, Sex, and Property in Oscar Micheaux's 'God's Stepchildren,'" critic Marilyn Jimenez says of his films:

> There is in them the true mark of the "auteur," the unmistakable stamp of a personality, the obsessions of a visionary; this all generally under the surface, for the distinctive mark of a Micheaux film is the relationship between text and subtext, between what the film says and what it really says. In so doing, Micheaux more

than any other filmmaker, embodies the ancient characteristic of black artistic creation: the trope of reversal, the use of "indirections to find directions out."

Micheaux, fascinated by what I call "a politics of pleasure and danger" focused both on racialized sexual politics as they informed the construction and expression of desire between black heterosexual couples as well as interracial sexual bondings. Though he was involved in a romantic liaison with a white woman in South Dakota, Micheaux felt marriage to her was tantamount to a betrayal of his race. Desire expressed sexually, a constant theme in his films, became a site where loyalty and solidarity are tested. Much of his work explores passions aroused in response to acts of betrayal. Attempting to express and convey the particular forms desire and courtship take within a racial context of color caste, a society where black male and female sexuality is constructed as dangerous and threatening, Micheaux's work offers an extended cinematic narrative of black sexual politics. Focusing on womanizing and vamping, Micheaux's work "exploits" conventional constructions of good and bad sexuality as he simultaneously "toys" with the idea of transgression.

The l932 Micheaux film *Ten Minutes To Live* problematized the location of black heterosexual pleasure within a rigid color caste system that makes the desired object the body most resembling whiteness. In a series of narrative reversals challenging assumptions that whiteness/light skin should be interpreted as signifying innocence, the question of who is good or bad is rendered far more complex than the issue of color. Calling into question the Western metaphysical dualism which associates whiteness with purity and blackness with taint, the subtext of Micheaux's seemingly simple melodrama interrogates internalized racism and the color caste system.

Superficially, *Ten Minutes To Live* conforms to the cinematic paradigm already set by Hollywood and gives his audience a bad guy. Addressing the black public's need to have race movies reproduce aspects of white mainstream cinema that denied their presence, Micheaux incorporates into his work familiar melodramatic narratives. Just as the white "master" narratives of cinema insisted that plots be structured around conflicts between good and evil, this became the usual ground of conflict in race movies. Responding to what Clyde Taylor calls in "The Master Text and The Jeddi Doctrine" an insistence on "the sense of the presence and identity of corruption" which then "embodies the need for a menacing Manichean adversary," Micheaux

used this model to generate suspense, a cinematic tension that fascinated audiences.

Ironically, even though *Ten Minutes To Live* will interrogate the
audience's need for a "bad guy," Micheaux structures the film's opening
scenes so that they stimulate the audience's interest in identifying a
villain. First we are shown the image of a distressed black woman
boarding a train, the glamorous Letha. A male voice-over poses the
question: "What mystery here? Why has this beautiful girl been put on
the spot?" The film proceeds to explain the scenes we have just seen.
Initially jolted into a state of defamiliarization, the audience sees images
that they know but do not understand in the film context. Micheaux
works to establish film as a site for the production of narratives that are
structured to be more compelling than ordinary life, after all race
movies were, like their Hollywood counterparts, about business. An
audience had to be captivated so that they would return to see more.
Using the camera to disrupt fixed notions of subject and place, to create
an aura of intrigue, Micheaux aggressively insists that viewers be "glued
to their seats" if they want to solve the mystery. (His shooting of this
scene is really technologically spectacular when viewed within the
context of early film production.) Disrupting the audiences capacity to
"read" familiar signs, Micheaux delights in the pleasure of manipulation, excessively subordinating everything to the narration. Though a
"race man" eager to work for the uplift of black people, he refused to
accept the notion that black cultural production should simply be a
response to white representations of blackness, and thereby only
portray blackness in a positive light. Insisting on diversity and complexity of image, his films set an example.

After the train scene, which opens the film in the middle of the
story, strategically shifting the focus away from linear narrative,
Micheaux breaks with convention and lets the audience know from the
onset who the villain is. Identified by a snapshot from a police blotter,
the villain Marvin is described as:

> Forty, deaf and mute—but cunning, formerly an actor known on
> the stage as the "escape" king due to his ability to pick any lock,
> open any door...lost his voice and hearing about 5 years ago and
> developed strange hallucinations.

Though appearing to "identify" the bad guy, this description does not
really say what crimes have been committed. Presented as official
information even though it says nothing specific, this representation
undercuts the stereotype of the black male as criminal, hinting at the

possibility that all representation is constructed and therefore subject to manipulation (Marvin as actor), and that nothing is as it appears.

Unable to speak or hear, Marvin must rely solely on sight as a means to perceive reality. Concurrently, since he has no voice (a symbolic mirroring of the voicelessness of black masculinity in racist culture during the 1930s) he must think and feel through the body. Richard Dyer's critical assessment of Paul Robeson in *Heavenly Bodies: Film Stars and Society* calls attention to the way representations of black folks in the white imagination are a "site where the problem of the body is worked through":

> Representations of blacks then function as the site of remembering and denying the inescapability of the body in the economy. Hence, on the one hand, the black body as a reminder of what the body can do, its vitality, its strength, its sensuousness, and yet, simultaneously, the denial of all that bodily energy and delight as creative and productive...

Conversely, to subvert the negation of the black body that is imposed by white supremacy, representations by black people claim that creative potential, glorifying it. Even though the fair-skinned, handsome Marvin, is the bad guy, his body is constructed as the object of a desiring black female gaze. Challenging dominant cinematic practices that position woman as the object of male gaze, Micheaux acknowledges female desire, exploiting it to create interest in Marvin's character. His body is excessively objectified, all the more so because he does not speak. Asserting a masculine presence that is profoundly physical, embodying a sense of threat and menace, he is a seductive villain. Micheaux both critiques and celebrates this black male physicality. Beginning his professional life as a Pullman porter, respectable employment (the train scene represents the inclusion in the film of his personal history), he is identified with that organization of black men who militantly resisted racist discrimination in the work force. Yet Micheaux knew all too well that it was easy within a racist society for black men to fall into disrepute, to end up like Marvin on the chain gang. It is only when the film is about to end that we learn from a letter Marvin's mother writes, rebuking him for persecuting the beautiful Letha, that he has been on the chain gang, a site where white domination over the black male body is expressed by excessive exploitation of their physical labor. Many chain gangs composed solely of black men did the arduous labor on railroads, laying tracks, making repairs. Micheaux's inclusion of these historical references (that would have been immediately understood by his audience) situate representations of black male "criminality" in a social and political context, contesting notions of inherent biological propensity of evil perpetuated in racist ideology, in white cinema.

Even though Marvin is a sympathetic character, he is depicted as dangerous, exhibiting all the characteristics of "the demon lover." He has returned to old haunts to kill the woman who betrayed him by turning him over to the authorities. Robin Morgan's description of "the deadly hero" in *The Demon Lover* could be a profile of Marvin:

> Valorous, abnegating his own selfhood and severed from that of others, disconnected from a living logic and the pathos of emotional commitments, recognizing only the redeeming ecstasy of a tragic death, *the hero already lives as a dead man*. As a dead man he is fearless, because as a dead man he is unconquerable by any life force.

Throughout *Ten Minutes To Live,* Marvin resurfaces as though from the dead. His inability to speak reinforces the sense that he has no ties with human community, as it is language that affirms this bonding. Able to express himself to others only by writing, he terrorizes Letha by sending her threatening messages, "death warrants," to let her know that she is his prey, hunted by an old love who intends to show no mercy. Inverting the popular myth of embittered revengeful womanhood betrayed and scorned by man, Micheaux implies that it is really the black male, personified by Marvin, who will be betrayed and manipulated.

In keeping with his critique of a color caste that sees the fair-skinned black woman as more desirable and worthy of love, Micheaux's "vamp" Charlotte could pass for white. Jewish-American actress Theda Bara, whose real name was Theodosia Goodman, brought the image of the vamp to Hollywood and popularized it. Woman as "vamp" was depicted as an adventuress, alluring, enticing, dangerous; vamp was short for vampire. She had the power to seduce and destroy men. In *Girls on Film,* Julie Burchill critically examines the cinematic portrait of woman as vamp, emphasizing that this character was often portrayed as dark in contrast to white:

> The vamp was a beacon and a blessing in the cinema, the apex of what a woman on the screen can be. The vamp was beautiful *and* strong; she made helplessness, which previously and ever since has been the desirable norm for girls on film, look insipid and

uninspiring. She came from nowhere and she walked alone. The vamp was a rhapsody and a revolution.

Micheaux offers the viewers images of woman as "vamp" and as helpless damsel in distress through his juxtaposition of the characters Charlotte and Letha. Again, as though to counter the racism of mainstream cinema, his vamp is the fair-skinned, white-woman-look-alike.

Marvin's inability to distinguish between Charlotte and Letha, to know which woman is vamping and betraying him, is Micheaux's way to once again problematize the question of representation and our capacity to know reality *via* the senses. How can we judge good and evil if so much that appears to be one thing is really the other? His answer of course is to sharpen and intensify one's capacity for perception, to learn to be more aware. Employing diverse images of black womanhood, Micheaux encourages audiences to resist the urge to construct a totalizing vision of woman, one that sees the female as embodying all that is evil, licentious, and morally corrupt. An advocate of rights for women, Micheaux created a space in cinema where black women could be portrayed as desiring subjects; he countered the demeaning images of black femaleness in Hollywood cinema. In his films, black women's bodies are celebrated—plump or thin, light or dark (though they were never "too" dark), they are sensual and desirable.

Careful in *Ten Minutes to Live* to distinguish between the image of woman as "vamp" who uses her body as a seductive weapon to exert power over men, and the representation of a liberated image of the sensual/sexual black woman who is at home in her body, Micheaux remains one of the few filmmakers to portray black women's bodies in a manner that does not invite a phallocentric violating gaze. Without allying himself with idealized representations of "innocent" womanhood, he portrays Letha as a virtuous woman who is also glamorous, and therefore desirable. In "Living dolls and 'real' Women," published in *The Power of the Image*, Annette Kuhn offers this account of glamour's allure:

> Glamour is understood generally to imply a sense of deceptive fascination, of groomed beauty, of charm enhanced by means of illusion. A glamorous/glamorized image then is one manipulated, falsified perhaps, in order to heighten or even idealize. A glamorous image of a woman (or an image of a glamorous woman) is peculiarly powerful in that it plays on the desire of the spectator in a particularly pristine way: beauty or sexuality is desirable to the extent that it is idealized and unattainable.

Micheaux employs this notion of glamour in his representation of Letha. One of longest scenes in *Ten Minutes to Live* shows Letha returning to her bedroom in a boarding house to change clothes. There, fully made-up, gazing at herself in the mirror of her vanity table (all images that identify her as using cosmetics to create glamour), attired in beautiful lingerie and dressing gown, she dresses for an evening out. Unself-consciously adorned, Letha maintains an aura of naïveté even though she is not innocent. That aura is not disrupted by the presence of Marvin, who has entered her space, violating her privacy, for she does not know that her integrity is threatened until the front door slams as he escapes.

Fully adorned, the glamorous Letha meets her current dark-skinned male admirer, Anthony, in a nightclub. She shows him another terrorizing message from Marvin, one that says she has only "ten minutes to live." That they should go nightclubing when her life is endangered seems outrageously melodramatic, yet Micheaux's tactic is always to reproduce an image of the real in the context of the bizarre. Such is the nature of intrigue. It requires a combination of the ordinary and the fantastic. In his films, nightclubs are the perfect settings to introduce this mixture, representing as they do sites of transgression, existing on the boundaries of morally sanctioned social life. Seeing nightclubs as non-hegemonic, non-homogenous spaces where class/caste barriers were crossed in the realm of pleasure, Jimenez comments:

> The song-dance sequences in black films lifted the film out of social reality, relieved the tensions of having to maintain racial consciousness, and broke the chains of unrealistic, narrative developments. The nightclub was a playspace, a dystopia, not a space that was no-where, but a disassociated, discontinuous realm.

In *Ten Minutes To Live* Micheaux includes a song and dance sequence in the nightclub scene that at first glance seems in no way connected to the suspenseful drama. It is however as much a clue hinting at the film's subtext as any other scene in the movie.

In the nightclub, Letha talks quietly to Anthony, encouraging him to wait, even though they are waiting for death. He replies, "Are you mad enough to think I'm going to sit here and let you, the woman I love—the woman I've always loved, be killed by this madman?" This melodramatic, passionate declaration and its underlying eroticism can be expressed in the nightclub setting as the sexual tension it arouses; the desire can be displaced onto the dancers. Letha and Anthony's passionate talk is interrupted by the master of ceremonies' announcement: "And now we introduce you to a little bit of the jungle—'Spirit of the Jungle.'" Suddenly, skimpily dressed black women of all sizes and shades appear and begin to dance. Their body movements resemble those of Josephine Baker, calling attention to their breasts, legs, and ·asses. Yet this display does not evoke pornographic gazes from folks in the nightclub, it is presented not as exposure of the taboo sexuality but as comfortable expression of bodily delight. Like Baker, Micheaux sees the black body as a site where nakedness and eroticism are not considered shameful realities to be hidden and masked.

Though the biography *Jazz Cleopatra* by Phyllis Rose assaults Baker's life and work, now and then, it offers tidbits of useful information. This is particularly so in passages that address Baker's theorizing of the body and its relation to eroticism. Attempting to describe Baker's sense of the body, particularly the rear end, and documenting Baker's words, Rose comments:

> She handled it as though it were an instrument, a rattle something apart from herself that she could shake. One can hardly overemphasize the importance of the rear end. Baker herself declared that people had been hiding their asses too long. 'The rear end exists. I see no reason to be ashamed of it. It's true that there are rear ends so stupid, so pretentious, so insignificant that they're good only for sitting on.' With Baker's triumph, the erotic gaze of a nation moved downward: she had uncovered a new region for desire.

Rose lacks the knowledge of black culture that would enable her to decode the subtext of Baker's comments as well as an informed perspective on race that would have enabled her to understand that "asses" have always been eroticized in black sexual iconography, that within black folk culture the asses that are ridiculed and mocked are those of whites, called names like "ironing board butts." Hence, only the gaze of the white segment of the nation was transformed by Baker's assertion of bodily passion in dance.

Though associated with the "jungle," all the dancers in Micheaux's sequence are light-skinned, some white enough to pass. Yet by connecting this image with a jungle experience, he affirms an unbroken diasporic bond with Africa that has not been severed by assimilation. Atavism, as expressed in this dance routine, glorifies the connection to Africa. As Dyer put it in his essay on Robeson, atavism is often rooted in "the idea of the black race as a repository of uncontaminated feelings." Though he acknowledges that the atavistic image in the white imagination is similar to that in black folk culture, as a sign it has different meanings in the black context. In the black imagination, atavism was primarily connected to a counter-hegemonic sense of history, wherein the African past, which white supremacy had taught blacks to despise, was now revered and seen as a site for "the recovery of qualities and values held by one's ancestors."

After the dancers evoke an atavism that is about ancestor acknowledgment, Letha emphasizes her familial legacy. She explains to Anthony that she has received spiritual guidance from her mother in a dream:

> Last night, I dreamed of mother, my poor dear mother, who is dead. She came to me in my sleep and told me not to run away. "Be calm my baby. Place your trust in God. Something terrible is going to happen. Have faith my daughter, have faith."

Trusting in the wisdom of her mother, Letha refuses to listen to either the patriarchal voice that threatens or the one that encourages her to flee, offering to Anthony a paradigm for romantic love that is rooted in trust.

Contrary to the Freudian conceptualization of subjectivity wherein, as Jane Gallop describes it in *Thinking Through The Body,* "universal ambivalence toward the mother is made up of a universal primary attachment to the mother as nurturer and universal disappointment in the mother," Micheaux's drama suggests that it is only by maintaining a connection to the mother that is not tainted by suspicion that the adult child receives her unmediated wisdom and guidance. Both Letha and Marvin are rescued after they listen to the mothers' voices. The possibility of disappointment rests not with the mother but with the child who may lack the ability to recognize "truth" and therefore reality. Marvin's mother informs him in a letter that Charlotte is the vamp who has betrayed him for monetary rewards even as she castigates him for being a "fool." As in other Micheaux films that have feminist implications, his representations of maleness challenge the patriarchal construction of masculinity as powerful and all knowing. The men in *Ten Minutes To Live* lack insight. They can only apprehend the world fully, grasp the true nature of reality by learning from women. Letha and Marvin are spiritually renewed when they listen to the mother's voice. Escaping after he has revenged himself against Charlotte, Marvin writes a note of apology to Letha. This expression of regret enables him to reconnect with human community. His representation as "villain" is mediated by this confession of wrongdoing.

Ten Minutes To Live exploits all the conventions of simplistic melodrama even as it interrogates, on multiple levels, issues of representation. Nothing appears on the screen to be as simplistic as it often seems in everyday life. The capacity of individuals to discern good and evil, to distinguish that which is desirable and that which threatens is interrogated. Micheaux lets the audience know how easily perceptions are manipulated. Representing the ultimate villain, Charlotte, who is white enough to pass, stands in contrast to the romantic trusting lover Anthony who is dark-skinned. Micheaux subtly urges black spectators to re-evaluate the internalized racism that leads them to respect white or light skin and devalue blackness. Simultaneously, he urges us to claim the past, symbolized by the body of the mother—the mother tongue, the mother land. It is a call for a celebration of blackness in all its diversity and complexity—for that level of collective self-recognition that brings clarity and insight, that allows for reunion and reconciliation.

Chapter 9

Is Paris Burning?

There was a time in my life when I liked to dress up as a male and go out into the world. It was a form of ritual, of play. It was also about power. To cross-dress as a woman in patriarchy—then, more so than now—was also to symbolically cross from the world of powerlessness into a world of privilege. It was the ultimate, intimate, voyeuristic gesture. Searching old journals for passages documenting that time, I found this paragraph:

> She pleaded with him, "Just once, well every now and then, I just want us to be boys together. I want to dress like you and go out and make the world look at us differently, make them wonder about us, make them stare and ask those silly questions like is he a woman dressed up like a man, is he an older black gay man with his effeminate boy/girl lover flaunting same-sex love out in the open. Don't worry I'll take it all very seriously, I want to let them laugh at you. I'll make it real, keep them guessing, do it in such a way that they will never know for sure. Don't worry when we come home I will be a girl for you again but for now I want us to be boys together."

Cross-dressing, appearing in drag, transvestism, and transsexualism emerge in a context where the notion of subjectivity is challenged, where identity is always perceived as capable of construction, invention, change. Long before there was ever a contemporary feminist movement, the sites of these experiences were subversive places where gender norms were questioned and challenged.

Within white supremacist, capitalist patriarchy the experience of
men dressing as women, appearing in drag, has always been regarded
by the dominant heterosexist cultural gaze as a sign that one is symbolically crossing over from a realm of power into a realm of powerlessness. Just to look at the many negative ways the word "drag" is defined
reconnects this label to an experience that is seen as burdensome, as
retrograde and retrogressive. To choose to appear as "female" when
one is "male" is always constructed in the patriarchal mindset as a loss,
as a choice worthy only of ridicule. Given this cultural backdrop, it is
not surprising that many black comedians appearing on television
screens for the first time included as part of their acts impersonations
of black women. The black woman depicted was usually held up as
an object of ridicule, scorn, hatred (representing the "female" image
everyone was allowed to laugh at and show contempt for). Often the
moment when a black male comedian appeared in drag was the most
successful segment of a given comedian's act (for example, Flip Wilson,
Redd Foxx, or Eddie Murphy).

I used to wonder if the sexual stereotype of black men as overly
sexual, manly, as "rapists," allowed black males to cross this gendered
boundary more easily than white men without having to fear that they
would be seen as possibly gay or transvestites. As a young black female,
I found these images to be disempowering. They seemed to both allow
black males to give public expression to a general misogyny, as well as
to a more specific hatred and contempt toward black woman. Growing
up in a world where black women were, and still are, the objects of
extreme abuse, scorn, and ridicule, I felt these impersonations were
aimed at reinforcing everyone's power over us. In retrospect, I can see
that the black male in drag was also a disempowering image of black
masculinity. Appearing as a "woman" within a sexist, racist media was
a way to become in "play" that "castrated" silly childlike black male that
racist white patriarchy was comfortable having as an image in their
homes. These televised images of black men in drag were never
subversive; they helped sustain sexism and racism.

It came as no surprise to me that Catherine Clement in her book
Opera, or the Undoing of Women would include a section about black
men and the way their representation in opera did not allow her to
neatly separate the world into gendered polarities where men and
women occupied distinctly different social spaces and were "two
antagonistic halves, one persecuting the other since before the dawn
of time." Looking critically at images of black men in operas she found
that they were most often portrayed as victims:

Eve is undone as a woman, endlessly bruised, endlessly dying and coming back to life to die even better. But now I begin to remember hearing figures of betrayed, wounded men; men who have women's troubles happen to them; men who have the status of Eve, as if they had lost their innate Adam. These men die like heroines; down on the ground they cry and moan, they lament. And like heroines they are surrounded by real men, veritable Adams who have cast them down. They partake of femininity: excluded, marked by some initial strangeness. They are doomed to their undoing.

Many heterosexual black men in white supremacist patriarchal culture have acted as though the primary "evil" of racism has been the refusal of the dominant culture to allow them full access to patriarchal power, so that in sexist terms they are compelled to inhabit a sphere of powerlessness, deemed "feminine," hence they have perceived themselves as emasculated. To the extent that black men accept a white supremacist sexist representation of themselves as castrated, without phallic power, and therefore pseudo-females, they will need to overly assert a phallic misogynist masculinity, one rooted in contempt for the female. Much black male homophobia is rooted in the desire to eschew connection with all things deemed "feminine" and that would, of course, include black gay men. A contemporary black comedian like Eddie Murphy "proves" his phallic power by daring to publicly ridicule women and gays. His days of appearing in drag are over. Indeed it is the drag queen of his misogynist imagination that is most often the image of black gay culture he evokes and subjects to comic homophobic assault—one that audiences collude in perpetuating.

For black males to take appearing in drag seriously, be they gay or straight, is to oppose a heterosexist representation of black manhood. Gender bending and blending on the part of black males has always been a critique of phallocentric masculinity in traditional black experience. Yet the subversive power of those images is radically altered when informed by a racialized fictional construction of the "feminine" that suddenly makes the representation of whiteness as crucial to the experience of female impersonation as gender, that is to say when the idealized notion of the female/feminine is really a sexist idealization of white womanhood. This is brutally evident in Jennie Livingston's new film *Paris Is Burning*. Within the world of the black gay drag ball culture she depicts, the idea of womanness and femininity is totally personified by whiteness. What viewers witness is not black men longing to impersonate or even to become like "real" black women but their obsession with an idealized fetishized vision of femininity that is white. Called out in the film by Dorian Carey, who names it by saying no black drag queen of his day wanted to be Lena Horne, he makes it clear that the femininity most sought after, most adored, was that perceived to be the exclusive property of white womanhood. When we see visual representations of womanhood in the film (images torn from magazines and posted on walls in living space) they are, with rare exceptions, of white women. Significantly, the fixation on becoming as much like a white female as possible implicitly evokes a connection to a figure never visible in this film: that of the white male patriarch. And yet if the class, race, and gender aspirations expressed by the drag queens who share their deepest dreams is always the longing to be in the position of the ruling-class woman then that means there is also the desire to act in partnership with the ruling-class white male.

This combination of class and race longing that privileges the "femininity" of the ruling-class white woman, adored and kept, shrouded in luxury, does not imply a critique of patriarchy. Often it is assumed that the gay male, and most specifically the "queen," is both anti-phallocentric and anti-patriarchal. Marilyn Frye's essay, "Lesbian Feminism and Gay Rights," remains one of the most useful critical debunkings of this myth. Writing in *The Politics of Reality,* Frye comments:

> One of things which persuades the straight world that gay men are not really men is the effeminacy of style of some gay men and the gay institution of the impersonation of women, both of which are associated in the popular mind with male homosexuality. But as I read it, gay men's effeminacy and donning of feminine apparel displays no love of or identification with women or the womanly. For the most part, this femininity is affected and is characterized by theatrical exaggeration. It is a casual and cynical mockery of women, for whom femininity is the trapping of oppression, but it is also a kind of play, a toying with that which is taboo...What gay male affectation of femininity seems to be is a serious sport in which men may exercise their power and control over the feminine, much as in other sports...But the mastery of the feminine is not feminine. It is masculine...

Any viewer of *Paris is Burning* can neither deny the way in which its contemporary drag balls have the aura of sports events, aggressive competitions, one team (in this case "house") competing against another etc., nor ignore the way in which the male "gaze" in the audience is directed at participants in a manner akin to the objectifying phallic stare straight men direct at "feminine" women daily in public spaces. *Paris is Burning* is a film that many audiences assume is inherently oppositional because of its subject matter and the identity of the filmmaker. Yet the film's politics of race, gender, and class are played out in ways that are both progressive and reactionary.

When I first heard that there was this new documentary film about black gay men, drag queens, and drag balls I was fascinated by the title. It evoked images of the real Paris on fire, of the death and destruction of a dominating white western civilization and culture, an end to oppressive Eurocentrism and white supremacy. This fantasy not only gave me a sustained sense of pleasure, it stood between me and the unlikely reality that a young white filmmaker, offering a progressive vision of "blackness" from the standpoint of "whiteness," would receive the positive press accorded Livingston and her film. Watching *Paris is Burning,* I began to think that the many yuppie-looking, straight-acting, pushy, predominantly white folks in the audience were there because the film in no way interrogates "whiteness." These folks left the film saying it was "amazing," "marvelous," "incredibly funny," worthy of statements like, "Didn't you just love it?" And no, I didn't just love it. For in many ways the film was a graphic documentary portrait of the way in which colonized black people (in this case black gay brothers, some of whom were drag queens) worship at the throne of whiteness, even when such worship demands that we live in perpetual self-hate, steal, lie, go hungry, and even die in its pursuit. The "we" evoked here is all of us, black people/people of color, who are daily bombarded by a powerful colonizing whiteness that seduces us away from ourselves, that negates that there is beauty to be found in any form of blackness that is not imitation whiteness.

The whiteness celebrated in *Paris is Burning* is not just any old brand of whiteness but rather that brutal imperial ruling-class capitalist patriarchal whiteness that presents itself—its way of life—as the only meaningful life there is. What could be more reassuring to a white public fearful that marginalized disenfranchised black folks might rise any day now and make revolutionary black liberation struggle a reality than a documentary affirming that colonized, victimized, exploited, black folks are all too willing to be complicit in perpetuating the fantasy that ruling-class white culture is the quintessential site of unrestricted joy, freedom, power, and pleasure. Indeed it is the very "pleasure" that so many white viewers with class privilege experience when watching this film that has acted to censor dissenting voices who find the film and its reception critically problematic.

In Vincent Canby's review of the film in the *New York Times* he begins by quoting the words of a black father to his homosexual son. The father shares that it is difficult for black men to survive in a racist society and that "if you're black and male and gay, you have to be stronger than you can imagine." Beginning his overwhelmingly positive review with the words of a straight black father, Canby implies that the film in some way documents such strength, is a portrait of black gay pride. Yet he in no way indicates ways this pride and power are evident in the work. Like most reviewers of the film, what he finds most compelling is the pageantry of the drag balls. He uses no language identifying race and class perspectives when suggesting at the end of his piece that behind the role-playing "there is also a terrible sadness in the testimony." Canby does not identify fully the sources of this sadness; instead he states, "The queens knock themselves out to imitate the members of a society that will not have them." This makes it appear that the politics of ruling-class white culture are solely social and not political, solely "aesthetic" questions of choice and desire rather than expressions of power and privilege. Canby does not tell readers that much of the tragedy and sadness of this film is evoked by the willing-ness of black gay men to knock themselves out imitating a ruling-class culture and power elite that is one of the primary agents of their oppression and exploitation. Ironically, the very "fantasies" evoked emerge from the colonizing context, and while marginalized people often appropriate and subvert aspects of the dominant culture, *Paris is Burning* does not forcefully suggest that such a process is taking place.

Livingston's film is presented as though it is a politically neutral documentary providing a candid, even celebratory, look at black drag balls. And it is precisely the mood of celebration that masks the extent to which the balls are not necessarily radical expressions of subversive imagination at work undermining and challenging the *status quo*. Much of the film's focus on pageantry takes the ritual of the black drag ball and makes it spectacle. Ritual is that ceremonial act that carries with it meaning and significance beyond what appears, while spectacle func-tions primarily as entertaining dramatic display. Those of us who have grown up in a segregated black setting where we participated in diverse pageants and rituals know that those elements of a given ritual that are empowering and subversive may not be readily visible to an outsider looking in. Hence it is easy for white observers to depict black rituals as spectacle.

Jennie Livingston approaches her subject matter as an outsider looking in. Since her presence as white woman/lesbian filmmaker is "absent" from *Paris is Burning* it is easy for viewers to imagine that they are watching an ethnographic film documenting the life of black gay "natives" and not recognize that they are watching a work shaped and formed by a perspective and standpoint specific to Livingston. By cinematically masking this reality (we hear her ask questions but never see her), Livingston does not oppose the way hegemonic whiteness "represents" blackness, but rather assumes an imperial overseeing position that is in no way progressive or counter-hegemonic. By shooting the film using a conventional approach to documentary and not making clear how her standpoint breaks with this tradition, Livingston assumes a privileged location of "innocence." She is represented both in interviews and reviews as the tender-hearted, mild-mannered, virtuous white woman daring to venture into a contemporary "heart of darkness" to bring back knowledge of the natives.

A review in the *New Yorker* declares (with no argument to substantiate the assertion) that "the movie is a sympathetic observation of a specialized, private world." An interview with Livingston in *Outweek* is titled "Pose, She Said" and we are told in the preface that she "discovered the Ball world by chance." Livingston does not discuss her interest and fascination with black gay subculture. She is not asked to speak about what knowledge, information, or lived understanding of black culture and history she possessed that provided a background for her work or to explain what vision of black life she hoped to convey and to whom. Can anyone imagine that a black woman lesbian would make a film about white gay subculture and not be asked these questions? Livingston is asked in the *Outweek* interview, "How did you build up the kind of trust where people are so open to talking about their personal experiences?" She never answers this question. Instead she suggests that she gains her "credibility" by the intensity of her spectatorship, adding, "I also targeted people who were articulate, who had stuff they wanted to say and were very happy that anyone wanted to listen." Avoiding the difficult questions underlying what it means to be a white person in a white supremacist society creating a film about any aspect of black life, Livingston responds to the question, "Didn't the fact that you're a white lesbian going into a world of Black queens and street kids make that [the interview process] difficult?" by implicitly evoking a shallow sense of universal connection. She responds, "If you know someone over a period of two years, and they still retain their sex and their race, you've got to be a pretty sexist, racist person." Yet it

is precisely the race, sex, and sexual practices of black men who are
filmed that is the exploited subject matter.

So far I have read no interviews where Livingston discusses the
issue of appropriation. And even though she is openly critical of
Madonna, she does not convey how her work differs from Madonna's
appropriation of black experience. To some extent it is precisely the
recognition by mass culture that aspects of black life, like "voguing,"
fascinate white audiences that creates a market for both Madonna's
product and Livingston's. Unfortunately, Livingston's comments about
Paris is Burning do not convey serious thought about either the
political and aesthetic implications of her choice as a white woman
focusing on an aspect of black life and culture or the way racism might
shape and inform how she would interpret black experience on the
screen. Reviewers like Georgia Brown in the *Village Voice* who suggest
that Livingston's whiteness is "a fact of nature that didn't hinder her
research" collude in the denial of the way whiteness informs her
perspective and standpoint. To say, as Livingston does, "I certainly
don't have the final word on the gay black experience. I'd love for a
black director to have made this film" is to oversimplify the issue and
to absolve her of responsibility and accountability for progressive
critical reflection and it implicitly suggests that there would be no
difference between her work and that of a black director. Underlying
this apparently self-effacing comment is cultural arrogance, for she
implies not only that she has cornered the market on the subject matter
but that being able to make films is a question of personal choice, like
she just "discovered" the "raw material" before a black director did. Her
comments are disturbing because they reveal so little awareness of the
politics that undergird any commodification of "blackness" in this society.

Had Livingston approached her subject with greater awareness
of the way white supremacy shapes cultural production—determining
not only what representations of blackness are deemed acceptable,
marketable, as well worthy of seeing—perhaps the film would not so
easily have turned the black drag ball into a spectacle for the entertainment of those presumed to be on the outside of this experience looking
in. So much of what is expressed in the film has to do with questions
of power and privilege and the way racism impedes black progress (and
certainly the class aspirations of the black gay subculture depicted do
not differ from those of other poor and underclass black communities).
Here, the supposedly "outsider" position is primarily located in the
experience of whiteness. Livingston appears unwilling to interrogate
the way assuming the position of outsider looking in, as well as

interpreter, can, and often does, pervert and distort one's perspective. Her ability to assume such a position without rigorous interrogation of intent is rooted in the politics of race and racism. Patricia Williams critiques the white assumption of a "neutral" gaze in her essay "Teleology on the Rocks" included in her new book *The Alchemy of Race and Rights*. Describing taking a walking tour of Harlem with a group of white folks, she recalls the guide telling them they might "get to see some services" since "Easter Sunday in Harlem is quite a show." William's critical observations are relevant to any discussion of *Paris is Burning*:

> What astonished me was that no one had asked the churches if they wanted to be stared at like living museums. I wondered what would happen if a group of blue-jeaned blacks were to walk uninvited into a synagogue on Passover or St. Anthony's of Padua during high mass—just to peer, not pray. My feeling is that such activity would be seen as disrespectful, at the very least. Yet the aspect of disrespect, intrusion, seemed irrelevant to this well-educated, affable group of people. They deflected my observation with comments like "We just want to look," "No one will mind," and "There's no harm intended." As well-intentioned as they were, I was left with the impression that no one existed for them who could not be governed by their intentions. While acknowledging the lack of apparent malice in this behavior, I can't help thinking that it is a liability as much as a luxury to live without interaction. To live so completely impervious to one's own impact on others is a fragile privilege, which over time relies not simply on the willingness but on the inability of others—in this case blacks—to make their displeasure heard.

This insightful critique came to mind as I reflected on why whites could so outspokenly make their pleasure in this film heard and the many black viewers who express discontent, raising critical questions about how the film was made, is seen, and is talked about, who have not named their displeasure publicly. Too many reviewers and interviewers assume not only that there is no need to raise pressing critical questions about Livingston's film, but act as though she somehow did this marginalized black gay subculture a favor by bringing their experience to a wider public. Such a stance obscures the substantial rewards she has received for this work. Since so many of the black gay men in the film express the desire to be big stars, it is easy to place Livingston in the role of benefactor, offering these "poor black souls" a way to realize their dreams. But it is this current trend in producing colorful ethnicity for the white consumer appetite that makes it possible for blackness to be commodified in unprecedented ways, and for whites to appropriate black culture without interrogating whiteness or showing concern for the displeasure of blacks. Just as white cultural imperialism informed and affirmed the adventurous journeys of colonizing whites into the countries and cultures of "dark others," it allows white audiences to applaud representations of black culture, if they are satisfied with the images and habits of being represented.

Watching the film with a black woman friend, we were disturbed by the extent to which white folks around us were "entertained" and "pleasured" by scenes we viewed as sad and at times tragic. Often individuals laughed at personal testimony about hardship, pain, loneliness. Several times I yelled out in the dark: "What is so funny about this scene? Why are you laughing?" The laughter was never innocent. Instead it undermined the seriousness of the film, keeping it always on the level of spectacle. And much of the film helped make this possible. Moments of pain and sadness were quickly covered up by dramatic scenes from drag balls, as though there were two competing cinematic narratives, one displaying the pageantry of the drag ball and the other reflecting on the lives of participants and value of the fantasy. This second narrative was literally hard to hear because the laughter often drowned it out, just as the sustained focus on elaborate displays at balls diffused the power of the more serious critical narrative. Any audience hoping to be entertained would not be as interested in the true life stories and testimonies narrated. Much of the individual testimony makes it appear that the characters are estranged from any community beyond themselves. Families, friends, etc., are not shown, which adds to the representation of these black gay men as cut off, living on the edge.

It is useful to compare the portraits of their lives in *Paris is Burning* with those depicted in Marlon Riggs' compelling film *Tongues Untied*. At no point in Livingston's film are the men asked to speak about their connections to a world of family and community beyond the drag ball. The cinematic narrative makes the ball the center of their lives. And yet who determines this? Is this the way the black men view their reality or is this the reality Livingston constructs? Certainly the degree to which black men in this gay subculture are portrayed as cut off from a "real" world heightens the emphasis on fantasy, and indeed gives *Paris is Burning* its tragic edge. That tragedy is made explicit when we are told that the fair-skinned Venus has been murdered, and yet there is no mourning of him/her in the film, no intense focus on the sadness of this murder. Having served the purpose of "spectacle" the film abandons him/her. The audience does not see Venus after the murder. There are no scenes of grief. To put it crassly, her dying is upstaged by spectacle. Death is not entertaining.

For those of us who did not come to this film as voyeurs of black gay subculture, it is Dorian Carey's moving testimony throughout the film that makes *Paris is Burning* a memorable experience. Carey is both historian and cultural critic in the film. He explains how the balls enabled marginalized black gay queens to empower both participants and audience. It is Carey who talks about the significance of the "star" in the life of gay black men who are queens. In a manner similar to critic Richard Dyer in his work *Heavenly Bodies*, Carey tells viewers that the desire for stardom is an expression of the longing to realize the dream of autonomous stellar individualism. Reminding readers that the idea of the individual continues to be a major image of what it means to live in a democratic world, Dyer writes:

> Capitalism justifies itself on the basis of the freedom (separateness) of anyone to make money, sell their labor how they will, to be able to express opinions and get them heard (regardless of wealth or social position). The openness of society is assumed by the way that we are addressed as individuals—as consumers (each freely choosing to buy, or watch, what we want), as legal subjects (equally responsible before the law), as political subjects (able to make up our minds who is to run society). Thus even while the notion of the individual is assailed on all sides, it is a necessary fiction for the reproduction of the kind of society we live in...Stars articulate these ideas of personhood.

This is precisely the notion of stardom Carey articulates. He emphasizes the way consumer capitalism undermines the subversive power of the drag balls, subordinating ritual to spectacle, removing the will to display unique imaginative costumes and the purchased image. Carey speaks profoundly about the redemptive power of the imagination in black life, that drag balls were traditionally a place where the aesthetics of the image in relation to black gay life could be explored with complexity and grace.

Carey extols the significance of fantasy even as he critiques the use of fantasy to escape reality. Analyzing the place of fantasy in black gay subculture, he links that experience to the longing for stardom that is so pervasive in this society. Refusing to allow the "queen" to be Othered, he conveys the message that in all of us resides that longing to transcend the boundaries of self, to be glorified. Speaking about the

importance of drag queens in a recent interview in *Afterimage,* Marlon
Riggs suggests that the queen personifies the longing everyone has for
love and recognition. Seeing in drag queens "a desire, a very visceral
need to be loved, as well as a sense of the abject loneliness of life where
nobody loves you," Riggs contends "this image is real for anybody who
has been in the bottom spot where they've been rejected by everybody
and loved by nobody." Echoing Carey, Riggs declares: "What's real for
them is the realization that you have to learn to love yourself." Carey
stresses that one can only learn to love the self when one breaks
through illusion and faces reality, not by escaping into fantasy. Emphasizing that the point is not to give us fantasy but to recognize its
limitations, he acknowledges that one must distinguish the place of
fantasy in ritualized play from the use of fantasy as a means of escape.
Unlike Pepper Labeija who constructs a mythic world to inhabit,
making this his private reality, Carey encourages using the imagination
creatively to enhance one's capacity to live more fully in a world beyond
fantasy.

Despite the profound impact he makes, what Riggs would call "a
visual icon of the drag queen with a very dignified humanity," Carey's
message, if often muted, is overshadowed by spectacle. It is hard for
viewers to really hear this message. By critiquing absorption in fantasy
and naming the myriad ways pain and suffering inform any process of
self-actualization, Carey's message mediates between the viewer who
longs to voyeuristicly escape into film, to vicariously inhabit that lived
space on the edge, by exposing the sham, by challenging all of us to
confront reality. James Baldwin makes the point in *The Fire Next Time*
that "people who cannot suffer can never grow up, can never discover
who they are." Without being sentimental about suffering, Dorian Carey
urges all of us to break through denial, through the longing for an
illusory star identity, so that we can confront and accept ourselves as
we really are—only then can fantasy, ritual, be a site of seduction,
passion, and play where the self is truly recognized, loved, and never
abandoned or betrayed.

Chapter 10

Madonna

Plantation Mistress or Soul Sister?

Subversion is contextual, historical, and above all social. No matter how exciting the "destabilizing" potential of texts, bodily or otherwise, whether those texts are subversive or recuperative or both or neither cannot be determined by abstraction from actual social practice.

—Susan Bordo

White women "stars" like Madonna, Sandra Bernhard, and many others publicly name their interest in, and appropriation of, black culture as yet another sign of their radical chic. Intimacy with that "nasty" blackness good white girls stay away from is what they seek. To white and other non-black consumers, this gives them a special flavor, an added spice. After all it is a very recent historical phenomenon for any white girl to be able to get some mileage out of flaunting her fascination and envy of blackness. The thing about envy is that it is always ready to destroy, erase, take-over, and consume the desired object. That's exactly what Madonna attempts to do when she appropriates and commodifies aspects of black culture. Needless to say this kind of fascination is a threat. It endangers. Perhaps that is why so many of the grown black women I spoke with about Madonna had no interest in her as a cultural icon and said things like, "The bitch can't even sing." It was only among young black females that I could find die-hard Madonna fans. Though I often admire and, yes at times, even envy Madonna because she has created a cultural space where she can invent

and reinvent herself and receive public affirmation and material reward,
I do not consider myself a Madonna fan.

Once I read an interview with Madonna where she talked about
her envy of black culture, where she stated that she wanted to be black
as a child. It is a sign of white privilege to be able to "see" blackness
and black culture from a standpoint where only the rich culture of
opposition black people have created in resistance marks and defines
us. Such a perspective enables one to ignore white supremacist domination and the hurt it inflicts *via* oppression, exploitation, and everyday
wounds and pains. White folks who do not see black pain never really
understand the complexity of black pleasure. And it is no wonder then
that when they attempt to imitate the joy in living which they see as the
"essence" of soul and blackness, their cultural productions may have
an air of sham and falseness that may titillate and even move white
audiences yet leave many black folks cold.

Needless to say, if Madonna had to depend on masses of black
women to maintain her status as cultural icon she would have been
dethroned some time ago. Many of the black women I spoke with
expressed intense disgust and hatred of Madonna. Most did not respond
to my cautious attempts to suggest that underlying those negative
feelings might lurk feelings of envy, and dare I say it, desire. No black
woman I talked to declared that she wanted to "be Madonna." Yet we
have only to look at the number of black women entertainers/stars
(Tina Turner, Aretha Franklin, Donna Summer, Vanessa Williams,
Yo-Yo, etc.) who gain greater cross-over recognition when they demonstrate that, like Madonna, they too, have a healthy dose of "blonde
ambition." Clearly their careers have been influenced by Madonna's
choices and strategies.

For masses of black women, the political reality that underlies
Madonna's and our recognition that this is a society where "blondes"
not only "have more fun" but where they are more likely to succeed in
any endeavor is white supremacy and racism. We cannot see
Madonna's change in hair color as being merely a question of aesthetic
choice. I agree with Julie Burchill in her critical work *Girls on Film,*
when she reminds us: "What does it say about racial purity that the best
blondes have all been brunettes (Harlow, Monroe, Bardot)? I think it
says that we are not as white as we think. I think it says that Pure is a
Bore." I also know that it is the expressed desire of the non-blonde
Other for those characteristics that are seen as the quintessential markers
of racial aesthetic superiority that perpetuate and uphold white
supremacy. In this sense Madonna has much in common with the

masses of black women who suffer from internalized racism and are forever terrorized by a standard of beauty they feel they can never truly embody.

Like many black women who have stood outside the culture's fascination with the blonde beauty and who have only been able to reach it through imitation and artifice, Madonna often recalls that she was a working-class white-girl who saw herself as ugly, as outside the mainstream beauty standard. And indeed what some of us like about her is the way she deconstructs the myth of "natural" white girl beauty by exposing the extent to which it can be and is usually artificially constructed and maintained. She mocks the conventional racist defined beauty ideal even as she rigorously strives to embody it. Given her obsession with exposing the reality that the ideal female beauty in this society can be attained by artifice and social construction it should come as no surprise that many of her fans are gay men, and that the majority of non-white men, particularly black men, are among that group. Jennie Livingston's film *Paris Is Burning* suggests that many black gay men, especially queens/divas, are as equally driven as Madonna by "blonde ambition." Madonna never lets her audience forget that whatever "look" she acquires is attained by hard work—"it ain't natural." And as Burchill comments in her chapter "Homosexual Girls":

> I have a friend who drives a cab and looks like a Marlboro Man but at night is the second best Jean Harlow I have ever seen. He summed up the kind of film star he adores, brutally and brilliantly, when he said, "I like actresses who look as if they've spent hours putting themselves together—and even then they don't look right."

Certainly no one, not even die-hard Madonna fans, ever insists that her beauty is not attained by skillful artifice. And indeed, a major point of the documentary film *Truth or Dare: In Bed With Madonna* was to demonstrate the amount of work that goes into the construction of her image. Yet when the chips are down, the image Madonna most exploits is that of the quintessential "white girl." To maintain that image she must always position herself as an outsider in relation to black culture. It is that position of outsider that enables her to colonize and appropriate black experience for her own opportunistic ends even as she attempts to mask her acts of racist aggression as affirmation. And no other group sees that as clearly as black females in this society. For we have always known that the socially constructed image of innocent white womanhood relies on the continued production of the racist/sexist sexual myth that black women are not innocent and never can be. Since we are coded always as "fallen" women in the racist cultural iconography we can never, as can Madonna, publicly "work" the image of ourselves as innocent female daring to be bad. Mainstream culture always reads the black female body as sign of sexual experience. In part, many black women who are disgusted by Madonna's flaunting of sexual experience are enraged because the very image of sexual agency that she is able to project and affirm with material gain has been the stick this society has used to justify its continued beating and assault on the black female body. The vast majority of black women in the United States, more concerned with projecting images of respectability than with the idea of female sexual agency and transgression, do not often feel we have the "freedom" to act in rebellious ways in regards to sexuality without being punished. We have only to contrast the life story of Tina Turner with that of Madonna to see the different connotations "wild" sexual agency has when it is asserted by a black female. Being represented publicly as an active sexual being has only recently enabled Turner to gain control over her life and career. For years the public image of aggressive sexual agency Turner projected belied the degree to which she was sexually abused and exploited privately. She was also materially exploited. Madonna's career could not be all that it is if there were no Tina Turner and yet, unlike her cohort Sandra Bernhard, Madonna never articulates the cultural debt she owes black females.

In her most recent appropriations of blackness, Madonna almost always imitates phallic black masculinity. Although I read many articles which talked about her appropriating male codes, no critic seems to have noticed her emphasis on black male experience. In his *Playboy* profile, "Playgirl of the Western World," Michael Kelly describes Madonna's crotch grabbing as "an eloquent visual put-down of male phallic pride." He points out that she worked with choreographer Vince Paterson to perfect the gesture. Even though Kelly tells readers that Madonna was consciously imitating Michael Jackson, he does not contextualize his interpretation of the gesture to include this act of appropriation from black male culture. And in that specific context the groin grabbing gesture is an assertion of pride and phallic domination that usually takes place in an all male context. Madonna's imitation of this gesture could just as easily be read as an expression of envy.

Throughout much of her autobiographical interviews runs a thread of expressed desire to possess the power she perceives men have. Madonna may hate the phallus, but she longs to possess its power. She is always first and foremost in competition with men to see who has the biggest penis. She longs to assert phallic power, and like every other group in this white supremacist society, she clearly sees black men as embodying a quality of maleness that eludes white men. Hence, they are often the group of men she most seeks to imitate, taunting white males with her own version of "black masculinity." When it comes to entertainment rivals, Madonna clearly perceives black male stars like Prince and Michael Jackson to be the standard against which she must measure herself and that she ultimately hopes to transcend.

Fascinated yet envious of black style, Madonna appropriates black culture in ways that mock and undermine, making her presentation one that upstages. This is most evident in the video "Like a Prayer." Though I read numerous articles that discussed public outrage at this video, none focused on the issue of race. No article called attention to the fact that Madonna flaunts her sexual agency by suggesting that she is breaking the ties that bind her as a white girl to white patriarchy, and establishing ties with black men. She, however, and not black men, does the choosing. The message is directed at white men. It suggests that they only labeled black men rapists for fear that white girls would choose black partners over them. Cultural critics commenting on the video did not seem at all interested in exploring the reasons Madonna chooses a black cultural backdrop for this video, i.e., black church and religious experience. Clearly, it was this backdrop that added to the video's controversy.

In her commentary in the *Washington Post,* "Madonna: Yuppie Goddess," Brooke Masters writes: "Most descriptions of the controversial video focus on its Catholic imagery: Madonna kisses a black saint, and develops Christ-like markings on her hands. However, the video is also a feminist fairy tale. Sleeping Beauty and Snow White waited for their princes to come along, Madonna finds her own man and wakes him up." Notice that this writer completely overlooks the issue of race and gender. That Madonna's chosen prince was a black man is in part what made the representation potentially shocking and provocative to a white supremacist audience. Yet her attempt to exploit and transgress traditional racial taboos was rarely commented on. Instead critics concentrated on whether or not she was violating taboos regarding religion and representation.

In the United States, Catholicism is most often seen as a religion that has little or no black followers and Madonna's video certainly perpetuates this stereotype with its juxtaposition of images of black non-Catholic representations with the image of the black saint. Given the importance of religious experience and liberation theology in black life, Madonna's use of this imagery seemed particularly offensive. For she made black characters act in complicity with her as she aggressively flaunted her critique of Catholic manners, her attack on organized religion. Yet, no black voices that I know of came forward in print calling attention to the fact that the realm of the sacred that is mocked in this film is black religious experience, or that this appropriative "use" of that experience was offensive to many black folk. Looking at the video with a group of students in my class on the politics of sexuality where we critically analyze the way race and representations of black-ness are used to sell products, we discussed the way in which black people in the video are caricatures reflecting stereotypes. They appear grotesque. The only role black females have in this video is to catch (i.e., rescue) the "angelic" Madonna when she is "falling." This is just a contemporary casting of the black female as Mammy. Made to serve as supportive backdrop for Madonna's drama, black characters in *Like a Prayer* remind one of those early Hollywood depictions of singing black slaves in the great plantation movies or those Shirley Temple films where Bojangles was trotted out to dance with Miss Shirley and spice up her act. Audiences were not supposed to be enamored of Bojangles, they were supposed to see just what a special little old white girl Shirley really was. In her own way Madonna is a modern day Shirley Temple. Certainly her expressed affinity with black culture enhances her value.

Eager to see the documentary *Truth or Dare* because it promised to focus on Madonna's transgressive sexual persona, which I find interesting, I was angered by her visual representation of her domina-tion over not white men (certainly not over Warren Beatty or Alek Keshishian), but people of color and white working-class women. I was too angered by this to appreciate other aspects of the film I might have enjoyed. In *Truth or Dare* Madonna clearly revealed that she can only think of exerting power along very traditional, white suprem-acist, capitalistic, patriarchal lines. That she made people who were dependent on her for their immediate livelihood submit to her will was neither charming nor seductive to me or the other black folks that I spoke with who saw the film. We thought it tragically ironic that Madonna would choose as her dance partner a black male with dyed blonde hair. Perhaps had he appeared less like a white-identified black male consumed by "blonde ambition" he might have upstaged her. Instead he was positioned as a mirror, into which Madonna and her audience could look and see only a reflection of herself and the worship of "whiteness" she embodies—that white supremacist culture wants everyone to embody. Madonna used her power to ensure that he and the other non-white women and men who worked for her, as well as some of the white subordinates would all serve as the backdrop to her white-girl-makes-good drama. Joking about the film with other black folks, we commented that Madonna must have searched long and hard to find a black female that was not a good dancer, one who would not deflect attention away from her. And it is telling that when the film directly reflects something other than a positive image of Madonna, the camera highlights the rage this black female dancer was suppressing. It surfaces when the "subordinates" have time off and are "relaxing."

As with most Madonna videos, when critics talk about this film they tend to ignore race. Yet no viewer can look at this film and not think about race and representation without engaging in forms of denial. After choosing a cast of characters from marginalized groups— non-white folks, heterosexual and gay, and gay white folks—Madonna publicly describes them as "emotional cripples." And of course in the context of the film this description seems borne out by the way they allow her to dominate, exploit, and humiliate them. Those Madonna fans who are determined to see her as politically progressive might ask themselves why it is she completely endorses those racist/sexist/classist stereotypes that almost always attempt to portray marginalized groups as "defective." Let's face it, by doing this, Madonna is not breaking with any white supremacist, patriarchal *status quo;* she is endorsing and perpetuating it.

Some of us do not find it hip or cute for Madonna to brag that she has a "fascistic side," a side well documented in the film. Well, we did not see any of her cute little fascism in action when it was Warren Beatty calling her out in the film. No, there the image of Madonna was the little woman who grins and bears it. No, her "somebody's got to be in charge side," as she names it, was most expressed in her interaction with those representatives from marginalized groups who are most often victimized by the powerful. Why is it there is little or no discussion of Madonna as racist or sexist in her relation to other women? Would audiences be charmed by some rich white male entertainer telling us he must "play father" and oversee the actions of the less powerful, especially women and men of color? So why did so many people find it cute when Madonna asserted that she dominates the inter-racial casts of gay and heterosexual folks in her film because they are crippled and she "like[s] to play mother." No, this was not a display of feminist power, this was the same old phallic nonsense with white pussy at the center. And many of us watching were not simply unmoved—we were outraged.

Perhaps it is a sign of a collective feeling of powerlessness that many black, non-white, and white viewers of this film who were disturbed by the display of racism, sexism, and heterosexism (yes, it's possible to hire gay people, support AIDS projects, and still be biased in the direction of phallic patriarchal heterosexuality) in *Truth or Dare* have said so little. Sometimes it is difficult to find words to make a critique when we find ourselves attracted by some aspect of a performer's act and disturbed by others, or when a performer shows more interest in promoting progressive social causes than is customary. We may see that performer as above critique. Or we may feel our critique will in no way intervene on the worship of them as a cultural icon.

To say nothing, however, is to be complicit with the very forces of domination that make "blonde ambition" necessary to Madonna's success. Tragically, all that is transgressive and potentially empowering to feminist women and men about Madonna's work may be undermined by all that it contains that is reactionary and in no way unconventional or new. It is often the conservative elements in her work converging with the *status quo* that has the most powerful impact. For example: Given the rampant homophobia in this society and the concomitant heterosexist voyeuristic obsession with gay lifestyles, to what extent does Madonna progressively seek to challenge this if she insists on primarily representing gays as in some way emotionally handicapped or defective? Or when Madonna responds to the critique that she exploits gay men by cavalierly stating: "What does exploitation mean?… In a revolution, some people have to get hurt. To get people to change, you have to turn the table over. Some dishes get broken."

I can only say this doesn't sound like liberation to me. Perhaps when Madonna explores those memories of her white working-class childhood in a troubled family in a way that enables her to understand intimately the politics of exploitation, domination, and submission, she will have a deeper connection with oppositional black culture. If and when this radical critical self-interrogation takes place, she will have the power to create new and different cultural productions, work that will be truly transgressive—acts of resistance that transform rather than simply seduce.

Chapter 11

Representations of Whiteness in the Black Imagination

Although there has never been any official body of black people in the United States who have gathered as anthropologists and/or ethnographers to study whiteness, black folks have, from slavery on, shared in conversations with one another "special" knowledge of whiteness gleaned from close scrutiny of white people. Deemed special because it was not a way of knowing that has been recorded fully in written material, its purpose was to help black folks cope and survive in a white supremacist society. For years, black domestic servants, working in white homes, acting as informants, brought knowledge back to segregated communities—details, facts, observations, and psycho-analytic readings of the white Other.

Sharing the fascination with difference that white people have collectively expressed openly (and at times vulgarly) as they have traveled around the world in pursuit of the Other and Otherness, black people, especially those living during the historical period of racial apartheid and legal segregation, have similarly maintained steadfast and ongoing curiosity about the "ghosts," "the barbarians," these strange apparitions they were forced to serve. In the chapter on "Wild-ness" in *Shamanism, Colonialism, and The Wild Man*, Michael Taussig urges a stretching of our imagination and understanding of the Other to include inscriptions "on the edge of official history." Naming his critical project, identifying the passion he brings to the quest to know more deeply *you who are not ourselves*, Taussig explains:

> I am trying to reproduce a mode of perception—a way of seeing
> through a way of talking—figuring the world through dialogue
> that comes alive with sudden transformative force in the crannies
> of everyday life's pauses and juxtapositions, as in the kitchens of
> the Putumayo or in the streets around the church in the Niña Maria.
> It is always a way of representing the world in the roundabout
> "speech" of the collage of things...It is a mode of perception that
> catches on the debris of history...

I, too, am in search of the debris of history. I am wiping the dust off past conversations to remember some of what was shared in the old days when black folks had little intimate contact with whites, when we were much more open about the way we connected whiteness with the mysterious, the strange, and the terrible. Of course, everything has changed. Now many black people live in the "bush of ghosts" and do not know themselves separate from whiteness. They do not know this thing we call "difference." Systems of domination, imperialism, colonialism, and racism actively coerce black folks to internalize negative perceptions of blackness, to be self-hating. Many of us succumb to this. Yet, blacks who imitate whites (adopting their values, speech, habits of being, etc.) continue to regard whiteness with suspicion, fear, and even hatred. This contradictory longing to possess the reality of the Other, even though that reality is one that wounds and negates, is expressive of the desire to understand the mystery, to know intimately through imitation, as though such knowing worn like an amulet, a mask, will ward away the evil, the terror.

Searching the critical work of post-colonial critics, I found much writing that bespeaks the continued fascination with the way white minds, particularly the colonial imperialist traveler, perceive blackness, and very little expressed interest in representations of whiteness in the black imagination. Black cultural and social critics allude to such representations in their writing, yet only a few have dared to make explicit those perceptions of whiteness that they think will discomfort or antagonize readers. James Baldwin's collection of essays, *Notes of A Native Son,* explores these issues with a clarity and frankness that is no longer fashionable in a world where evocations of pluralism and diversity act to obscure differences arbitrarily imposed and maintained by white racist domination. Addressing the way in which whiteness exists without knowledge of blackness even as it collectively asserts control, Baldwin links issues of recognition to the practice of imperialist racial domination. Writing about being the first black person to visit a

Swiss village with only white inhabitants in his essay "Stranger in the Village," Baldwin notes his response to the village's yearly ritual of painting individuals black who were then positioned as slaves and bought so that the villagers could celebrate their concern with converting the souls of the "natives":

> I thought of white men arriving for the first time in an African village, strangers there, as I am a stranger here, and tried to imagine the astounded populace touching their hair and marveling at the color of their skin. But there is a great difference between being the first white man to be seen by Africans and being the first black man to be seen by whites. The white man takes the astonishment as tribute, for he arrives to conquer and to convert the natives, whose inferiority in relation to himself is not even to be questioned, whereas I, without a thought of conquest, find myself among a people whose culture controls me, has even, in a sense, created me, people who have cost me more in anguish and rage than they will ever know, who yet do not even know of my existence. The astonishment with which I might have greeted them, should they have stumbled into my African village a few hundred years ago, might have rejoiced their hearts. But the astonishment with which they greet me today can only poison mine.

My thinking about representations of whiteness in the black imagination has been stimulated by classroom discussions about the way in which the absence of recognition is a strategy that facilitates making a group the Other. In these classrooms there have been heated debates among students when white students respond with disbelief, shock, and rage, as they listen to black students talk about whiteness, when they are compelled to hear observations, stereotypes, etc., that are offered as "data" gleaned from close scrutiny and study. Usually, white students respond with naive amazement that black people critically assess white people from a standpoint where "whiteness" is the privileged signifier. Their amazement that black people watch white people with a critical "ethnographic" gaze, is itself an expression of racism. Often their rage erupts because they believe that all ways of looking that highlight difference subvert the liberal belief in a universal subjectivity (we are all just people) that they think will make racism disappear. They have a deep emotional investment in the myth of "sameness," even as their actions reflect the primacy of whiteness as a sign informing who they are and how they think. Many of them are shocked that black people think critically about whiteness because racist thinking perpetuates the fantasy that the Other who is subjugated, who is subhuman, lacks the ability to comprehend, to understand, to see the working of the powerful. Even though the majority of these students politically consider themselves liberals and anti-racist, they too unwittingly invest in the sense of whiteness as mystery.

In white supremacist society, white people can "safely" imagine that they are invisible to black people since the power they have historically asserted, and even now collectively assert over black people, accorded them the right to control the black gaze. As fantastic as it may seem, racist white people find it easy to imagine that black people cannot see them if within their desire they do not want to be seen by the dark Other. One mark of oppression was that black folks were compelled to assume the mantle of invisibility, to erase all traces of their subjectivity during slavery and the long years of racial apartheid, so that they could be better, less threatening servants. An effective strategy of white supremacist terror and dehumanization during slavery centered around white control of the black gaze. Black slaves, and later manumitted servants, could be brutally punished for looking, for appearing to observe the whites they were serving, as only a subject can observe, or see. To be fully an object then was to lack the capacity to see or recognize reality. These looking relations were reinforced as whites cultivated the practice of denying the subjectivity of blacks (the better to dehumanize and oppress), of relegating them to the realm of the invisible. Growing up in a Kentucky household where black servants lived in the same dwelling with the white family who employed them, newspaper heiress Sallie Bingham recalls, in her autobiography *Passion and Prejudice,* "Blacks, I realized, were simply invisible to most white people, except as a pair of hands offering a drink on a silver tray." Reduced to the machinery of bodily physical labor, black people learned to appear before whites as though they were zombies, cultivating the habit of casting the gaze downward so as not to appear uppity. To look directly was an assertion of subjectivity, equality. Safety resided in the pretense of invisibility.

Even though legal racial apartheid no longer is a norm in the United States, the habits that uphold and maintain institutionalized white supremacy linger. Since most white people do not have to "see" black people (constantly appearing on billboards, television, movies, in magazines, etc.) and they do not need to be ever on guard nor to observe black people to be safe, they can live as though black people are invisible, and they can imagine that they are also invisible to blacks. Some white people may even imagine there is no representation of whiteness in the black imagination, especially one that is based on concrete observation or mythic conjecture. They think they are seen by black folks only as they want to appear. Ideologically, the rhetoric of white supremacy supplies a fantasy of whiteness. Described in Richard Dyer's essay "White," this fantasy makes whiteness synonymous with goodness:

> Power in contemporary society habitually passes itself off as embodied in the normal as opposed to the superior. This is common to all forms of power, but it works in a peculiarly seductive way with whiteness, because of the way it seems rooted, in common-sense thought, in things other than ethnic difference...Thus it is said (even in liberal textbooks) that there are inevitable associations of white with light and therefore safety, and black with dark and therefore danger, and that this explains racism (whereas one might well argue about the safety of the cover of darkness, and the danger of exposure to the light); again, and with more justice, people point to the Jewish and Christian use of white and black to symbolize good and evil, as carried still in such expressions as "a black mark," "white magic," "to blacken the character" and so on. Socialized to believe the fantasy, that whiteness represents goodness and all that is benign and non-threatening, many white people assume this is the way black people conceptualize whiteness. They do not imagine that the way whiteness makes its presence felt in black life, most often as terrorizing imposition, a power that wounds, hurts, tortures, is a reality that disrupts the fantasy of whiteness as representing goodness.

Collectively black people remain rather silent about representations of whiteness in the black imagination. As in the old days of racial segregation where black folks learned to "wear the mask," many of us pretend to be comfortable in the face of whiteness only to turn our backs and give expression to intense levels of discomfort. Especially talked about is the representation of whiteness as terrorizing. Without evoking a simplistic essentialist "us and them" dichotomy that suggests black folks merely invert stereotypical racist interpretations so that black becomes synonymous with goodness and white with evil, I want to focus on that representation of whiteness that is not formed in reaction to stereotypes but emerges as a response to the traumatic pain and anguish that remains a consequence of white racist domination, a psychic state that informs and shapes the way black folks "see" whiteness. Stereotypes black folks maintain about white folks are not the only representations of whiteness in the black imagination. They emerge primarily as responses to white stereotypes of blackness. Lorraine Hansberry argues that black stereotypes of whites emerge as a trickle-down process of white stereotypes of blackness, where there is the projection onto an Other all that we deny about ourselves. In *Young, Gifted, and Black,* she identifies particular stereotypes about white people that are commonly cited in black communities and urges us not to "celebrate this madness in any direction":

> Is it not "known" in the ghetto that white people, as an entity, are "dirty" (especially white women—who never seem to do their own cleaning); inherently "cruel" (the cold, fierce roots of Europe; who else could put all those people into ovens *scientifically);* "smart" (you really have to hand it to the m.f.'s), and anything *but* cold and passionless (because look who has had to live with little else than their passions in the guise of love and hatred all these centuries)? And so on.

Stereotypes, however inaccurate, are one form of representation. Like fictions, they are created to serve as substitutions, standing in for what is real. They are there not to tell it like it is but to invite and encourage pretense. They are a fantasy, a projection onto the Other that makes them less threatening. Stereotypes abound when there is distance. They are an invention, a pretense that one knows when the steps that would make real knowing possible cannot be taken or are not allowed.

Looking past stereotypes to consider various representations of whiteness in the black imagination, I appeal to memory, to my earliest recollections of ways these issues were raised in black life. Returning to memories of growing up in the social circumstances created by racial apartheid, to all black spaces on the edges of town, I reinhabit a location where black folks associated whiteness with the terrible, the terrifying, the terrorizing. White people were regarded as terrorists, especially those who dared to enter that segregated space of blackness. As a child, I did not know any white people. They were strangers, rarely seen in our neighborhoods. The "official" white men who came across the tracks were there to sell products, Bibles and insurance. They terrorized by economic exploitation. What did I see in the gazes of those white men who crossed our thresholds that made me afraid, that made black children unable to speak? Did they understand at all how strange their whiteness appeared in our living rooms, how threatening? Did they journey across the tracks with the same "adventurous" spirit that other white men carried to Africa, Asia, to those mysterious places they would one day call the "third world?" Did they come to our houses to meet the Other face-to-face and enact the colonizer role, dominating us on our own turf?

Their presence terrified me. Whatever their mission, they looked too much like the unofficial white men who came to enact rituals of terror and torture. As a child, I did not know how to tell them apart, how to ask the "real white people to please stand up." The terror that I felt is one black people have shared. Whites learn about it second-hand. Confessing in *Soul Sister* that she too began to feel this terror after changing her skin to appear "black" and going to live in the south, Grace Halsell described her altered sense of whiteness:

> Caught in this climate of hate, I am totally terror-stricken, and I search my mind to know why I am fearful of my own people. Yet they no longer seem my people, but rather the "enemy" arrayed in large numbers against me in some hostile territory...My wild heartbeat is a secondhand kind of terror. I know that I cannot possibly experience what *they,* the black people, experience...

Black folks raised in the North do not escape this sense of terror. In her autobiography, *Every Good-bye Ain't Gone,* Itabari Njeri begins the narrative of her northern childhood with a memory of southern roots. Traveling south as an adult to investigate the murder of her grandfather by white youth who were drag racing and ran him down in the streets, Njeri recalls that for many years "the distant and accidental violence that took my grandfather's life could not compete with the psychological terror that had begun to engulf my own." Ultimately, she begins to link that terror with the history of black people in the United States, seeing it as an imprint carried from the past to the present:

> As I grew older, my grandfather assumed mythic proportions in my imagination. Even in absence, he filled my room like music and watched over me when I was fearful. His fantasized presence diverted thoughts of my father's drunken rages. With age, my fantasizing ceased, the image of my grandfather faded. What lingered was the memory of his caress, the pain of something missing in my life, wrenched away by reckless white youths. I had a growing sense—the beginning of an inevitable comprehension—that this society deals blacks a disproportionate share of pain and denial.

Njeri's journey takes her through the pain and terror of the past, only the memories do not fade. They linger as does the pain and bitterness:

"Against a backdrop of personal loss, against the evidence of history that fills me with a knowledge of the hateful behavior of whites toward blacks, I see the people of Bainbridge. And I cannot trust them. I cannot absolve them." If it is possible to conquer terror through ritual reenactment, that is what Njeri does. She goes back to the scene of the crime, dares to face the enemy. It is this confrontation that forces the terror of history to loosen its grip.

To name that whiteness in the black imagination is often a representation of terror. One must face written histories that erase and deny, that reinvent the past to make the present vision of racial harmony and pluralism more plausible. To bear the burden of memory one must willingly journey to places long uninhabited, searching the debris of history for traces of the unforgettable, all knowledge of which has been suppressed. Njeri laments that "nobody really knows us." She writes, "So institutionalized is the ignorance of our history, our culture, our everyday existence that, often, we do not even know ourselves." Theorizing black experience, we seek to uncover, restore, as well as to deconstruct, so that new paths, different journeys, are possible. Indeed, Edward Said, in "Traveling Theory," argues that theory can "threaten reification, as well as the entire bourgeois system on which reification depends, with destruction." The call to theorize black experience is constantly challenged and subverted by conservative voices reluctant to move from fixed locations. Said reminds us:

> Theory…is won as the result of a process that begins when consciousness first experiences its own terrible ossification in the general reification of all things under capitalism; then when consciousness generalizes (or classes) itself as something opposed to other objects, and feels itself as contradiction to (or crisis within) objectification, there emerges a consciousness of change in the *status quo;* finally, moving toward freedom and fulfillment, consciousness looks ahead to complete self-realization, which is of course the revolutionary process stretching forward in time, perceivable now only as theory or projection.

Traveling, moving into the past, Njeri pieces together fragments. Who does she see staring into the face of a southern white man who was said to be the murderer? Does the terror in his face mirror the look of the unsuspecting black man whose death history does not name or record? Baldwin wrote that "people are trapped in history and history is trapped in them." There is then only the fantasy of escape, or the promise that what is lost will be found, rediscovered, and returned. For black folks, reconstructing an archaeology of memory makes return possible, the journey to a place we can never call home even as we reinhabit it to make sense of present locations. Such journeying cannot be fully encompassed by conventional notions of travel.

Spinning off from Said's essay, James Clifford, in "Notes on Travel and Theory," celebrates the idea of journeying, asserting:

> This sense of worldly, "mapped" movement is also why it may be worth holding on to the term "travel," despite its connotations of middle class "literary" or recreational journeying, spatial practices long associated with male experiences and virtues. "Travel" suggests, at least, profane activity, following public routes and beaten tracks. How do different populations, classes and genders travel? What kinds of knowledges, stories, and theories do they produce? A crucial research agenda opens up.

Reading this piece and listening to Clifford talk about theory and travel, I appreciated his efforts to expand the travel/theoretical frontier so that it might be more inclusive, even as I considered that to answer the questions he poses is to propose a deconstruction of the conventional sense of travel, and put alongside it, or in its place, a theory of the journey that would expose the extent to which holding on to the concept of "travel" as we know it is also a way to hold on to imperialism.

For some individuals, clinging to the conventional sense of travel allows them to remain fascinated with imperialism, to write about it, seductively evoking what Renato Rosaldo aptly calls, in *Culture and Truth*, "imperialist nostalgia." Significantly, he reminds readers that "even politically progressive North American audiences have enjoyed the elegance of manners governing relations of dominance and subordination between the 'races.' " Theories of travel produced outside conventional borders might want the Journey to become the rubric within which travel, as a starting point for discourse, is associated with different headings—rites of passage, immigration, enforced migration, relocation, enslavement, and homelessness. Travel is not a word that can be easily evoked to talk about the Middle Passage, the Trail of Tears, the landing of Chinese immigrants, the forced relocation of Japanese-Americans, or the plight of the homeless. Theorizing diverse journeying is crucial to our understanding of any politics of location. As Clifford asserts at the end of his essay:

> Theory is always written from some "where," and that "where" is less a place than itineraries: different, concrete histories of dwelling, immigration, exile, migration. These include the migration of

third world intellectuals into the metropolitan universities, to pass
through or to remain, changed by their travel but marked by places
of origin, by peculiar allegiances and alienations.

Listening to Clifford "playfully" evoke a sense of travel, I felt such
an evocation would always make it difficult for there to be recognition
of an experience of travel that is not about play but is an encounter with
terrorism. And it is crucial that we recognize that the hegemony of one
experience of travel can make it impossible to articulate another
experience or for it to be heard. From certain standpoints, to travel is
to encounter the terrorizing force of white supremacy. To tell my
"travel" stories, I must name the movement from racially segregated
southern community, from rural black Baptist origin, to prestigious
white university settings. I must be able to speak about what it is like
to be leaving Italy after I have given a talk on racism and feminism,
hosted by the parliament, only to stand for hours while I am interrogated by white officials who do not have to respond when I enquire as
to why the questions they ask me are different from those asked the
white people in line before me. Thinking only that I must endure this
public questioning, the stares of those around me, because my skin is
black, I am startled when I am asked if I speak Arabic, when I am told
that women like me receive presents from men without knowing what
those presents are. Reminded of another time when I was stripped
searched by French officials, who were stopping black people to make
sure we were not illegal immigrants and/or terrorists, I think that one
fantasy of whiteness is that the threatening Other is always a terrorist.
This projection enables many white people to imagine there is no
representation of whiteness as terror, as terrorizing. Yet it is this representation of whiteness in the black imagination, first learned in the
narrow confines of poor black rural community that is sustained by my
travels to many different locations.

To travel, I must always move through fear, confront terror. It
helps to be able to link this individual experience to the collective
journeying of black people, to the Middle Passage, to the mass migration of southern black folks to northern cities in the early part of the
20th century. Michel Foucault posits memory as a site of resistance. As
Jonathan Arac puts it in his introduction to *Postmodernism and Politics,*
the process of remembering can be a practice which "transforms history
from a judgement on the past in the name of a present truth to a
'counter-memory' that combats our current modes of truth and justice,
helping us to understand and change the present by placing it in a new
relation to the past." It is useful, when theorizing black experience, to

examine the way the concept of "terror" is linked to representations of whiteness.

In the absence of the reality of whiteness, I learned as a child that to be "safe," it was important to recognize the power of whiteness, even to fear it, and to avoid encounter. There was nothing terrifying about the sharing of this knowledge as survival strategy, the terror was made real only when I journeyed from the black side of town to a predominantly white area near my grandmother's house. I had to pass through this area to reach her place. Describing these journeys "across town" in the essay "Homeplace: A Site of Resistance," I remembered:

> It was a movement away from the segregated blackness of our community into a poor white neighborhood. I remember the fear, being scared to walk to Baba's, our grandmother's house, because we would have to pass that terrifying whiteness—those white faces on the porches staring us down with hate. Even when empty or vacant those porches seemed to say *danger*, you do not belong here, you are not safe.

Oh! that feeling of safety, of arrival, of homecoming when we finally reached the edges of her yard, when we could see the soot black face of our grandfather, Daddy Gus, sitting in his chair on the porch, smell his cigar, and rest on his lap. Such a contrast, that feeling of arrival, of homecoming—this sweetness and the bitterness of that journey, that constant reminder of white power and control. Even though it was a long time ago that I made this journey, associations of whiteness with terror and the terrorizing remain. Even though I live and move in spaces where I am surrounded by whiteness, there is no comfort that makes the terrorism disappear. All black people in the United States, irrespective of their class status or politics, live with the possibility that they will be terrorized by whiteness.

This terror is most vividly described by black authors in fiction writing, particularly the recent novel by Toni Morrison, *Beloved*. Baby Suggs, the black prophet, who is most vocal about representations of whiteness, dies because she suffers an absence of color. Surrounded by a lack, an empty space, taken over by whiteness, she remembers: "Those white things have taken all I had or dreamed and broke my heartstrings too. There is no bad luck in the world but white folks." If the mask of whiteness, the pretense, represents it as always benign, benevolent, then what this representation obscures is the representation of danger, the sense of threat. During the period of racial apartheid, still known by many folks as Jim Crow, it was more difficult for black people to internalize this pretense, hard for us not to know that the shapes under white sheets had a mission to threaten, to terrorize. That representation of whiteness, and its association with innocence, which engulfed and murdered Emmett Till was a sign; it was meant to torture with the reminder of possible future terror. In Morrison's *Beloved,* the memory of terror is so deeply inscribed on the body of Sethe and in her consciousness, and the association of terror with whiteness is so intense that she kills her young so that they will never know the terror. Explaining her actions to Paul D., she tells him that it is her job "to keep them away from what I know is terrible." Of course Sethe's attempt to end the historical anguish of black people only reproduces it in a different form. She conquers the terror through perverse reenactment, through resistance, using violence as a means of fleeing from a history that is a burden too great to bear.

It is the telling of our history that enables political self-recovery. In contemporary society, white and black people alike believe that racism no longer exists. This erasure, however mythic, diffuses the representation of whiteness as terror in the black imagination. It allows for assimilation and forgetfulness. The eagerness with which contemporary society does away with racism, replacing this recognition with evocations of pluralism and diversity that further mask reality, is a response to the terror. It has also become a way to perpetuate the terror by providing a cover, a hiding place. Black people still feel the terror, still associate it with whiteness, but are rarely able to articulate the varied ways we are terrorized because it is easy to silence by accusations of reverse racism or by suggesting that black folks who talk about the ways we are terrorized by whites are merely evoking victimization to demand special treatment.

I was reminded of the way in which the discourse of race is increasingly divorced from any recognition of the politics of racism when I attended a recent conference on Cultural Studies. Attending the conference because I was confident that I would be in the company of like-minded, "aware," progressive intellectuals, I was disturbed when the usual arrangements of white supremacist hierarchy were mirrored both in terms of who was speaking, of how bodies were arranged on the stage, of who was in the audience. All of this revealed the underlying assumptions of what voices were deemed worthy to speak and be heard. As the conference progressed, I began to feel afraid. If these progressive people, most of whom were white, could so blindly reproduce a version of the *status quo* and not "see" it, the thought of how racial politics would be played out "outside" this arena was horrifying.

That feeling of terror that I had known so intimately in my childhood surfaced. Without even considering whether the audience was able to shift from the prevailing standpoint and hear another perspective, I talked openly about that sense of terror. Later, I heard stories of white women joking about how ludicrous it was for me (in their eyes I suppose I represent the "bad" tough black woman) to say I felt terrorized. Their inability to conceive that my terror, like that of Sethe's, is a response to the legacy of white domination and the contemporary expressions of white supremacy is an indication of how little this culture really understands the profound psychological impact of white racist domination.

At this same conference, I bonded with a progressive black woman and her companion, a white man. Like me, they were troubled by the extent to which folks chose to ignore the way white supremacy was informing the structure of the conference. Talking with the black woman, I asked her: "What do you do, when you are tired of confronting white racism, tired of the day-to-day incidental acts of racial terrorism? I mean, how do you deal with coming home to a white person?" Laughing she said, "Oh, you mean when I am suffering from White People Fatigue Syndrome? He gets that more than I do." After we finish our laughter, we talk about the way white people who shift locations, as her companion has done, begin to see the world differently. Understanding how racism works, he can see the way in which whiteness acts to terrorize without seeing himself as bad, or all white people as bad, and all black people as good. Repudiating us-and-them dichotomies does not mean that we should never speak of the ways observing the world from the standpoint of "whiteness" may indeed distort perception, impede understanding of the way racism works both in the larger world as well as in the world of our intimate interactions.

In *The Post-Colonial Critic,* Gayatri Spivak calls for a shift in locations, clarifying the radical possibilities that surface when positionality is problematized. She explains that "what we are asking for is that the hegemonic discourses, and the holders of hegemonic discourse, should dehegemonize their position and themselves learn how to occupy the subject position of the other." Generally, this process of repositioning has the power to deconstruct practices of racism and make possible the disassociation of whiteness with terror in the black imagination. As critical intervention it allows for the recognition that progressive white people who are anti-racist might be able to understand the way in which their cultural practice reinscribes white supremacy without promoting paralyzing guilt or denial. Without the capacity to inspire terror, whiteness no longer signifies the right to dominate. It truly becomes a benevolent absence. Baldwin ends his essay "Stranger in the Village" with the declaration: "This world is white no longer, and it will never be white again." Critically examining the association of whiteness as terror in the black imagination, deconstructing it, we both name racism's impact and help to break its hold. We decolonize our minds and our imaginations.

Chapter 12

Revolutionary "Renegades"

Native Americans, African Americans, and Black Indians

We are drawn by our origins as well as our destiny in this country to seek out some real communion with you, our oldest ancestors on this land, Native Americans, Indians, the People...you are unique among us, partly because of the millennia of your tenure here, the power of your teaching in words and deeds, the ancient wisdom which assists our own search, and because of your truth which reminds us that "our first teacher is our own heart"...We pause with you before ending, before beginning, simply because our integrity allows nothing else... We dare to seek forgiveness from you, from ourselves, for the greed and madness which led (and still leads) to our participation in decimation and imprisonment of your ancestors, our ancestors...whose names are now remembered only by the winds (but that is a mighty remembering)...You are close to our hearts. We pause to thank you, rejoin you in hope and solidarity. We promise to stand with you in your continuing quest for justice. As we rebuild this nation, as we seek to begin again, we need you...to be teachers and vision seekers with us.

—Vincent Harding
Hope and History

The Africans who came before Columbus to these Americas that we now call home did not come as strangers. According to historian Ivan Van Sertima in *They Came Before Columbus*, these Africans brought with them ways of knowing akin to that of Native American

people—a reverence for nature, for life, for ancestors. Face to face with
their difference, African and Native American eagerly communicated
all that was common, shared, and familiar. To share habits of being,
ways of living in the world, was a way to establish kinship, not ties of
blood but bonds of affinity—longlasting and sustained. Let us remember the words attributed to Chinook leader Chief Seattle disavowing
commonality with whites: "We are two distinct races with separate
origins and separate destinies. There is little in common between us."
Even before the Africans journeyed to the "new world," their destiny
was linked to that of Native Americans. Red and black people shared
a common way. Not just because, as Jose Martí had written, "the same
blow that paralyzes the Indian, cripples us," but because similar ontological understandings of the world united the two groups. Aware
always that ancestor acknowledgment was vital to the sustaining of
culture and community, "new world" Africans and Native Americans
shared belief systems.

In the old days, Native Americans, Africans, and African Americans
believed that the dead stay among us so that we will not forget.
Explaining to whites as late as 1853 their different understanding of the
dead, Chief Seattle shared this vision:

> To us the ashes of our ancestors are sacred and their resting
> place is hallowed ground. You wander far from the graves of
> your ancestors and seemingly without regret. Your religion was
> written upon tablets of stone by the iron finger of your God so
> that you could not forget. The Red Man could never compre-
> hend nor remember it. Our religion is the traditions of our
> ancestors—the dreams of our old men, given them in solemn
> hours of night by the Great Spirit; and the visions of our
> sachems; and it is written in the hearts of our people. Your dead
> cease to love you and the land of their nativity as soon as they
> pass the portals of the tomb and wander beyond the stars. They
> soon are forgotten and never return. Our dead never forget the
> beautiful world that gave them being.

The dead call us to remember. Some of us have not forsaken these
teachings. We hear the voice of our African past urging us to remember
that "a people without ancestors are like a tree without roots." Let us
remember, then, that in the beginning of their meeting, Native Americans
and Africans were different, but One, among the same world family.
We know this.

The Africans who journeyed to the "new world" before Columbus
recognized their common destiny with the Native peoples who gave

them shelter and a place to rest. They did not come to command, to take over, to dominate, or to colonize. They were not eager to sever their ties with memory; they had not forgotten their ancestors. These African explorers returned home peaceably after a time of communion with Native Americans. Contrary to colonial white imperialist insistence that it was "natural" for groups who are different to engage in conflict and power struggle, the first meetings of Africans and Native Americans offer a counter-perspective, a vision of cross-cultural contact where reciprocity and recognition of the primacy of community are affirmed, where the will to conquer and dominate was not seen as the only way to confront the Other who is not ourselves. This same generosity of spirit later informed contact between free or enslaved black people and Native Americans. Explaining the way this sense of community shaped contact between the black slave and the Native in his essay "The Caribbean Writers and Exile," Jan Carew writes:

> When the African arrived in the New World, he knew that the colonizer who had brought him there was a usurper who had seized the land of the Indians, desecrated the graves and the altars of their ancestors, and sent countless of the ones who welcomed them to the Forest of the Long Night. It was clear to the slave from Africa, that in order to escape the terrible retribution that was certain to overtake their masters, they had to make peace with both the living and dead in this new land...The African had to recreate his vision of himself in the universe often being violently uprooted...to have seen himself only through his master's eyes and to have even appeared to be an accomplice in his obnoxious deeds, would have left him with a permanent heritage of self-hatred, distorted self-images and guilt. In order to reconstruct his ontological system, the African was compelled by the logic of his own cultural past, to establish relations with his Indian host independent of the white man.

In keeping with the spirit of ancestor acknowledgment, the memory of earlier communion between African and Native American lay the groundwork of an interaction based in mutual respect and reciprocity. Even though Carew only emphasizes relations among men in his text, African women and Native American women were of course active agents in the effort to establish and maintain affinity between the two groups.

Over time, white supremacist constructions of history have effectively erased from public collective cultural memory the recognition of solidarity and communion among Native Americans, Africans, and

African Americans. Even though books like Jack Forbes' *Black Africans and Native Americans* and William Katz' *Black Indians* document interactions between the two groups, they do not emphasize shared sensibility or shared vision. Yet, it is this bond that most intimately connected the two groups. Shared sensibility made other more pragmatic bondings (marriage, joining together to struggle against white enemies, the sharing of medicinal knowledge, etc.) possible. When white armies sought to destroy the Seminole nation they found that blacks and Native Americans were "identified in interests and feelings," that black leaders mapped out strategies for their red comrades and influenced decisionmaking. As Katz documents in *Black Indians,* African Americans who lived among Native peoples, when given options, preferred to stay with these communities. Katz reports that a group of Black Cherokees, petitioning for equal rights in 1879, adamantly declared their solidarity and kinship with Native peoples: "The Cherokee nation is our country; there we were born and reared; there are our homes made by the sweat of our brows; there are our wives and children, whom we love as dearly as though we were born with red, instead of black, skin." Echoing these sentiments in 1884, black members of the Chickasaw nation declared, "As natives, we are attached to the people among whom we have been born and bred."

Disturbed by political solidarity and bonds of affinity between blacks and Native Americans, racist white people both then and now strategically work to separate the two groups. An important strategy has been their historical erasure and suppression of documents and information affirming the depth of these ties or their perverse rewriting of history from the colonizing standpoint. Ward Churchill emphasizes in his recent study *Fantasies of the Master Race:*

> It is a given in any colonial situation that the colonizing power presumes that its culture is inherently superior to that of the colonized. Hence it assumes the right…to explain this to its subjects, rendering the colonized ever more accommodating to the "material condition" of their domination by the colonial master, ever more compliant to the inevitability of material exploitation by the colonizer. This has been the clear purpose, historically, of the interpretation of indigenous cultures by their conquerors.

True for both Native and African Americans, it has been hard for the two groups to recover from this colonizing process and assert full agency in documenting and interpreting their reality, their mutual bond. Identifying this problem in *Spirit Woman,* Bonita Wa Wa

Calachaw laments: "Few American authors have ever written a true insight into the Life of the American Indian...I have become skeptical of many of the White Man's tales. Their historical writings of My people were written by mad-Minded Men and Women whose Hates so warped them that I think they were suffering from some type of psychic determinism..." Even though progressive contemporary scholars are working to uncover facts about ties between African Americans and Native Americans, to gather extensive documentation, their work is often presented solely as a corrective about the past and in no way seeks to affirm a continuum of affinity between African Americans and Native Americans.

In truth, sacred bonds between blacks and Native Americans, bonds of blood and metaphysical kinship, cannot be documented solely by factual evidence confirming extensive interaction and intermingling—they are also matters of the heart. These ties are best addressed by those who are not simply concerned with the cold data of history, but who have "history written in the hearts of our people" who then feel for history, not just because it offers facts but because it awakens and sustains connections, renews and nourishes current relations. Before the history that is in our hearts can be spoken, remembered with passion and love, we must discuss the myriad ways white supremacy works to impose forgetfulness, creating estrangement between red and black peoples, who though different lived as One.

Even the most progressive scholarship by white people on the subject of blacks and Native Americans usually reflects, to a greater or lesser degree, a white supremacist standpoint. This contradiction is evident in William Katz' *Black Indians*. On the one hand, he makes the progressive gesture of uncovering buried history about blacks and Native Americans even as he addresses that work to an audience presumed to be either white or white-identified. In his introduction to *Black Indians,* Katz begins:

> Black Indians? The very words make most people shake their heads in disbelief or smile at what appears to be a joke, a play on words. No one remembers any such person in a school text, history book, or western novel. None ever appeared.

Who are the "most people" he is talking about? Certainly not Native American blacks or African Americans with Native ancestry. Why is it that his introduction includes no words, no welcoming invitation, for those who hold in their heart-memory the history of Native American blacks, whose contemporary loved ones are "black Indians," who look in mirrors daily and bear witness to the legacy of this great connection? Clearly, this opening paragraph illustrates how a white supremacist sensibility (the belief that all that is white is superior, more "civilized," more intelligent, and destined to dominate) may be shared by non-white people, hence increasing the destructive power of the habits of thought and being perpetuated by white supremacist ideology.

Speaking primarily to those folks who have always denied the many truths of U.S. history that tell of imperialist expansion, cultural genocide, and racism, Katz makes it seem that it is most important to convince this audience that "black Indians" ever even existed. This desire, as well as a refusal to take an overtly political stand against racism, may explain why Katz does not critically examine the ways white supremacy, as it is advanced by whites and by all groups who internalize racism, strategically orchestrates this ignorance. Institutionalized white supremacy puts in place structures for the dissemination of knowledge, whether elementary schools, universities, or the mass media, whereby all connections between African and Native Americans are erased and the knowledge of our shared history is suppressed.

In a different context, Winona LaDuke of the Anishinabé nation reminds contemporary critical thinkers that we must "relearn" ways of thinking based on a shared sensibility. In her essay "Natural to Synthetic and Back Again," LaDuke reminds us that "we are in this together, we must rebuild, redevelop, and reclaim an understanding/analysis which is uniquely ours." Her words ring true in a context where we must reconceptualize and change the way most people think about the identity of Native Americans and all black people irrespective of our ethnic groups. (Just as there are Native American black people, there are Asian black people, etc.) For Native Americans, especially those who are black, and for African Americans, it is a gesture of resistance to the dominant culture's ways of thinking about history, identity, and community for us to decolonize our minds, reclaim the word that is our history as it was told to us by our ancestors, not as it has been interpreted by the colonizer.

In the old days, black elders (even those who were not raised in Native American communities) remembered their ties to the first culture (that we now call Native Americans). When they spoke history, they identified these ties, called their ancestors red and black by name. My grandmother told me "they were the people of the first snow." I explained to her that at school we learned that they should just be called Indians. Proud that she had been taken out of school because her labor was needed to work the land, she told me "you go to school to learn the white man's ways—we have our own way." I was reminded of her words when I first read about the 1890 reawakening of Native religious ritual centered around the ghost dance—the way whites interpreted it as a sign of madness. Wovoka, a member of the Paiutes, had spread the message that the dead would come if called by dancing spirits, bringing with them the buffalo, and all that was lost would be recovered. When the Sioux began to dance in 1890, white government agents responded with hysteria, telegraphing distraught messages to the commissioner of Indian Affairs: "Indians are dancing in the snow and are wild and crazy. I have fully informed you that employees and government property at this agency have no protection and are at the mercy of these dancers." It must have been truly shocking to racist whites that, after experiencing grave genocidal attack, distinct cultural rituals could be used to awaken a resisting spirit in a ravaged and devastated people. Even when so much was lost, Native Americans, like their African American counterparts, held to redemptive life-sustaining visions.

To understand fully how bonds with ancestors are broken, how our visions are lost, it is necessary that we name without shame or fear the way white imperialist racist domination and its ideological base, white supremacy, strategically worked to sever bonds between Africans, African Americans, and Native Americans. Two historical moments, both shaped by white imperialism, greatly affected the ties that had been established between red and black people: the forced relocation of Native Americans into camps (reservations) and the later mass migration of black people from rural areas to northern cities. In both cases, ties with the land were, to a large extent, broken. Black people in cities, no longer farming, began to lose their reverence for nature. Southern rural ways of sharing oral testimony about the past lost ground. Sadly, since racist white people often ridiculed and mocked black people who gave oral testimony documenting Native American ancestry, black folks learned to "hold their tongue" on such matters. When colonized black people also began to suggest that black folks who claimed Native American ancestry were self-hating, wanting to deny blackness, it became a stigma to speak of this past. Concurrently, Native Americans who internalized racism also sought to disassociate themselves from blackness (the racial color caste systems which became a norm in black communities also were established in many Native communities and darker-skinned groups were seen as inferior, ugly, etc.). Even black-skinned Native Americans, whose hair was a mixture of straight and coarse, like many of the Lumbee, did not want to be seen as "black."

Mass media representations of Native Americans have been a major "colonizing" force. On television and in movies, Native Americans are depicted as fair-skinned with dark straight hair. This look conveys an accurate image of many Native Americans, but it is only one type. Like all other groups, there are diverse skin-colors and features that characterize Native Americans. No one has yet done extensive scholarly work on the extent to which representations of Native Americans have been influenced by white perceptions of what an "Indian" should look like. Both African and Native Americans have been deeply affected by the degrading representations of red and black people that continue to be the dominant images projected by movies and television. Portrayed as cowardly, cannibalistic, uncivilized, the images of "Indians" mirror screen images of Africans. When most people watch degrading images of red and black people daily on television, they do not think about the ways these images cause pain and grief.

During the heyday of westerns on U.S. television, anyone watching saw spectacle after spectacle of white men destroying hundreds of Native Americans. No psychoanalytic studies have been done exploring the psychological impact on individuals (especially Native Americans) who have suffered holocaust and genocidal attack only to live in a culture where the major medium of mass communication reenacts this tragedy for "entertainment." Yet this has always been the case with Native Americans. When westerns were regularly shown on television, one could daily witness the slaughter of nations by white people. Children naturally mimic this genocidal drama and play cowboys and Indians. Even the contemporary Hollywood film *Mississippi Masala*, directed by South Asian filmmaker Mira Nair, reproduces the childhood fascination with the narrative of cowboys and Indians. In the film, viewers see South Asian children living in the southern United States "playing" cowboys and Indians.

When I was a child, my grandmother taught me to identify with "the people of the first snow"—to recognize our shared destiny. Thus, in my cowgirl fantasies, I knew that my frontier mission was to protect Indians from the enemy white man. However, this decolonized stand-point made it impossible for me to watch passively, without anguish or grief, images of Native peoples in Westerns. Although it was presented as an "alternative" to Hollywood's traditional slaughter of Native peoples, the movie *Dances with Wolves* was also painful to watch. Any viewer who recognizes that this slaughter is an ongoing tragedy, though it now takes different forms, cannot be entertained by these images.

Globally, survivors of holocaust (whether it be the Japanese who suffered nuclear attack, Jews and Gypsies in the Nazi concentration camps, or African slaves in the Middle Passage) found it difficult, if not downright impossible, to speak about the horrors they had experienced. While there is current interest in the way children of Jewish survivors are affected by the torture and persecution of their ancestors, there have been few attempts to understand how the horrors of slavery and the genocidal assault on Native Americans has affected the children of survivors. Since much racialized genocidal assault against both these groups continues in less aggressive forms than all-out massacre, it is easy for everyone in this society to act as though red and black people do not suffer ongoing trauma. No one speaks of how the pain that our ancestors endured is carried in our hearts and psyches, shaping our contemporary worldview and social behavior. In the United States it is rare for anyone to publicly acknowledge that African Americans and Native Americans are the survivors of holocaust, of genocidal warfare waged against red and black people by white imperialist racism. Often it is only in the realm of fiction that this reality can be acknowledged, that the unspeakable can be named. Toni Morrison's novel *Beloved* seeks to acknowledge the trauma of slavery holocaust, the pain that lingers, wounds, and perverts the psyche of its victims, leaving its mark on the body forever.

White scholars writing about the Native American past rarely acknowledge the ongoing experience of psychic trauma that afflicts survivors, their children, and their children's children. Specific moments in forced relocation, for example "The Trail of Tears," are acknowledged to have been terrible, horrific, yet they are seen as exceptional race events. All American history, as it is shaped by racist whites, seeks to erase the horrors perpetrated against red people. Ravaged by genocidal attack and invasion, by white imperialist colonization, all Native American nations and surviving communities suffered. When retelling the past, the colonizer invariably minimizes this suffering.

Theodora Kroeber's work *Ishi: In Two Worlds* is a perfect example of this tendency. Subtitled "a biography of the last wild Indian," the front cover of the first paperback edition is illustrated with a photograph of a Native man, clear-eyed, no emotion on his face, framed against a light background, wearing a suit and tie. The back cover shows Ishi as he was when he was first "captured" by white people. This photo is placed against a dark background. He is shown with no visible clothing and an anguished look on his face. His eyes are nearly closed and his hair is unkempt. This dark-skinned Native man was the only survivor of the white world's genocidal attack on the Yahi tribe in California. Witnessing the tragic death of kin and loved ones, Ishi's presence was a living reminder of "the world before the coming of the white man." The visual text presented on the cover of Kroeber's book does not convey this tragedy; the story it presents is a contrast between Ishi as "civilized" and Ishi as "wild man." When he was first imprisoned after wandering into a white town, he was called "the wild man of Oroville." This cover affirms white conquest and domination of the "wild man" and his people even as it laments *via* imperialist nostalgia all that was lost. Though the book tells of holocaust, the back cover announces that it is a work that "combines the ghastly atrocity of the extermination of the Yahis with the touching and melancholy comedy of Ishi in San Francisco." Ishi's tragedy is reinscribed as an entertaining spectacle for the colonizing white imagination.

Though Kroeber acknowledges that the trauma Ishi had experienced was damaging, she makes no connection between his survival of holocaust and the fears that tormented him in his new life. Attempting to describe Ishi's worldview, Kroeber writes:

> His aloneness was not that of temperament but of cultural chance, and one early evidence of his sophisticated intelligence was his awareness of this. He felt himself so different, so distinct, that to regard himself or to have others regard him as "one of them" was not to be thought. "I am one; you are others; this is in the inevitable nature of things," is an English approximation of his judgment on himself. It was a harsh judgment, arousing in his friends compassion, then respect. He was fearful and timid at first, but never unobservant, nor did his fear paralyze his thinking as it paralyzed his gesturing. He faced the areas of his total ignorance, of the disparity between Yahi culture and white, and the knowledge that he could not begin from so far behind and come abreast.

Reflecting the racist mindset of her times, Kroeber never acknowledges that the San Francisco world Ishi inhabited was not all white—that there might have been groups of people with habits of being and values that might not have seemed so strange and other as the white world.

Kept as a "living specimen" in the San Francisco Museum of Anthropology, Ishi did not speak of his past. His silence was always interpreted by whites as culturally-based (Indians, afterall, do not openly express their feelings). It was never interpreted as a response to horrible trauma or as profound psychic suppression in the interest of survival. Had Ishi maintained the memories of the extermination of the Yahi community by white people by giving constant oral testimony, he might have been unable to live among whites with goodwill. It is not that Ishi did not remember. He never forgot himself or his history. He simply refused to share it. Such sharing would have mocked the intensity of his pain, would have made him complicit with his oppressors. For with what words can one describe to the white colonizer how they have ravaged and destroyed one's beloved community, one's most intimate kin? Ishi chose to "hold his tongue" refusing even to share his Yahi name. Reflecting on this refusal, Kroeber explains: "He *never* revealed his own, private, Yahi name. It was as though it had been consumed in the funeral pyre of the last of his loved ones." One could interpret the withholding of his name as a gesture of resistance, whereby Ishi kept separate the world of his ancestors from this new world he inhabited.

Imperialist nostalgia, which expresses itself as yearning on the part of the colonizer for the ways of life they have destroyed or altered, best describes the attitude of whites towards Ishi. In *Culture and Truth,* Renato Rosaldo suggests that imperialist nostalgia "revolves around a paradox":

> A person kills somebody, and then mourns the victim. In more attenuated form, someone deliberately alters a form of life, and then regrets that things have not remained as they were prior to the intervention. At one more remove, people destroy their environment, and then they worship nature. In any of its versions, imperialist nostalgia uses a pose of "innocent yearning" both to capture people's imaginations and to conceal its complicity with often brutal domination.

Perhaps more intensely than at any other time in the history of the United States, imperialist nostalgia informs contemporary thinking about Native Americans. While white people are more inclined to give expression to this nostalgia, other groups of people, including African Americans, who have no knowledge of Native American history and struggle also indulge in simplistic nostalgic romanticization. They know only what the representations that appear in mass media show them.

Before mass migration to the urban north, before racial integration, much African American history, particularly family history (ancestor acknowledgment), was shared through oral testimony and storytelling by elders who often could not read or write. These elders kept alive the memories of bonds and ties with Native American cultures. They were proud of those connections. Even though that pride was at times evoked to mask shame felt about African heritage, about blackness, this contradiction does not alter the reality that the two groups intermingled. Living in Oberlin, Ohio and teaching at the college where Wildfire, a.k.a. Edmonia Lewis, studied has been an inspiration for me to write this piece as she grappled with an insensitive white environment that was not able to fully respect her artistic ambitions or her desire to remain in touch with the Chippewa world of her mother and the African American world of her father.

Few contemporary black people speak publicly about the need for political solidarity between Native Americans and African Americans that would emerge from an understanding of a shared history and destiny. Instead, the two groups are often perceived by whites, and perceive themselves, as having no common interests or basis for shared cultural bonding. When I was a girl, my grandmother talked to me about Native American culture, taught me to respect that there was much to learn in the way of wisdom from Indian people. Raised in Kentucky where Shawnee, Cherokee, and at times Chickasaw communities dwelled, the elders remembered times when red and black people lived and worked together. My grandmother told me that her mother, my ancestor Bell Blair Hooks, whose memory I keep alive by taking her name as my writing name, had left her Native community to marry my grandfather who "looked like a white man but was a nigga." Telling me stories about the way Bell Hooks fused her ways of living in the world with black traditions, my grandmother talked to me about the spirits that reside in all living things and the need to respect those spirits. She talked about hunting and planting, about quiltmaking, about the respect we owe the dead.

I learned early not to repeat these stories, not to come home with my head "full of nonsense" for fear that our visits would be limited. In her special room there was a framed reproduction of a Native man sitting on his horse at the top of a mountain, his arms spread out towards the sky, his head uplifted. This image conveyed harmony, a oneness with nature and the power that comes to us when we stretch out our hands in supplication. The Native presence is a part of Nature in the picture. It is a scene of true communion. No one knows what happened to this picture when she died. These days when I ask about the "truth" of her words, no one says anything, no one remembers. They want to forget this past.

Within white supremacist capitalist patriarchy, forgetfulness is encouraged. When people of color remember ourselves, remember the myriad ways our cultures and communities have been ravaged by white domination, we are often told by white peers that we are "too bitter," that we are "full of hate." Memory sustains a spirit of resistance. Too many red and black people live in a state of forgetfulness, embracing a colonized mind so that they can better assimilate into the white world. In such a state, cultivating solidarity with one another is no longer valued. Competition for the attention of whites, for material reparations, has led some Native Americans to believe that their cause is best addressed if it is not linked to the liberation struggles of other people of color, particularly black people. Concurrently, many black people make no effort to understand and support the politics of Native American struggle.

Sadly, for Native Americans this means that they are often victimized by a racialized color caste system within Native culture that has its roots in internalized racism. White people who can trace and document Native ancestry may be more readily accepted than black folks whose lineage is more direct, who may even have spent their entire lives within a Native community. In the preface to the most recent edition of *Black Indians,* Katz shares that the title "stirred controversy among people with African ancestors who had long accepted themselves as Indians." Again, this insistence on "ethnic purity" is an inheritance of white supremacy, the refusal to acknowledge mixture and kinship. Native American blacks I know are often eager to deny any connection to black people because blackness is still considered a mark of shame. Katz also states that the work "raised concerns among Native Americans still battling a government that traditionally seizes any excuse (e.g., mixture with Africans) to violate treaties, land claims, and human rights." Katz does not identify this government as white supremacist or link the proscriptions it seeks to place on Native Americans to institutionalized racism. (One example of this ongoing racist repression is the outlawing of many Native American religious rituals, which has been particularly enforced during the Reagan and Bush administrations.) Yet, the U.S. government puts in place a bargaining structure that demands that Native people do not demonstrate allegiance, solidarity, and kinship with other non-whites.

Despite civil rights movement and changes in the nature of racial apartheid in the United States, white supremacist thinking continues to inform and shape the way most people think about race, ethnicity, skin color, and identity. Why did so many critics respond with hostility and

rage when *Black Indians* first appeared? What stake does the collective
culture have in the continued denial of connections between red and
black people? Why do people doubt that Native American black people
exist, that many African Americans have similar ancestry?

Apparently most people can accept that black "buffalo soldiers"
existed and fought alongside of the U.S. government against Native
Americans, even if such soldiers were a very small group. Just as there
were Native Americans who owned black slaves, who were complicit
with maintaining white imperialism, the buffalo soldiers aided the
extermination of diverse Native American communities. The fact that
Bob Marley's song "Buffalo Soldier" could have a transnational popularity indicates public acceptance of this reality. Marley's lyrics declare:
"If you know your history, you will know where I am coming from and
you would not have to ask me, who the hell I think I am. I'm just a
buffalo soldier in the war for America." What is unthinkable is that the
very Native people who bestowed the title "buffalo soldier" on black
men who fought against them were very possibly, given Native American reverence and respect for the Buffalo, according their black
opponents a recognition and respect not given their white enemies.
This would suggest a historic sense of solidarity between African and
Native Americans.

Just as we should not celebrate slave-owning Native Americans,
even though they were likely to be less harsh than white owners, we
should not celebrate the buffalo soldier even as we acknowledge the
forces that drove African Americans to participate in white imperialist
wars of extermination. My complaint is simply that these acts tend to
be focused on more than the gestures of solidarity between red and
black people because they not only deny our connections but implicitly
justify white domination by making racist exploitation appear as a
universal human behavior. When black buffalo soldiers slaughtered
Native Americans, they were slaughtering a part of themselves. This
history is important to remember, for it reminds us of how easy it is for
the colonized to be co-opted, to compromise in the interests of material
survival, to forget themselves. The red and black history which shows
both groups acting in complicity with white domination is often far
more widely known than any facts documenting solidarity.

When solidarity between red and black is declared, when we
celebrate shared history we are most often asked to "prove" that such
connections exist. There will never be enough proof, enough documentation, since so much data has been lost that can never be recovered.
The need for "proof" must be interrogated, however. Often it is the

voice of the biased and prejudiced who demand proof. What really changes when racist minds read *Black Indians* and find documentation of bonds between Native Americans and African Americans? Saundra Sharp's short film *Picking Tribes* depicts the confusion and anguish of a young black girl who longs to identify with both her Native American and African American ancestry. When she tells a group of little black girls at school that her ancestors are also Native American, they demand that she prove it. The burden of proof weighs heavily on the hearts of those who do not have written documentation, who rely on oral testimony passed from generation to generation. Within a white supremacist culture, to be without documentation is to be without a legitimate history. In the culture of forgetfulness, memory alone has no meaning.

As red and black people decolonize our minds we cease to place value solely on the written document. We give ourselves back memory. We acknowledge that the ancestors speak to us in a place beyond written history. Poetically evoking the insurrection of these subjugated knowledges in her most recent novel *The Temple of My Familiar,* Alice Walker uses fiction to create awareness of the ties between red and black people. When a black woman character is asked why she loves Native Americans, she responds:

> They open doors inside me. It's as if they're keys. To rooms inside myself. I find a door inside and it's as if I hear a humming from behind it, and then I get inside somehow, with the key the old ones give me, and as I stumble about in the darkness of the room, I begin to feel the stirring in myself, the humming of the room, and my heart starts to expand with the absolute feeling of bravery, or love, or audacity, or commitment. It becomes a light, and that light enters me, by osmosis, and a part of me that was not clear before is clarified.

Walker evokes a process of remembering that is essential for the political self-recovery of colonized and oppressed peoples.

Nostalgia for a lost past is useless if it paralyzes and keeps us so trapped in the memory of grief that we cannot engage in active struggle. To allow our ancestors to dwell among us and to invite their wisdom to enter us is powerful. We are nurtured by their presence. This truth has been passed through generations. Given the grave crises facing us in modern society, we need more than ever to draw on oppositional resources. Though supposedly speaking to white people, Chief Seattle calls all of us to remember our ancestors, to cherish their presence and their power. Agreeing to forced relocation, he requests that the right to visit at the tombs of ancestors be respected. Sharing the knowledge that the ancestors dwell among us, he made this proclamation:

> Every part of this soil is sacred in the estimation of my people. Every hillside, every valley, every plain and grove has been hallowed by some sad or happy event in days long vanished...the very dust upon which you now stand responds more lovingly to their footsteps than to yours, because it is rich with the dust of our ancestors and our bare feet are conscious of the sympathetic touch...even the little children who lived here and rejoiced here for a brief season, still love these somber solitudes and at even-time they grow wary of returning spirits. And when the last Red Man shall have perished, the memory of my tribe shall have become a myth among the white man, these shores will swarm with the invisible dead of my tribe...the dead are not powerless. Dead—I say? There is no death, only a change of worlds.

Within changing worlds, black and red people look once again to the spirit of our ancestors, recovering worldviews and life-sustaining values that renew our spirit and restore in us the will to resist domination. Though certainly not a perfect work, *Black Indians,* like all the other scholarship that seeks to recover buried history, can aid this process. Stressing the need for such work in his preface, Katz states:

> Clearly the 1920's estimate that a third of African Americans have Indian blood requires new research. Today just about every African American family tree has an Indian branch. While Europeans forcefully entered the African blood stream, Native Americans and Africans merged by choice, invitation and love. This profound difference cannot be understated—and it explains why families who share this bi-racial inheritance feel so much solace and pride.

Celebration of shared history between African American and Native American will have lasting impact only if it is linked to efforts to construct and maintain ongoing political solidarity. We affirm the ties of the past, the bonds of the present, when we relearn our history, nurture the shared sensibility that has been retained in the present, linking these gestures to resistance struggle, to liberation movement that seeks to eradicate domination and transform society.

Selected Bibliography

Aidoo, Christina Ama Ata. *Our Sister Killjoy: or Reflections from a Black-eyed Squint*. New York: NOK Pub., International, 1979.

Arac, Jonathan, ed., *Postmodernism and Politics*. Minneapolis, MN: University of Minnesota Press, 1986.

Ali, Shahrazad. *The Blackman's Guide to Understanding the Blackwoman*. Philadelphia, PA: Civilized Publications, 1990.

Argueta, Manlio. *One Day of Life*. New York: Vintage, 1983.

Baldwin, James. *The Fire Next Time*. New York: Dell, 1988.

—*No Name in the Street*. New York: Dell, 1986.

—*Notes of a Native Son*. Boston: Beacon, 1990.

Bambara, Toni Cade. *The Salt Eaters*. New York: Random House, 1980.

—ed., *The Black Woman*. New York: New American Library, 1970.

Baudrillard, Jean. *Fatal Strategies*. New York: Autonomedia, 1990.

Beam, Joseph. "No Cheek to Turn." In *Brother to Brother: New Writings by Black Gay Men,* edited by Essex Hemphill. Boston: Alyson Publications, 1991.

Bingham, Sallie. *Passion and Prejudice: A Family Memoir*. New York: Applause Theatre Book Publishers, 1991.

Brooks, Peter. *The Melodramatic Imagination: Balzac, Henry James, Melodrama, and the Mode of Excess*. New York: Columbia University Press, 1984.

Brown, Cynthia Stokes, ed., *Ready From Within: Septima Clark and the Civil Rights Movement*. Navarro, CA: Wild Trees Press, 1986.

Burchill, Julie. *Girls on Film*. New York: Pantheon, 1986.

Butler, Johnella. "Difficult Dialogues." *Women's Review of Books,* Feb. 1989.

Carew, Jan. "The Caribbean Writer and Exile." *Komparatistische Hefte,* Vol. 9, No. 10 (1984), pp. 23-39.

Carter, Angela. *The Sadeian Woman*. New York: Pantheon, 1988.

Chisholm, Shirley. *Unbought and Unbossed*. New York: Avon, 1970.

Churchill, Ward. *Fantasies of the Master Race*. Monroe, ME: Common Courage Press, 1992.

Clement, Catherine. *Opera, or the Undoing of Women*. Minneapolis: University of Minnesota Press, 1988.

Cliff, Michelle. *No Telephone to Heaven*. New York: Dutton, 1988.

—"Women Warriors: Black Women Writers Load the Canon." *Voice Literary Supplement,* May 1990.

Clifford, James. "Notes on Travel and Theory." In *Traveling Theorist's Inscriptions,* Vol. 5 (1989).

Clifford, James. *The Predicament of Culture*. Cambridge: Harvard University Press, 1988.

Cocks, Joan. *The Oppositional Imagination*. New York: Routledge, 1989.

Cone, James. *A Black Theology of Liberation*. New York: Orbis, 1990.

—*My Soul Looks Back*. New York: Orbis, 1986.

Crouch, Stanley. *Notes of a Hanging Judge*. New York: Oxford University Press, 1990.

Davis, Angela. *Angela Davis: An Autobiography*. New York: Random House, 1974.

de Lauretis, Teresa. *Technologies of Gender: Essays on Theory, Film, and Fiction*. Bloomington, IN: Indiana University Press, 1987.

Delaney, Martin. *The Condition, Elevation, Immigration and Destiny of the Colored People of the United States, Politically Considered*. New Hampshire: Ayer Company Publishers, 1968.

Diawara, Manthia. "Black British Cinema: Spectatorship and Identity Formation in Territories." *Public Culture,* Vol. 1, No. 3 (Summer 1989).

—"Black Spectatorship: Problems of Identification and Resistance." *Screen,* Vol. 29, No. 4 (1988).

Doane, Mary Ann. "Remembering Women: Psychical and Historical Constructions in Film Theory." In *Psychoanalysis and Cinema,* edited by E. Ann Kaplan. London: Routledge, 1990.

—"Woman's Stake: Filming the Female Body." In *Feminism and Film Theory,* edited by Constance Penley. New York: Routledge, 1988.

Douglass, Frederick. *Narrative of the Life of Frederick Douglass*. Edited by Benjamin Quarles. Cambridge, MA: Belknap Press, 1969.

Ehrenreich, Barbara. *The Hearts of Men: American Dreams and the Flight from Commitment*. New York: Doubleday, 1984.

Eisenstein, Zillah. *The Female Body and the Law*. Berkeley: University of California Press, 1988.

Ewen, Stuart. *All Consuming Images: The Politics of Style in Contemporary Culture*. New York: Basic, 1990.

Ewen, Stuart and Elizabeth Ewen. *Channels of Desire: Mass Images and the Shaping of American Consciousness*. New York: McGraw Hill, 1982.

Fanon, Franz. *Black Skin, White Masks*. New York: Monthly Review, 1967.

Faurshou, Gail. "Fashion and the Cultural Logic of Postmodernity." In *Body Invaders*, edited by Arthur and Marilouise Kroker. Canada: New Word Perspectives, 1988.

Forbes, Jack. *Black Africans and Native Americans*. Cambridge, MA: Blackwell, 1980.

Foster, Hal. *Recoding: Art, Spectacle, Cultural Politics*. Seattle: Bay Press, 1985.

Foucault, Michel. *Language, Counter-memory, Practice: Selected Essays and Interviews*. Edited by Donald F. Bouchard, translated by Bouchard and Sherry Simon. Ithaca, NY: Cornell University Press, 1977.

—*Power/Knowledge: Selected Interviews and Other Writings*. Edited by Colin Gordon, translated by Gordon et al. New York: Pantheon, 1980.

Friedberg, Anne. "A Denial of Difference: Theories of Cinematic Identification." In *Psychoanalysis & Cinema*, edited by E. Ann Kaplan. London: Routledge, 1990.

Frye, Marilyn. "The Problem that Has No Name." In *Politics of Reality: Essays in Feminist Theory*. Trumansburg, NY: The Crossing Press, 1983.

Fuss, Diana. *Essentially Speaking: Feminism, Nature and Difference*. New York: Routledge, 1989.

Gallop, Jane. *Thinking Through the Body*. New York: Columbia University Press, 1990.

Gamman, Lorraine and Margaret Marshment. *Female Gaze: Women as Viewers of Popular Culture*. Seattle, WA: Real Comet Press, 1989.

García Marquez, Gabriel. *Fragrance of Guava*. Translated by by Ann Wright. London: Verso, 1983.

Gilman, Sander. L. "Black Bodies, White Bodies: Toward an Iconography of Female Sexuality in Late Nineteenth-Century Art, Medicine, and Literature." *Critical Inquiry* 12 (Autumn 1985), pp. 204-242.

Giovanni, Nikki. "Woman Poem." In *The Black Woman*, edited by Toni Cade Bambara. New York: New American Library, 1970.

Gutierrez, Gustavo. *On Job: God Talk & The Suffering of the Innocent*. Translated by Matthew J. O'Connell. New York: Orbis Books, 1987.

Halsell, Grace. *Soul Sister*. Connecticut: Fawcett, 1969.

Hansberry, Lorraine. *Les Blancs: The Collected Last Plays of Lorraine Hansberry*. Edited by Robert Nemiroff. New York: Random House, 1972.

—*To Be Young, Gifted, and Black*. New York: Signet, 1970.

Haraway, Donna. "A Manifesto for Cyborgs." In *Feminism/Postmodernism.* Edited by Linda J. Nicholson. New York: Routledge, 1990.

Haraway, Donna. *Primate Visions.* New York: Routledge, 1989.

Harding, Vincent. *Hope and History: Why We Must Share the Story of the Movement.* Maryknoll, NY: Orbis, 1987.

Hoch, Paul. *White Hero, Black Beast: Racism, Sexism and the Mask of Masculinity.* London: Pluto Press, 1979.

hooks, bell. *Ain't I A Woman: Black Women and Feminism.* Boston: South End Press, 1981.

—*Feminist Theory: From Margin to Center.* Boston: South End Press, 1984.

—*Talking Back: Thinking Feminist, Thinking Black.* Boston: South End Press, 1989.

—*Yearning: Race, Gender, and Cultural Politics.* Boston: South End Press, 1990.

hooks, bell and Cornel West. *Breaking Bread: Insurgent Black Intellectual Life.* Boston: South End Press, 1991.

Jackson, George. *Blood in My Eye.* Baltimore: Black Classic Press, 1990.

—*Soledad Brother: The Prison Letters of George Jackson.* New York: Bantam Books, 1970.

Jacobs, Harriet. *Incidents in the Life of a Slave Girl.* New York: Harcourt Brace Jovanovich, 1973.

Jimenez, Marilyn. "The Changeling: Race, Sex and Property." Unpublished manuscript.

Kaplan, E. Ann, ed., *Psychoanalysis & Cinema: AFI Film Readers.* New York: Routledge, 1989.

Katz, William. *Black Indians.* New York: Macmillan Children's Book Group, 1986.

Keen, Sam. *The Passionate Life.* San Francisco: Harper, 1983.

Kroeber, Theodora. *Ishi in Two Worlds: A Biography of the Last Wild Indian in North America.* Berkeley, CA: University of California Press, 1961.

Kuhn, Annette. *Power of the Image: Essays on Representation and Sexuality.* New York: Routledge, 1985.

LaDuke, Winona. "Natural to Synthetic and Back Again." In *Marxism and Native Americans,* edited by Ward Churchill. Boston: South End Press, 1983.

Larsen, Nella. *Quicksand and Passing.* New Brunswick, NJ: Rutgers University Press, 1989.

Lewis, Victor. "Healing the Heart of Justice." *Creation Spirituality* (March/April 1991).

Lorde, Audre. *Sister Outsider.* Trumansburg, New York: Crossing Press, 1984.

Madhubuti, Haki R. *Black Men: Obsolete, Single, Dangerous?: Afrikan American Families in Transition: Essays in Discovery, Solution and Hope.* Chicago: Third World Press, 1990.

Majors, Richard and Janet Mancini Billson. *Cool Pose: The Dilemmas of Black Manhood in America.* New York: MacMillan, 1991.

Marcus, Greil. *Lipstick Traces.* Cambridge: Harvard University Press, 1989.

Marshall, Paule. *Praisesong for the Widow.* New York: Dutton, 1984.

Mehrez, Samia. *The Bounds of Race.* Ithaca: Cornel University Press, 1991.

Menchu, Rigoberta. *I, Rigoberta Menchu: An Indian Woman in Guatemala.* New York: Routledge, Chapman and Hall, 1985

Micheaux, Oscar. *Philadelphia Afro-American,* Jan. 24, 1925.

Minh-ha, Trinh. "Outside In, Inside Out." In *Questions of Third World Cinema,* edited by Jim Pines. London: British Film Institute, 1989.

Morrison, Toni. *Beloved.* New York: Knopf, 1987.

—*The Bluest Eye.* New York: Holt, Rinehart and Winston, 1970.

—*Sula.* New York: Knopf, 1973.

Mulvey, Laura. *Feminism and Film Theory.* New York: Routledge, 1988.

—*Visual and Other Pleasures.* Bloomington, IN: Indiana University Press, 1989.

Naylor, Gloria. *Mama Day.* New York: Ticknor and Fields, 1988.

O'Neale, Sondra. "Inhibiting Midwives, Usurping Creators: The Struggling of Black Women in American Fiction." In *Feminist Studies/Critical Studies,* edited by Teresa de Lauretis. Bloomington, IN: Indiana University Press, 1986.

Penley, Constance. *Feminism and Film Theory.* New York: Routledge, 1988.

Penley, Constance. *The Future of an Illusion.* Minneapolis: University of Minnesota Press, 1989.

Podhoretz, Norman. "My Negro Problem And Ours." *Commentary* (1963).

Radford-Hill, Sheila. "Considering Feminism as a Model for Social Change." In *Feminist Studies/Critical Studies,* edited by Teresa de Lauretis. Bloomington, IN: Indiana University Press, 1986.

Rorty, Richard. *Contigency, Irony, and Solidarity.* New York: Cambridge University Press, 1989.

Rosaldo, Renato. *Culture & Truth: The Remaking of Social Analysis.* Boston: Beacon, 1989.

Rose, Phyllis. *Jazz Cleopatra: Josephine Baker in Her Time.* New York: Harper Collins, 1989.

Ross, Andrew. *No Respect: Intellectuals and Popular Culture.* New York: Routledge, 1989.

Saadawi, Nawal El. *Women At Point Zero*. New Jersey: Humanities Press International, 1983.

Said, Edward. "Traveling Theory." *Raritan* 1 (Winter 1982), pp. 41-67.

Scott, James. *Domination and the Arts of Resistance*. New Haven: Yale University Press, 1990.

Shange, Ntozake. *For Colored Girls Who Have Considered Suicide When the Rainbow is Enuf*. San Lorenzo, CA: Shameless Hussy Press, 1975.

Spivak, Gayatri. *In Other Worlds: Essays in Cultural Politics*. New York: Methuen, 1987.

Spivak, Gayatri. *The Post-Colonial Critic: Interviews, Strategies, Dialogues*. New York: Routledge, 1990.

Staples, Brent. "White Girl Problem." *New York Magazine* (1989).

Steele, Shelby. *The Content of Our Character: A New Vision of Race in America*. New York: Harper Perennial, 1991.

Taussig, Michael T. *Shamanism, Colonialism and the Wild Man: A Study in Terror and Healing*. Chicago: University of Chicago Press, 1986.

Thiong'o, Ngugi. *Decolonising the Mind*. London: Heinemann, 1986.

Torgovnick, Marianna. *Gone Primitive: Savage Intellects, Modern Lives*. Chicago: University of Chicago Press, 1990.

Turner, Tina. *I, Tina: My Life Story*. New York: Avon, 1987.

Van Sertima, Ivan. *They Came Before Columbus*. New York: Random House, 1976.

Walker, Alice. *The Color Purple*. New York: Washington Square Press, 1982.

—*Meridian*. San Diego, CA: Harcourt Brace Jovanovich, 1976.

—*The Temple of My Familiar*. San Diego: Harcourt Brace Jovanovich, 1989.

—*The Third Life of Grange Copeland*. New York: Harcourt Brace Jovanovich, 1970.

Wallace, Michele. *Black Macho and the Myth of the Superwoman*. New York: Dial Press, 1970.

Ware, Vron. *Beyond the Pale: White Women, Racism, and History*. London: Verso, 1992.

White, E. Frances. "Africa on My Mind: Gender, Counter Discourse and African-American Nationalism." *Journal of Women's History,* Vol. 2, No. 1 (Summer 1990).

White, Evelyn C., ed., *The Black Women's Health Book: Speaking for Ourselves*. Seattle, WA: Seal Press, 1990.

Wright, Richard. *Native Son*. New York: Harper Collins, 1969.

About South End Press

South End Press is a nonprofit, collectively run book publisher with over 175 titles in print. Since our founding in 1977, we have tried to meet the needs of readers who are exploring, or are already committed to, the politics of radical social change.

Our goal is to publish books that encourage critical thinking and constructive action on the key political, cultural, social, economic, and ecological issues shaping life in the United States and in the world. In this way, we hope to give expression to a wide diversity of democratic social movements and to provide an alternative to the products of corporate publishing.

If you would like a free catalog of South End Press books or information about our membership program—which offers two free books and a 40% discount on all titles—please write us at South End Press, 116 Saint Botolph Street, Boston, MA 02115.

Other titles of interest from South End Press: